8 KEYS TO RECOVERY FROM AN EATING DISORDER

8 Keys to Mental Health Series

Babette Rothschild, Series Editor

The 8 Keys series of books provides consumers with brief, inexpensive, and high-quality self-help books on a variety of topics in mental health. Each volume is written by an expert in the field, someone who is capable of presenting evidence-based information in a concise and clear way. These books stand out by offering consumers cutting-edge, relevant theory in easily digestible portions, written in an accessible style. The tone is respectful of the reader and the messages are immediately applicable. Filled with exercises and practical strategies, these books empower readers to help themselves.

8 KEYS TO RECOVERY FROM AN EATING DISORDER

Effective Strategies from Therapeutic Practice and Personal Experience

---

CAROLYN COSTIN
GWEN SCHUBERT GRABB

W. W. Norton & Company
New York • London

Important Note: 8 *Keys to Recovery From an Eating Disorder* is intended to provide general information on the subject of health and well-being; it is not a substitute for medical or psychological treatment and may not be relied upon for purposes of diagnosing or treating any illness. Please seek out the care of a professional healthcare provider if you are pregnant, nursing, or experiencing symptoms of any potentially serious condition.

Copyright © 2012 by Carolyn Costin and Gwen Schubert Grabb

All rights reserved
Printed in the United States of America
First Edition

For information about permission to reproduce selections from this book, write to Permissions, W. W. Norton & Company, Inc., 500 Fifth Avenue, New York, NY 10110

For information about special discounts for bulk purchases, please contact W. W. Norton Special Sales at specialsales@wwnorton.com or 800-233-4830

Manufacturing by Sheridan Books
Production manager: Leeann Graham

Library of Congress Cataloging-in-Publication Data

Costin, Carolyn.
   8 keys to recovery from an eating disorder : effective strategies from therapeutic practice and personal experience / Carolyn Costin, Gwen Schubert Grabb.
      pages cm. — (8 keys to mental health series)
   Includes bibliographical references and index.
   ISBN 978-0-393-70695-6 (pbk. : alk. paper)
 1. Eating disorders—Treatment. 2. Mind and body.
 I. Grabb, Gwen Schubert. II. Title. III. Title: Eight keys to recovery from an eating disorder.
RC552.E18C666 2013
616.85'26—dc23

                       2013015936

ISBN 978-0-393-70695-6 (pbk. : alk. paper)

W. W. Norton & Company, Inc.
500 Fifth Avenue, New York, N.Y. 10110
www.wwnorton.com

W. W. Norton & Company Ltd.
15 Carlisle Street, London W1D 3BS

Gwen: I would like to dedicate this book to all those who helped me recover, to my brave clients who trust me with so much every day, and to those who continue to suffer from this devastating illness.

Carolyn: I share Gwen's sentiment exactly and also dedicate this book to the 14th Dalai Lama who announced his retirement this year, to the newest addition to my family, Amelia Rose, and to Lita.

A Note to Professionals

Although 8 *Keys* is a self-help book for clients, we believe the information and assignments can enhance your practice and provide useful tools for your work in this field. We have included assignments throughout the keys and worksheets in the appendix that we have found effective and successful in our own practice.

Contact Information

If you are interested in more information or professional trainings, you may contact Carolyn Costin at her Web site, www.montenido.com, by calling (310) 457-9958, or follow her on Twitter at Carolyn_Costin. Gwen Grabb may be reached via her Web site, www.gwenschubertgrabb.com, or by joining "8 Keys to Recovery from an Eating Disorder Book Group" on Facebook.

Contents

Acknowledgments ix
Foreword xi
Introduction 1
KEY 1: Motivation, Patience, and Hope 11
KEY 2: Your Healthy Self Will Heal Your
Eating Disorder Self 37
KEY 3: It's Not About the Food 63
KEY 4: Feel Your Feelings, Challenge Your Thoughts 93
KEY 5: It *Is* About the Food 125
KEY 6: Changing Your Behaviors 159
KEY 7: Reach Out to People Rather
Than Your Eating Disorder 191
KEY 8: Finding Meaning and Purpose 219

Epilogue 255
References 261
Resources 265
Appendix 267
Index 269

Acknowledgments

In a project of this nature, there are far more people who deserve acknowledgment and thanks than we have room for, but there are a few directly involved whom we cannot fail to mention. Babette Rothschild, thank you for giving us this amazing opportunity and paving the way. To W. W. Norton and all the people there who supported this book and helped to make it happen, thank you. Jennifer Dale zealously read our first drafts and provided valuable feedback; Tim Brewerton, Ralph Carson, Debra Gelbart, Jennie Nash, and Kate Schluter assisted with fact-checking and editing. We also each have a few personal appreciations.

Carolyn

This book and my life in general require several often unacknowledged support crew members. I could not be who I am or do what I do without them. I am filled with endless gratitude, appreciation, and love for:

- My staff, who carry on the mission of love, healing, and hope at all times.
- Bruce, who has never failed to see more in me than I see in myself.

- My many teachers along the way, some of whom are mentioned in the text or resource section.
- My soul sisters, who know the sacredness of tears and the moon (you know who you are).
- My loved ones, who see me, feed my body and soul, and remind me of what is truly important; and
- Gwen, who over the last fifteen years turned from client, to colleague, to friend, saying, "Yes" to recovery so many years ago and "Yes" again to co-authoring this book.

Gwen

I will forever be grateful to my husband Albert for his love, support, and patience through everything; and to my children, Ari, Jacob, and Chloe, for reminding me every day what is truly important; and to my beloved friends, my walking partners, and my confidantes. Thank you for always being there and willing to listen.

I am also deeply grateful to the people who helped me through my illness, especially: Nancy Sokolow, for her unwavering kindness, excellent care, and devotion; Erin Naimi, for helping me find freedom with more than just food; and Carolyn Costin, for always loving me, believing in me, and for continuing to inspire me with her courage, wisdom, and infinite heart.

Finally, of course, our greatest gratitude for this book goes to our clients, for teaching us, trusting us, and inspiring us to be better therapists, and for willingly sharing their experiences in our sessions and in this book.

Foreword

The 8 *Keys* series was conceived to provide a library of intelligent, highly accessible books—written by specialists in their fields—for consumers who may not want or be able to afford psychotherapy. The series aims to provide these readers with readily applicable techniques to aid the recovery of the condition being discussed. Each series volume can be easily used as a self-help tool or as an adjunct to psychotherapy itself. (From a wealth of reader feedback, I know that my own book, *8 Keys to Safe Trauma Recovery*, the first in this series, is used in both of these ways.) In addition, each book in the series includes background theory relevant to the featured topic to ensure that both consumer and helping professional are similarly informed. Knowledgeable consumers make better decisions about what does and does not help them. Therefore, any seeker of improved psychological health or personal growth should have access to the same information as the professionals; the theories and techniques that the psychotherapists use should not be kept a secret.

According to the Web site of the National Association of Anorexia Nervosa and Associated Disorders (ANAD), more than 20 million people in the U.S. alone suffer from an eating disorder. Moreover, they report, eating disorders account for the "highest mortality rate of any mental illness." From the series inception, I hoped to include a book to help those with eating disorders. Given the prevalence of sufferers, I felt a resource for those affected was critical. Moreover, just about every helping professional encounters clients and patients with eating disorders in the course of dealing with a multitude of other presenting problems. Often an eating disorder is at the core of diagnoses such as depression or anxiety. Consumers and professionals need to consider the role of eating disorders on their own *and* as companions to other difficulties. Both well- and less-experienced professionals need guidelines, a logical framework, and highly usable tools to address eating disorders alone or in combination with treatment for other issues. And, finally, consumers and professionals alike need guidance to decide when seeking additional professional consultation might be in order.

Written by two psychotherapist colleagues, Carolyn Costin and Gwen Grabb, *8 Keys to Recovery from an Eating Disorder* outstandingly meets all of these criteria. Costin has been a prominent figure among eating disorders professionals for decades. Her previous books, *Your Dieting Daughter* and *The Eating Disorders Sourcebook*, are both well known and valued in the field. She wisely chose Grabb, a former client-turned-colleague, to co-write the book, creating a writing team and voice that is totally unique—not only to books about eating disorders, but books about psychotherapy altogether. By offering the dual reflections of therapist and patient, this book may remind some readers of Irving Yalom's *Every Day Gets a Little Closer*, with the added benefit that the client in this book has become a professional herself and has a clear and valuable perspective from "both sides of the couch," so to speak. In *8 Keys to Recovery*, Costin and Grabb courageously disclose details of their own eating disorder histories and engage in revealing dialogue about Grabb's successful (if sometimes difficult) treatment by Costin. In doing so, they expose the most intimate challenges of living with and healing an eating disorder, both personally and professionally. Costin and Grabb enlighten the reader with the knowledge they gained from failure as well as success, literally, from the inside out.

FOREWORD

Those suffering from eating disorders (in addition to their families and friends) will feel immensely calmed by reading this book. They will feel in good hands with credible authors and therapists who have been where they are and made it through. Professionals will find sound information and a recovery structure that is logical and manageable.

Reading manuscripts fresh from the minds of authors is one of the privileges of being a series editor. Looking over Costin and Grabb's work for the first time, I found myself more excited and engaged with every page. Early on I knew this would be a special book, and working with the authors has been a pleasure. I cannot remember reading any book where I felt—all at the same time—securely informed, emotionally comforted, gently confronted, and realistically reassured. I hope you have a similar experience.

Babette Rothschild
Series Editor

8 KEYS TO RECOVERY FROM AN EATING DISORDER

INTRODUCTION

This book is about getting over an eating disorder, how we did it, how we helped thousands of others do it, and how we hope to help you do it, too. We took on this project because we want to share what we have learned, provide practical strategies and examples of what really works, and offer our own experience and that of our clients to facilitate your recovery process. *8 Keys to Recovery from an Eating Disorder: Effective Strategies from Therapeutic Practice and Personal Experience* is for anyone with an eating or body image problem. You don't have to meet any formal diagnosis to benefit from this book. If you restrict, binge, purge, excessively diet or weigh yourself, exercise compulsively, or engage routinely and obsessively in any other food- or weight-related behaviors, the eight keys can help you get on, and stay on, the road to recovery. Although *8 Keys* is a self-help book intended for those suffering from an eating disorder, it will also be informative and useful for family, friends, and professionals.

This is a personal book for you to use in your recovery process. You can read through the keys in order, skip around, or start with the ones that draw your attention the most. Our goal is to help you understand why you developed your eating disorder, and give you the necessary tools and strategies for change and healing. We do not offer diagnostic criteria, or details of medical complications, nor do we explain the various forms of treatment available. If you would like more information on those aspects of treatment and recovery, see the Resources section at the back of the book where we list suggestions for further reading. This book does not substitute for or replace medical, psychiatric, or therapeutic care. If you have not already done so, we highly encourage you to contact an eating disorder professional for help and obtain a thorough physical, as there are many medical consequences of eating disorders that may not be visible or obvious, but could be dangerous. We are aware that some readers may pick up this book instead of seeking professional help and if that describes you, we hope to help you get started on your path, and perhaps motivate you to seek whatever help is appropriate for you at this time.

Throughout this book you will hear personal accounts from others, including ours (the authors) who have struggled with an eating disorder and recovered. Research shows that working with someone who is recovered is a positive and significant experience for someone suffering with an eating disorder. This does not mean that you have to find a treatment professional who has recovered, but exposure to others who have gone before you and successfully overcome their eating disorder is vital. Revealing to our clients that we are "recovered" is somewhat controversial, as there are those who disagree with this practice. We acknowledge their concerns and understand that this kind of self-disclosure requires a great amount of responsibility and professional astuteness. We have found that our experience of suffering and triumphing over our own eating disorders has given us some of the most useful tools we have for helping others, and we consistently hear from clients that knowing that we recovered is one of the most helpful aspects of their treatment. Although we have chosen to share our own stories exactly as they occurred, some of the quotes and examples from clients are composites or we have changed a detail or two to ensure confidentiality.

In this book, we not only share examples from our personal stories, we also bring the reader into our work together as therapist and client, thus giving readers a glimpse into the process from both sides. Gwen Grabb was a patient at Monte Nido Eating Disorder Treatment Center when it first opened in 1996 and Carolyn Costin was owner, clinical director, and therapist. These narratives are intended to help you understand the therapeutic process, increase insight about your own resistance or fears, clarify issues, enhance your therapy, or provide you with the motivation to seek help if you have been discouraged, or afraid to do so. We hope that reading both of our perspectives will help reduce shame, increase trust, and show that you too can get well and live a normal, full life.

We begin our self-disclosure right here, as we conclude the introduction of the book with an introduction to us. The following is a brief overview to provide you with some needed context as you read though the keys and the personal reflections we provide.

Carolyn's Story

I developed my eating disorder around the age of 15. It all began with a diet that my friends and I went on in high school. I was the only one who never stopped the diet. At 16, when I was leaving for college (yes, I know, a bit young), I weighed 40 pounds less than I had before I started dieting, and was 40 times more screwed up than anyone knew. I did not know I had an illness. There were no books or television specials or treatment programs advertising help. My mom took me to a doctor to find out what was wrong, but my tests came back normal, validating my belief that I was OK and "Everyone should just leave me alone and let me eat what I want." I felt proud of my weight loss. It was a sign of success and willpower that I could control my hunger and pass up "fattening" foods, even though, it is more accurate to say that I was obsessed with food and thought about it day and night. Eventually, as often happens with an eating disorder, all foods became fattening in my mind and eventually eating itself felt like a weakness or failure. Still I persisted, due to an intense fear of what would happen to me if I relinquished my rigid control. The best way to describe it now is that I developed a phobia of gaining weight. As I got thinner and thinner, it seemed like I felt fatter. I noticed my stomach sticking out or my thighs looking too big no matter how much weight I lost. To get through the day eating as little as possible was the goal. It became so pervasive that I would not lick postage stamps for fear of the "extra" calories. Once I drank a sip of a regular soft drink that I thought was a diet soda, and when I realized my mistake, I felt panic. I felt like I was a disgrace, and like I had sinned. My mind had been completely taken over by an obsession with calories, weight, and food. I tell clients that it is like being brainwashed, but the good news is, you can be deprogrammed. I want others to know that back then I never would have imagined that I could turn it all around, that someday those behaviors would become old memories of a long-gone illness. I would never have imagined that one day I would be eating pasta and pizza, cake and candy bars, and whatever else I wanted without any hesitation or bother. I would not have believed I would stop counting calories or weighing myself. Yet all of these things are true, and they can be true for you, too.

People always ask, "What made you get better?" or "What turned you around?" Just as there are a myriad of things that come together in the development of an eating disorder, there are many things that have to come together to turn it around as well. There are a few moments that stand out in my mind as important and pivotal. One was an experience I had one morning in my college dorm room. I had been telling myself that I was *not* going to lose any more weight, but that I just did not want to gain any, either. I was sure that I was eating enough to maintain my weight. When I got on the scale for my routine morning weigh-in, I saw yet another unintended drop in weight. I heard myself say, "I am not in control of it anymore; it is in control of me." I knew I needed help and I began to look for it, but I could not find anyone who had ever heard of, much less treated, a person with an eating disorder. I was on my own to get better. It was a long hard struggle. I never wanted to gain weight; I wanted a better life, and I had to let weight gain happen as part of that process. When I did gain weight, I began compulsively exercising. This too had to be faced, dealt with, and let go.

There were many ingredients that helped along the way. My studies in psychology helped me to understand my mind, and pushed me to create behavior modification projects that helped me change. The love and unconditional support of my mother made me believe in myself and nourished me in times of desperation. I learned that I could tell people the truth and they would love me more, not less, so I reached out to others to help me. My work as a teacher gave me a sense of purpose. Finally, my exploration into the realm of philosophy and spirituality shifted my focus from the external to the internal, and brought new meaning to my life on a more soulful level. All of this helped me recover and helped make me who I am today. When I became a therapist in 1977, I began immediately disclosing to the few clients who came my way that I too had been there and understood what they were going through. I was "out of the closet" before I knew I was supposed to be in it! As it turned out, disclosing my own eating disorder and eventual recovery became a hallmark of my treatment philosophy. I became a pioneer in two important areas in the field of eating disorders: 1) that you can be fully recovered, and 2) that if you are recovered and you are a therapist, it is useful to share this with your clients, as it is valuable in your arsenal of therapeutic tools and role modeling.

Gwen's Story

I was only 11 years old when I went on my first diet. Up until that day, I hadn't thought much about food in relation to my body shape or weight. My mother was always talking about dieting and the social hazards of being overweight. Although her intentions were good, from the moment that I started dieting, my relationship with food and my body changed in very negative and ultimately destructive ways. I would spend the following seven years trying to lose weight and, as I saw it, failing miserably. Each diet failure confirmed my lack of self-discipline and reinforced my feelings of shame and hopelessness. Then, at 18, I moved away to begin college at my heaviest weight ever. Fearful of rejection, I avoided meeting people, joining groups, going to parties, or participating in campus activities. I didn't really want to be alone, but my decisions kept me that way. I believed that my weight was the root of my isolation and a desperate anger toward myself was brewing inside of me. I didn't know how to help myself and again my mother (who was extremely loving and truly trying to help) responded to my pain by suggesting I lose weight to improve my self-esteem, and sent me her latest diet. Neither of us could see that the weight was a symptom, rather than the problem itself. Due to my lack of friends and severe depression, this diet took hold of me and took over, leading me into what became a rapid descent into a full-blown eating disorder. I lost a lot of weight very quickly. My meals became more restrictive, rigid, and even ritualized. I started exercising compulsively and chronically weighing myself to make sure I was not gaining weight.

Back then, I had no way of knowing what I was doing to my mind and body, or that what I was doing would change me forever. It was 1980 and there was very little information available about eating disorders at that time. I had never even heard of anorexia or bulimia. Over the next two years, as my eating disorder progressed, I was able to keep it a secret and

INTRODUCTION

strongly dismissed any concerns about my weight loss. In fact, when people told me I was too thin, I was ecstatic and sentiments of worry or concern from others felt like a warm hug. That kind of concern felt great to me after years of feeling nothing but shame about my body. Soon, my behaviors started taking a toll on my health. After showing up at the health center weekly with numerous illnesses and ongoing infections, the doctor finally confronted me and used the word "anorexic" to describe me. I was shocked, confused, and thought he was just trying to scare me. After that appointment, I had moments of fear for my health, but my fear of gaining weight was much stronger. Finally, this same doctor recommended that I leave school until I got help and, if I wouldn't do it voluntarily, he threatened to proceed with a "formal dismissal." As I had no choice, I returned home and said nothing to my friends or family. I was terrified to stop what I was doing and to gain any weight. When I would try, my anxiety would skyrocket until I found a way to get rid of the food. Thankfully, just being back home around friends helped me feel less isolated and I started eating more and treating myself a little better. I returned to school, but I was far from well.

Shortly thereafter, I met Albert, whom I eventually married. I got pregnant very soon after our wedding, in spite of signs and warnings of possible infertility. Although being pregnant gave me short reprieves from my obsessions, as soon as I had each of my children, I quickly relapsed back into familiar rituals and fears about food and my body. After my third child, I fell back into the behaviors particularly intensively, and one day after running I had a seizure at the gym. This event was the catalyst to me finally seeking help. For the first time, I admitted everything to my husband and allowed him in. There wasn't very much help available at that time. I had no experience with therapy and didn't really know what kind of help I needed. Outpatient therapy was unsuccessful and the thought of going somewhere for inpatient treatment terrified me. I was almost ready to give up trying, when someone mentioned Carolyn being a recovered therapist with a house in Malibu where she helped others. The sound of that instilled some hope and I agreed to visit. I was very scared of getting well and all that would entail, but right away Carolyn made me feel safe, understood, and hopeful, and I agreed to treatment. Although I didn't realize it then, this decision was a major turning point in my life, and the moment when my recovery truly began. Recovery from my eating disorder was a slow process with many setbacks, and twists and turns. There was so much fear to overcome, but I did not give up. It's hard to say exactly when I got to the place where recovering turned into recovered, but it did. I have a good relationship with myself now, and have authentic and close relationships with the people around me. Having had such a serious illness, and being able to recover from it and heal, has helped me become a stronger and happier person than I ever could have imagined. Becoming a therapist was a natural evolution of this process, and I am very dedicated and passionate about helping others recover. I am honored and excited to bring all of the rich experiences and lessons I have learned along the way to the readers of this book. Through my words, may you find hope and healing.

Writing Assignment:

When you see this icon in the book, it means it is time for you to personalize the information. We strongly suggest that you get a journal and take time to do the assignments in order to make the material personal. Even though it is tempting to just read the assignments and move on, we can't stress enough how much more you will get out of this book if you do them. Writing in a journal is useful for clarifying your thoughts and feelings, getting to know yourself better, and managing over-

INTRODUCTION

whelming emotions associated with an experience. We know that writing down your account of an emotional situation can help you lower your reactivity to it even if you don't share your writing with anyone else. Recording your thoughts and feelings allows you to get them out and return to them later. You will be able to see your own progress or places when you are stuck. Sharing your journal with someone can also help you get feedback, clarification, and support. Finally, journaling is one of three things that most of our clients who have recovered have in common. The other two are not weighing and reaching out for support at the first sign of a problem. This is meaningful data and we stress the importance of journaling to all of our clients. Not weighing and reaching out for support are addressed thoroughly in the eight keys.

We have included a number of assignments in each key, but in order to avoid bogging down our readers or disrupting the flow of the reading, we sometimes list one or more of our assignments at the end of each key. Taking the time to do the assignments is important and worth it, but if you are not ready or willing to do this, don't worry, as you will benefit from the eight keys anyway.

KEY 1:

MOTIVATION, PATIENCE, AND HOPE

If you think you can do a thing or think you can't do a thing, you're right.
—Henry Ford

Hope was an incredible motivator for me. It is what kept me from giving up. It is what kept me on the road to recovery when I wanted to go back to my old ways. I had hope that the years ahead would hold a more joyful, fulfilling life for me and I didn't want to go back into all the pain and sickness. I knew that the eating disorder would not get me the things I dreamt of and hoped for.
—KK

Recovery from an eating disorder will not be an easy or short-term project. There will be times—perhaps when reading these pages—when you feel hopeful and motivated. There will be other times when your patience is gone or you are discouraged and feel like giving up. Several times throughout our own recovery both of us thought we would never get better. Sometimes, it seemed too hard, and sometimes it seemed impossible. But it is not! The truth is, recovery takes a long time and lots of work, but can turn out to be one of the biggest triumphs of your life. We are both proof of that, but if you could have seen us in the various stages of our own illnesses, you would no doubt wonder how we ever made it to where we are today. This is a good reason why you need to look beyond where you are now or how you feel today. If nothing else, our individual stories can offer hope. In this book you will find plenty of others who were also in your situation, and who are recovered today, which is where you can be too. Our first key will take you through the important issues of motivation, patience, and hope.

What motivated you to pick up, purchase, or read this book? Did you search online or in your neighborhood bookstore because you are ready to face and deal with your eating disorder? Did you accidentally stumble upon it and are simply curious to see how you might go about getting well once you are ready? Did a concerned person press these pages into your hands, even though you don't think you have that big of a problem? Or was it another factor altogether that motivated you to pick up this book? You may be unsure if you are fully ready or willing to recover, but on the other hand, you may be tired of obsessing about food and weight. You may be tired of avoiding social events and friends because of issues surrounding food, tired of feeling like you have to "pay" for every bite of food you eat, and tired of feeling as if life is passing you by. In essence, you might be tired of being *consumed* by your eating disorder.

You don't have to be ready to get rid of your eating disorder to benefit from this book. We have rarely met a client who was totally ready and willing to stop their eating disorder behaviors, even if he or she initially said this was the case. Our clients, probably like you, have ambivalence, and this ambivalence affects motivation. Dealing with your ambivalence is part of the recovery process. We don't consider lack of motivation a weakness or problem; we understand it and consider it a big part of our work as eating disorder therapists. It is our job to help motivate you and help you with the ambivalence we know is there.

Exploring where you are, discovering where you would like to go, and figuring out what it takes to get there involves an ongoing process. During recovery, your motivation, patience, and hope will come and go. This key is designed to help get

MOTIVATION, PATIENCE, AND HOPE

you started and get you past obstacles that prevent you from moving forward. We begin by helping you get a good picture of where you are and what your life with an eating disorder is like.

Writing Assignment:
Your Worst Eating Disorder Day

We have come to the first writing assignment, which means it is a good time to get your journal. Think back to the worst eating disorder day you can remember. Don't get caught up in trying to figure out which day was the worst. The idea is to pick a particularly bad day. Write down in very specific detail the day's events: what and how much you ate, any purging and the specific details involved, and any other eating disorder behaviors like body checking, laxatives, diet pills, or compulsive exercise. Write your feelings before, during, and after, any lies or dishonesty involved, how it affected you, and perhaps how it affected others. Be honest—this is only for you. We know that writing this down is something you probably never have done. It is also unlikely that you have shared this kind of detail with anyone or looked at it step-by-step yourself. After you are finished, read what you have written. Reading it may have a powerful effect on you. It might be hard to see yourself as the person you have become due to an eating disorder, but if you are able to face the truth and see how much your eating disorder has taken over, it could be the impetus for a new beginning. Know that this is not who you really are or who you want to be.

We asked you to reflect on your worst eating disorder day because we want you to be fully in touch with what your life with an eating disorder is really like. We want to show you on a personal level why you want to get better. If you feel overwhelmed afterwards, think of that energy as motivation to get better, so you don't have more days like your worst eating disorder day. On the other hand, if you believe your eating disorder is not that bad or is doing more *for* you than it is taking *from* you, think of the information in the rest of this key as designed to help you keep your eating disorder from getting any worse. No matter how bad you think your eating disorder is right now, the 8 keys will help you explore where you are and any thoughts, feelings, or fears you may have associated with change. Most importantly, try not to think of the process of recovery as giving up your eating disorder, but rather as getting yourself back.

Phases of Recovery from an Eating Disorder

We have identified several phases that people go through in their recovery from an eating disorder. You may have had an eating disorder for some time before you even realized that you had one. Once you became aware of the disorder, you might have gone on for some time before sharing this awareness with others. Maybe you believed your behaviors were not bad enough to warrant help or take action. Maybe you tried to get better, but it was too hard and you gave up. Knowing what the process looks like and what to expect can be very helpful. Below, we have outlined ten phases of recovery from an eating disorder, and under each we list some thoughts or feelings, which are typical for that phase.

Ten Phases of Eating Disorder Recovery

1. **I Don't Think I Have a Problem.**
   - It's my body so leave me alone.
   - There are people who are a lot thinner (worse) than I am.
2. **I Might Have a Problem But It's Not That Bad.**
   - I only throw up once in a while.
   - My physical didn't show anything wrong so I am OK.

MOTIVATION, PATIENCE, AND HOPE

3. **I Have a Problem But I Don't Care.**
   - I know throwing up isn't good for me, but it's working for me so I don't care.
   - I could change if I wanted to, but I don't.
4. **I Want To Change But I Don't Know How and I'm Scared.**
   - I want to eat normally, but I am afraid I will get fat (gain weight).
   - I want to stop bingeing, but I can't figure out where to start.
5. **I Tried To Change But I Couldn't.**
   - I told myself that I would not (fill in the blank) but I found myself doing it again.
   - I don't feel like I can really ever (change) get well, so why keep trying?
6. **I Can Stop Some of the Behaviors But Not All of Them.**
   - I could stop purging, but I will not be able to eat more.
   - My eating has gotten better, but my exercise is out of control.
7. **I Can Stop the Behaviors, But Not My Thoughts.**
   - I can't stop thinking about food and bingeing all the time.
   - I keep counting calories over and over in my head and still want to lose weight.
8. **I Am Often Free From Behaviors and Thoughts, But Not All the Time.**
   - I feel fine all day, but under stress I revert back to my unhealthy behaviors.
   - I was fine, but wearing a bathing suit triggered my eating disorder thoughts, and with it some related behaviors.
9. **I Am Free From Behaviors and Thoughts.**
   - I feel mostly OK in my body and am able to eat things I want and not feel guilty or anxious afterwards.

- Once I had stopped the behaviors for a period of time, at some point I realized that I was no longer having the thoughts or urges.
10. **I Am Recovered.**
    - For a long time now, I no longer have thoughts, feelings, or behaviors related to my eating disorder.
    - I accept my body's natural size. My eating disorder is a thing of the past.

What Does It Mean To Be Recovered?

Phase 10 of the process of recovery is when you are recovered. We both feel strongly about using the term "recovered" instead of "recovering" or "in recovery" to define the end goal. "Recovered" is how we feel and how we describe ourselves, and it is the end goal we pursue for all our clients.

The term and the concept of being "recovered" is important to us and we want to be clear regarding what we mean by it. There is no standard definition of what the term "recovered" means, and even researchers use varying definitions. One definition is when a person no longer meets the diagnostic criteria for an eating disorder. The problem with this definition is that a person can be symptomatic yet not meet the full criteria, and we would not consider that as being recovered. We prefer a definition that includes a variety of aspects we think are important to become recovered and stay that way.

Our definition of the term "recovered" is taken from Costin, *100 Questions & Answers About Eating Disorders*. Read the definition over a few times, write it down, post it on your mirror, or carry a copy with you, to remind you of where you are going, and where you can be.

> *Being recovered is when the person can accept his or her natural body size and shape and no longer has a self-destructive relationship with food or exercise. When you are recovered, food and*

MOTIVATION, PATIENCE, AND HOPE

weight take a proper perspective in your life, and what you weigh is not more important than who you are; in fact, actual numbers are of little or no importance at all. When recovered, you will not compromise your health or betray your soul to look a certain way, wear a certain size, or reach a certain number on the scale. When you are recovered, you do not use eating disorder behaviors to deal with, distract from, or cope with other problems. (pg. 164)

Writing Assignment: Exploring Your Phase of Recovery

Look at the 10 phases of recovery and try to determine which of the phases most accurately describes where you are today. Knowing the phase you are in can help you identify what is going on now, where you might be stuck, and where the recovery process will take you in the future. Write down the thoughts or behaviors you have that helped you determine what phase you are in as well as any feelings you have about it, where you have come from, and the road ahead.

Your Reasons for Change Will Change

We cannot know the reasons you might have for wanting to get better. Motivation to change comes in endless forms and changes over time. You might want to get better for someone else, or you might want to do it for yourself, or this might fluctuate. People sometimes start treatment because of a push or an ultimatum from a friend or loved one, but then later end up doing it for themselves. You might find yourself sick of being sick or you might be looking to the future and wanting a bigger life. You might be motivated by the desire to improve a current relationship or you might just want to get rid of your own incessant internal critic. Whatever your reasons for wanting to change are right now, just know that they may change over time. Clients often describe their shifts in motivation throughout the recovery process.

> *"I didn't want to change for a long time, but eventually I just got fed up with how things were. At first I was motivated by what I was trying to avoid like feeling sick, guilty, tired, cold, having no friends, and dying. After awhile I noticed that my motivation started being more about what I wanted to be able to do: concentrate, make friends, and go to parties again. Now I am noticing that I am motivated by what I want in the future. I want to travel, get married, and have children. Every change in motivation helped me along."*
>
> —CR

> *"It really helped to look at the things that I thought were motivating me a little bit closer . . . because it turned out I was really scared of those things, and getting better would mean I'd have to face them. They were all kind of double-edged swords—work, relationships, living back in a big city—I wanted them, but was so scared I'd fail at them, so even though I thought they were my motivation, being sick gave me an excuse to avoid them and the possibility of not getting what I wanted. When I realized that—and that really, in my old life I'd had all those things, I'd just been so empty inside that none of it had really mattered to me, and I was always going to want more and expect more from myself—I had to find something else."*
>
> —SL

When your reasons for changing change it can affect your motivation. For example, if your desire to get better stems from a wish to appease a friend or loved one, your motivation level might be low. If at some point you find a reason more compelling to you—for example, wanting to have a baby—your motivation might be very high. Everyone is different. Reasons for motivation and the degree of motivation vary from person to person and change over time.

Ready or Not

What brought you to these pages is important because whatever it was, it helps illuminate where you are in terms of your ambivalence and motivation. When reading this key, you can gauge your own readiness to change and modify the activities and exercises accordingly. If you know you are ready to overcome your eating disorder, you might, for example, dive into this book, complete every exercise, and share your progress with a trusted friend or therapist. If you still feel unsure, you might read through the whole book before you decide to complete a single exercise. Either approach—or any approach in between—is fine. Simply opening up this book suggests at least some small part of you is ready for something to be different in your life, and we believe that is enough to get started. You will take in what you are ready for and make changes in some areas, and at a pace that feels right for you. No matter how you came to this book, working through the keys will help you develop more insight and awareness into yourself as well as your situation. You can begin by assessing your own current level of motivation or readiness to change.

The Five Levels of Motivation for Change

DiClemente and Vasquez (1991) came up with a model for helping people understand and change addictive behavior, and Geller (2002) has used this model to research motivation and its relationship to eating disorders and success in treatment and recovery. Their work suggests that for any type of problem requiring change, your motivation or readiness to do so can be categorized into five main levels:

1. Pre-Contemplation: You don't think you have a problem and/or don't want to change.
2. Contemplation: You realize you have a problem and are thinking about changing, but you don't know how to start or what to do.
3. Preparation: You are getting ready for change. You look into different options, research online, or buy a self-help book.
4. Action: You know you want to change and you are taking action, making plans, and doing things differently.
5. Maintenance: You are working to continue doing the new behaviors, and not slip back.

When clients feel stuck, or can't find the motivation to keep trying, it is often because they are having difficulty moving from one level to the next. We use the following questions to help our clients evaluate their current situation and move forward. Read through them all and then do the assignment that follows.

Levels of Motivation: Asking the Important Questions

1. Pre-Contemplation
If you are reading this book, you are already past the pre-contemplation level. You might not be ready or want to change, but you know you have a problem.

2. Contemplation - If you are unsure whether you want to change:

MOTIVATION, PATIENCE, AND HOPE

- What are the pros and cons of staying the same vs. changing?
- What will your future likely be if you do change and what will it be like if you don't?
- How does continuing in your eating disorder help or hurt your health and happiness?
- What are the risks to your relationship(s) if you stay the same and what are the risks to your relationship(s) if you recover?
- Are there things that you know you will be giving up if you recover versus if you don't?

3. **Preparation - If you know you want to change, but can't get yourself started or don't know what to do:**
   - What are the obstacles you can see that keep you from trying? Or moving forward?
   - What would you need to overcome these obstacles?
   - Who are the people who are supportive to you in this process?
   - Who else might be a support? How could they help you?
   - Why do you want to recover?
   - What small step toward change could you take at this time? (Even the slightest movement is helpful.)

4. **Action - If you are stuck, feel defeated, and can't find the motivation to keep trying:**
   - What progress have you made so far, no matter how minimal you think it is? (Remember, it is hard to remain motivated if you never give yourself any credit or positive feedback.)
   - What progress might other people notice?
   - Can you remember a time when you didn't feel stuck or defeated? What were you doing then? Who helped you get there? How did you get there?
   - What are your fears or other feelings about giving up your eating disorder?

- What do you feel like you will lose by giving it up? (Even if you recognize your eating disorder is unhealthy, giving it up will feel like a loss, and losses bring up other feelings for everyone.)
- What do you want your relationship with food to ultimately look like?
- What do you need to practice in order to get there?
- What are you willing to give up for your eating disorder? What are you not willing to give up?
- Is there any small step or decision you could make right now that would support your recovery?
- Where can you get additional help?

5. **Maintenance - If you are struggling to figure out how you can continue or maintain your new behaviors once you have made changes:**
    - What kinds of situations—physical, situational, relational, or emotional—make you vulnerable to falling back into your behaviors?
    - Are there any similarities or patterns that you see when you find yourself struggling to maintain your recovery?
    - What tools or skills do you need to develop to maintain the progress that you worked so hard to achieve? What do you need to do to start working on those skills?
    - What kind of structure do you need to best support your recovery?
    - What would be the first behavior or feeling state that can signal to you that you are slipping?
    - What can you do now that will prevent you from falling backwards?
    - Who can you share this with? Who can you call when you are overwhelmed and need someone who can help you through it? How can you help yourself reach out to this person?

Writing Assignment: Identifying, Exploring, and Enhancing Your Motivation

Look back at the 10 phases of eating disorder recovery and be sure you have selected which phase best describes where you are right now. Now see which level of motivation best matches your recovery phase. For example, if you are in phase 5 of recovery, "Tried to change, but couldn't," the motivation level that most closely matches is level 3, because you are trying to take action, but feel stuck. In your journal, answer the questions for the motivation level that best matches your phase of eating disorder recovery. The questions are designed to help you evaluate your thoughts and feelings in areas where you feel stuck or unsure, gain insight into potential obstacles, or connect to some unexamined sources of motivation. Whenever you feel your motivation lagging, or if you think you need a little push to move further in your recovery process, come back to the levels of motivation and the questions associated and go through them to explore in detail how you can move forward. Exploring these issues, however long it takes, is most likely what is necessary for you to progress. Looking at your motivation and readiness begins to challenge you to think in new ways. You may already feel a bit frustrated, not know some of the answers, or feel like if you knew these things already you would not need this book. Have patience. As you go through the keys, you will gain new insights and skills, all of which will help your readiness and your reasons for wanting to change.

Personal Reflections:

Gwen: One of the biggest challenges for me in my recovery was maintaining the positive changes I made, thus I relapsed on three different occasions. It turned out that I was stuck in eating disorder recovery phase 6: "I am free from some of the behaviors, but not all of them." The motivation level that best matched where I was stuck was level 4 (maintenance), "Working to continue new behaviors," which addresses maintenance or preventing relapse. I would have enough motivation for long periods of time to free myself from the strict rules regarding what foods I allowed myself to eat, to resist the urge to lose more weight, to stop weighing myself, and many more, but I kept slipping. After going through and answering the questions related to maintenance level of motivation, I realized that there were other behaviors that I kept up, and kept private. I convinced myself that my workout schedule (compulsive exercise), my determination (perfectionism), and my propensity toward privacy (dishonesty when triggered or slipping) were harmless or actually helping me, when in reality they were really keeping me stuck.

It looked like this: Something would happen that would bring up thoughts and feelings of unworthiness, fear of judgment from others, or a fear of not measuring up. My thoughts would then trigger intense feelings of fear, insecurity, and self-doubt, which would catapult me back into my eating disorder thinking and the belief that losing weight was the solution instead of the problem. The situations which started me slipping were not that interesting or even unusual, but my habit of keeping my feelings to myself and handling my feelings "my own way" continued to lead me down the same road over and over.

Going through and answering the motivation questions is what helped me realize that all of my relapses started with a painful experience, which created painful feelings that were not shared with anyone. The belief that I should handle the feelings "my way" had to be reexamined honestly. When I did, I could see that I had several people ready and willing to be helpful and the only reason I wasn't sharing my feelings was because deep down I knew that "my way" wasn't really a way to help me work through my feelings as much as it was a way for me for me to avoid them or get rid of them. If I shared my feelings I would have to feel them and become "vulnerable," and I was afraid I wasn't strong enough for that. If I believed that I couldn't tolerate my feelings, it's easy to understand why I would want to protect myself and reduce my vulnerability by handling things in whatever way would help me avoid feeling: restricting food and compulsively exercising. After identifying this theme in my relapses, I realized that by not talking to anyone about my fear of the unknown, my deep-seated insecurities, and my desperate need to feel more in control, I was actually *fueling and protecting* my eating disorder. I needed to talk about my feelings instead of shutting down if I wanted to stay well. As I became more open in my therapy, and then with others, people were able to support me emotionally, reassure me when I needed it, and validate my feelings.

Carolyn: One of the things I helped Gwen do was remind her and continue to point out to her that restricting her food or doing anything else to change her weight or body was not going to "fix" the problem, or make her invulnerable to pain. In fact, Gwen had to begin to open up with me, in group, and with her husband, in order to learn that being vulnerable in this way actually helped her fight off her eating disorder voice, instead of listening to it and giving in to the behaviors it suggested would help her feel safe. Gwen learned that what she was most afraid of was exactly what she most needed.

Try and Try Again

Chances are you are in for a long journey and it will take trying many things many times. We say this not to discourage you, but to tell you the truth, so you don't expect too much of yourself or give up too soon. We have seen people get better in a few months, while others have taken many years. We have no way of knowing what the process will be like for you, but we do know that you can have some control over that. As you work through this book, you will be riding the ups and downs of motivation, the swings between determination and acquiescence, the vacillation between confidence and doubt, and a myriad of other feelings that go along with recovery. It is easy to become discouraged when you are trying to change your old eating disorder thoughts and behaviors. If your feelings become too overpowering, you might begin to believe it would be easier to just give up and stop trying. You might think if you don't try, you are protecting yourself from feeling like a failure or a disappointment. Truthfully, this might work, but only for a little while. You may retreat back to your eating disorder behaviors, back to what feels familiar and manageable, but very soon feelings of hopelessness will bubble up because now you feel bad about your eating disorder behaviors *and* you feel bad for giving up or not trying.

In addition to the feelings directly related to the eating disorder behaviors, people in recovery also have to work on *tolerating the feelings that are associated with trying*. This usually includes fear of failure or of facing an unpredictable outcome. These fears can provoke a lot of anxiety, but your life will be greatly improved when you learn how to tolerate this particular anxiety. Many of the most meaningful parts of life are dependent on learning the skill of tolerating your feelings. You will get specific help with this in Key 4.

Sometimes our clients come to therapy and gain insight into destructive eating or other weight-related behaviors, family of origin issues, difficult life experiences, and current fears and beliefs, but resist making any actual changes. To get better you will eventually have to *do* something different even if you are unsure, afraid, feel guilty, or in some other way are uncomfortable. Key 6 specifically deals with helping you make behavioral changes.

What is helpful to remember is that *even if you are not making any changes in your behaviors, you can still be making prog-*

ress. Sometimes it takes several attempts to accomplish a goal. Just by continuing to try—by not giving up—you are actually working on a very important aspect of recovery. Most everyone who recovers goes through periods of feeling discouraged and hopeless. After all, a change which requires you to completely reevaluate your current lifestyle, overcome significant obstacles, step out of your familiar patterns, and proceed into an uncertain future, could not occur without some self-doubt, fear, and setbacks along the way. It would be unrealistic to expect otherwise of yourself. To succeed you need to try and keep trying.

Recovery is Not a Linear Process

Don't be alarmed if your progress does not follow the identified phases in a linear fashion and you are not always moving forward. You will likely experience ups and downs, stalls, slips, and maybe even relapses. If you have been using your eating disorder behaviors to manage everything from food to feelings, it will not be easy to stop all at once. In fact, it's quite unlikely that you would be able to stop quickly and easily. You might make some progress, and feel OK about how your recovery is going, but then find yourself reverting back to old behaviors when life presents you with a new or stressful situation that you haven't learned to manage. You might find that you take care of yourself when with friends and coworkers, but then a visit home for the holidays throws you right back into old feelings and old ways of coping. Unfamiliar situations, like starting a new job or a new relationship, are likely to trigger or provoke feelings of insecurity and anxiety, which could lead to eating disorder behaviors if you haven't yet learned how to manage in healthier ways. All your experiences help to illuminate areas where you still need work. There is no way to know or predict how you will feel and react in every situation, so the best approach to adopt is trial and error. Slips and relapses can be very discouraging; they can also be informative because they show you where you are vulnerable in your recovery. Many people feel so badly when slips occur that they give up, but learning from your mistakes is the only way to know how to protect yourself the next time. Setbacks in recovery do not mean that you are back where you started, or that you should not try new things, or not go home for the holidays, but rather that you had an experience that you were unable to cope with *at that point in time*. Once you know that, you can start to look at the situation and figure out what happened. We want you to know that even if you are doing great and then end up falling back into your eating disorder behaviors, there is still plenty of reason to hold onto hope. We let all of our clients know that relapse is often part of recovery. We do not say this because we are trying to make excuses or make our clients feel better about slips or relapses, but because this is the truth.

We Have Been There

Our own recovery process came with good doses of resistance, doubts, fears, slips, and even relapse. There were many times when we ourselves experienced periods of no change, were filled with doubt, felt too afraid to take a step, became discouraged, believed we just couldn't do it, and worried we would never get better—and yet, we are both here today fully recovered. We made it through these periods of inaction or slipping back, and we offer ourselves as reminders of hope that you can too. Using our own recovery, our experiences as eating disorder therapists, and our past relationship with each other as therapist and client, we offer readers a very personal account of the process of going from disordered to recovered. We believe that sharing our own recovery will provide you with:

- A tangible example of someone who has recovered.
- Insider details of what the process of recovery is like.

- Warning signs for some of the common pitfalls people experience during recovery.
- Ideas and strategies that work to better prepare yourself for challenges.
- Patience, because our struggles were real, long, and hard.
- Motivation and hope, because if we can do it, you can too.

Working With Someone Who is Recovered

In the data collected from our clients in our private practices, graduates of the Monte Nido treatment program, and research studies on people who have recovered, one thing is clear: recovered people report that working with others who "have been there" was one of the most helpful aspects of their recovery. We are not saying you have to work with a recovered therapist. We do think that you need to find connection with someone recovered to help you in your journey whether it is a professional, friend, mentor, or otherwise. We hope the following quotes from clients will encourage you to find someone who has recovered.

> *"Working with people who were recovered gave me the motivation I wasn't capable of finding inside myself. When I was feeling absolutely horrible in the beginning stages of recovery, to hear someone whom I admire and respect tell me that they had gone through a similar feeling or situation, and by persevering they are now on the other side of it, helped me realize this feeling was only temporary. To be able to see people who have been scared or in pain, but have pushed through it, and are now some of the healthiest, wisest people I have come across in my life, is what made the difference for me."*
>
> —AA

> *"To make the commitment in my recovery, I needed more than a leap of faith; I needed to know that being recovered is possible. I needed to see real examples that there is a life of being recovered that is more rewarding than what the eating disorder allowed me, and that it is worth the pain of the recovery process to get there."*
>
> —LK

Looking Ahead

Just as there is not a day you can point to and say, "That is when I officially got an eating disorder," there is no specific day when you will be recovered. Getting and getting over an eating disorder involves a long process. You will have glimpses of being recovered along the way and then for increasingly longer periods of time you will feel free of your eating disorder. Eventually you will realize that you are living your life according to the definition of "recovered" we described earlier in this key. Nobody but you can decide this or determine if you are there. When you are fully recovered your eating disorder will feel totally gone, a thing of the past, but you will not be the exact same person you were before it started. Think about it—if you went back to being the exact same person you were prior to developing an eating disorder, if you thought the same and acted the same, you would develop an eating disorder again. Through the recovery process you will come to a new understanding of yourself, let things go, use new coping skills, engage in different behaviors, and discover how to lead a more authentic life.

Writing Assignment:
A Day In My Life When I Am Recovered

Try to create a picture in your mind of what being recovered might look like for you. It may help to read over our definition of being "recovered." Take some time to imagine a day in your life when you are fully recovered. Visualize in as much detail as possible what you are doing, what you are wearing, who you are with, how you feel about life, how you feel in your body, what profession you are in, what hobby or activities you enjoy, or whatever else you would like to be true for you. (Remember, sometimes we are afraid of the very same things that we want. Even if you are afraid of the recovered life, try to do this assignment anyway.) Imagining yourself as recovered is setting an intention for the future. Having a clear picture in your mind where you see yourself successful, happy, and doing something you love, such as having a child, hanging out with friends, or even just feeling comfortable, can provide helpful visuals and reminders when things feel tough. It might help you to know that research on visualization shows that it works. Visualization actually helps your brain to perform a task. Olympic skiers will repeatedly visualize themselves skiing down the mountain as a way to practice before the event because doing so actually enhances performance. Visualization helps set your mind up to accomplish what you want.

Personal Reflections:

Carolyn: Even before I was sure I could get better, I started taking time to visualize what it would be like. It was hard, but I had read about the power of visualization and thought I would give it a try. I would visualize myself doing specific things in relationship to my eating disorder that I found very hard to do, such as going out to dinner with friends and ordering whatever I wanted on the menu instead of the least caloric item. I visualized how I was dressed and who was there with me and how I would choose exactly what I liked, not what seemed "safe." I would see myself eating it and having fun with my friends. I also remember imagining myself ordering an appropriate meal on a date, right before the date took place. I also actually imagined myself teaching high school. I saw myself helping students and serving as a healthy role model and making a difference in people's lives. Teaching actually then did become my first job before I became a therapist. My visualization practice helped me go through some difficult times. I teach this technique to my clients today and continue to use it in my life.

Messages From Others

We offer the following quotes from clients to bring home messages of patience, motivation, and hope. We purposely have selected individuals who had long hard struggles with their eating disorders. Every one of them suffered with an eating disorder for over 10 years and had treatment failures and relapses. All of these individuals had loved ones who had lost their patience and given up on them. These are individuals who at one point had given up hope as well. The point is, all of them are well today! They offer words of encouragement that no matter how long it takes or how hard it is, it is possible.

"I would read stories of people who were in recovery or people who had got past the demeaning and controlling voice inside their head, but I did not and would not accept that I could be one of those people who survived and lived to tell the story. Don't let that voice tell you the same lie. Life is so good and if

MOTIVATION, PATIENCE, AND HOPE

I had known how good it could be and that full recovery was possible I would have changed a long time ago. I won't paint a pretty picture; going through the process is torturous at times. However, it is also the most rewarding and most insightful experience you will ever have. I feel lucky to have gone through it because I am a stronger, wiser, and healthier person now, and I feel I have skills to navigate this world that are far greater than those who have not had my experiences. I believe in myself now, and because of that I know I can continue into being fully recovered."

—JW

"When I first met Carolyn I told her I did not want to recover, that it was not possible for me because I knew that my eating disorder was stronger than I was. I was sure of it because, at 22, I had already been through three unsuccessful attempts at recovery in treatment programs and had been suffering from my eating disorder since I was nine. Carolyn told me then, and I came to see, that my eating disorder could not be stronger than me because it was me. Then I met many others, like me, who had also previously failed treatment, and yet were recovered. That gave me hope. I began to realize I could do it too and thinking otherwise was an excuse not to try."

—PM

"People often wonder how I got better after so many years and so many slips and lapses. There are a few things that stand out and I offer them as hope because if someone like me who suffered for 15 years can get better, I think anyone can. I had thought my eating disorder showed my strength and willpower, but I realized that the harder thing to do was not engage in behaviors and notice how much stronger I felt each time I disobeyed my disorder. When I noticed how much more people genuinely enjoyed my company when I was not using my eating disorder behaviors and how much more love I got when I

was doing the harder thing it was extremely motivating. I finally realized that I wanted to live and have relationships more than I wanted my eating disorder."

—MP

"Feeling hopeless didn't mean I was hopeless. The only difference between someone who gets better and someone who doesn't is whether or not that person gives up and stops trying. I had many opportunities to give up since I had multiple treatments that did not work. My parents stopped talking to me and I felt sure I would not recover, but I did not give up trying. After years of thinking I would never get better and looking for an answer outside myself, I finally realized it was up to me. I learned how to use my healthy self to fight off my eating disorder self and internalize the process, which I had needed all along. This helped me see that it was possible. Knowing that it was hard, and that hard times didn't mean I wasn't getting better, was also really helpful. People do get better. There's a point when you just have to start believing you can get better. I learned at Monte Nido that energy follows thought. When I thought I could do it and I started to see results, no matter how small, I gained more faith in myself and more strength to keep going."

—PK

Some Final Thoughts

Change is not easy, it is not a linear process, and your motivation to change or recover isn't something that you "get" once and then never have to work on again. We hope you are reassured that ambivalence or reluctance are normal and do not mean you cannot recover. We hope you have assessed where you are and where you want to go, accepting what is now and committing to not giving up. In our experience, people who

MOTIVATION, PATIENCE, AND HOPE

don't get better are the ones who, for whatever reason, stop trying. Stay with it and you can recover from your eating disorder, reclaim yourself, and create a life that includes peace, joy, and fulfillment. Of course, nobody will be able to force you to keep trying or make changes (at least lasting ones) unless you ultimately decide you want to change for yourself. Even if you are not completely ready to give up your eating disorder, there is some part of you that wants to get better, is interested in a better life, or at least is willing to explore the possibility. It is this part of you that is reading this book and it is the part of you that we call your "healthy self." Key 2 will discuss how to strengthen your healthy self so that it can be in charge and help you recover.

KEY 2:

YOUR HEALTHY SELF WILL HEAL YOUR EATING DISORDER SELF

No one can make you get better. The battle for recovery is not between you and me. It's not between your eating disorder and anyone else. The battle you have to fight to get better is inside of you. The battle you have to fight is between your healthy self and your eating disorder self.

—Carolyn to Gwen at the beginning of treatment

You Have an Eating Disorder Self and a Healthy Self

Chances are, you are aware of an internal battle going on in your head. If you want to eat dinner but hear yourself saying, "You can't eat or you will get fat," or if you are eating dinner and hear a voice saying, "You need to get rid of all this food right away," these directives are from a part of you we call your "eating disorder self." For various reasons that will be revealed throughout this book, some people more than others are susceptible to developing an eating disorder. If you have an eating disorder it means that over time, as you binged or dieted, made these comments to yourself and engaged in extreme weight loss behaviors, your thoughts and actions began to take on a life of their own. Soon there was a part of you that did things automatically. This part of yourself acts stronger and stronger and becomes a separate, adaptive, disordered self, the "eating disorder self," which is different from the core "healthy" part of you. The eating disorder self has different feelings, thoughts, and behaviors than your "healthy self." Your "eating disorder self" may tell you to get rid of your dinner, but your "healthy self" understands that vomiting your dinner is not an appropriate or healthy thing to do. Just ask yourself what you would say to someone else in your same situation. What would you say to a little girl who claims she must throw up her dinner to avoid becoming fat? We are pretty sure you would reassure her that she does not need to do so, and you would perhaps even try to explain the dangers of such behavior. Your healthy self comes forward to help others, but is quickly overpowered by your eating disorder self when it comes to you. It is your eating disorder self that will "talk you into" behaviors like vomiting, not eating all day, taking laxatives, cutting your food into tiny bits, or eating a whole box of cookies because you ate one.

We teach our clients about the concept of the eating disorder self and the healthy self. We believe that identifying and understanding these two aspects of yourself will help you understand your eating disorder, learn how to resist it, and ultimately get you well. The goal is not to try to *get rid* of your eating disorder self, but to learn from it, discover what it is doing for you, and then strengthen your healthy self to take over its job. When your healthy self is strong enough to deal with all that comes your way in life, your eating disorder self will no longer be useful or necessary. You will be able to handle your problems, even those concerning weight and shape, without resorting to eating disorder behaviors. Over time your eating disorder self will cease to exist and the two parts of your self will again be one. If this sounds silly, complicated, or like we're accusing you of having multiple personalities, hang in there and we're sure the concept will become clear as we go on.

Recognizing, Accepting, and Working With Your Two Selves

Usually by the time people come to our offices for help, they have developed a strong eating disorder self that is in charge and has taken over. Like most of our clients, you may find that the things you used to know, believe, and say to yourself have become suppressed, and your eating disorder thoughts have become who you think you are. Sometimes people become confused when first presented with the concept of eating disorder self and healthy self, but for others the idea immediately makes sense or resonates. For example, when one client with bulimia was presented with the concept of the eating disorder self, she responded by saying, "Oh, you mean Mr. Binge?" She then got out her journal and opened to a page where she had drawn pictures of a half-monster, half-girl creature who "took her over" during binge and purge episodes. If you binge eat, whether or not you purge, you are more likely to relate immediately to the idea of having an eating disorder self because you already identify with the feeling of having a part of you that is out of control and takes over. Most likely you want to regain control and get rid of the part of you that binges. On the other hand, if you have anorexia or are very restrictive with food, you are more likely to experience satisfaction, or even pride, in your ability to control your food intake and your weight. You may think your thoughts and behaviors around food and weight are "just who you are" and thus don't relate to the concept of having an eating disorder self and a healthy self. One client had this to say:

> *"The ability to distinguish and separate my eating disorder self from my healthy self is a vital part of my ability to continue to fight, heal, and recover. However, my initial reaction to the idea was a feeling of anger and resentment. This concept threatened the sense of wholeness and safety I felt as long as I*

identified completely with my disorder. Embracing two selves meant realizing that I was not bound by my eating disorder voice or its dictates, but that I had a choice, another part of me could choose to act differently. Initially this choice seemed threatening because if I was able to separate my healthy self from my eating disorder self then I risked what felt akin to losing my existence or what I thought was "my self" in the process. Ironically, however, it is this very concept that today is the cornerstone of my recovery."

—VE

We have found that most of our clients eventually come to appreciate and benefit from learning how to recognize the presence of both an eating disorder self and a healthy self inside. Recognizing these two parts of self creates a foundation for learning from the eating disorder self what it needs and strengthening the healthy self to take back control.

Taking Responsibility for Your Eating Disorder Self

We are not asking you to conceptualize your eating disorder self as a "bad" outside entity you have to eradicate. We have found that making enemies with your eating disorder self is not effective for long-term recovery. If you believe your eating disorder is "all bad" you might tend to feel ashamed and hide your behaviors rather than seeking help. If you see your eating disorder self as "all bad" you might never pay attention to its underlying messages. Furthermore, viewing your eating disorder self as an entity separate from yourself can lead to abdication of responsibility for your behaviors and your recovery, or, "My eating disorder made me do it!" If you take this perspective, you can be tricked into thinking that your eating disorder is more powerful than you. In truth, your eating disorder cannot possibly be more powerful than you because it *is a part of you.* It gets all its power from you, just as your healthy self does. Rather than, "My eating disorder made me do it," we would have you say, "My eating disorder *self* did it." It is a part of you for which you must take responsibility. Taking responsibility for it means you have to pay attention to it, listen to it, and learn what it might be doing for you.

Writing Assignment: A Thank You Letter to Your Eating Disorder Self

To begin to help you get clear on what purpose your eating disorder might be serving, write a letter to your eating disorder self thanking it for whatever you think it has done for you, such as keeping you thin or helping you deal with your anger, or assisting you in feeling unique or special. Write everything you can think of. Let your eating disorder self know what you think might have happened or might happen without it being there for you. Read over the letter. See if you can come up with and write about alternatives for how you could have handled or can handle situations instead of using your eating disorder. (This begins to bring out the healthy part of you.)

Distinguishing Between Your Eating Disorder Self and Healthy Self

To help you distinguish between your eating disorder self and your healthy self, let's look at examples of common statements from clients and begin to sort it out:

- *"Part of me wants to get better and part of me doesn't."* Ambivalent statements like these are one of the most common ways to recognize you have both a healthy self and an eating disorder self. You may claim there is nothing more important than ending the cycle of bingeing (healthy self), but then later that same night you binge (eating disorder self). You may agree to do something different with food that promotes or facilitates your recovery (healthy self), but when the time comes to do it, another part of you talks you out of it (eating disorder self). The goal is to recognize this internal battle and reinstate your healthy self as the one in charge.

- *"I feel like there's this monster inside of me."* Many clients with bulimia or binge-eating issues feel like there is some other monstrous aspect of them that takes over at times, leading them to binge and sometimes purge. It is important to understand that the monster is within, a part of the person that has gotten out of control (eating disorder self). The part of the person that knows there is a destructive force inside is the healthy self.
- *"I know I wear a size 4, but when I look in the mirror, I see a fat person staring back."* The healthy self of this client was a rational, bright person who knew a size 4 meant she was not fat. Yet, when she looked in the mirror, she saw herself through the eyes of her eating disorder self, which overshadowed her ability to reason and recognize her true body size. Her distorted perception came from her eating disorder self.
- *"I tell myself I'm not going to binge, and then something comes over me and I feel like it's out of my control."* As soon as you notice you are telling your "self" something, you know that part of you is doing the telling and part of you is doing the listening. In this case, the client's healthy self was telling her not to binge, but then her eating disorder self took over. With practice, you will get better and better at distinguishing your eating disorder self from your healthy self.
- *"I want to get better, but I don't want to gain weight."* Wanting to get better comes from the healthy part of you.

YOUR HEALTHY SELF WILL HEAL YOUR E.D. SELF

> Your eating disorder self will try to bargain in order to not have to gain weight or change other behaviors for fear of becoming fat, or some other fear.

You may never have thought about having an eating disorder self, but once you understand the concept and begin to take notice of your thoughts and actions, you will begin to recognize that part of yourself. When you begin to work with this concept and do some of the assignments you will gain increased understanding. Your healthy self used to be the only voice you heard in your head, but it is now being overshadowed by the voice of your louder and often more familiar eating disorder self, which says all kinds of things that keep you afraid or stuck.

One client explains her initial resistance to, and then acceptance of, the eating disorder versus healthy self-concept:

"When the concept of eating disorder self and healthy self was first mentioned to me I had no clue what was being talked about because I didn't see the two as separate, probably because I didn't have much of a healthy self. I thought the things I thought and did were just that, the things I thought and did. I woke up, I didn't eat, I worked out for hours, and then I binged and purged at night. I knew it wasn't normal, but for me it had become normal so there was no voice or side of me that ever really challenged it. Slowly, in therapy the healthy part of me was pointed out. What really helped was when I was in a situation and wanting to listen to what my eating disorder was telling me and I was asked what I would say to someone else in my situation. Coming up with what I would say to someone else helped me see that I did have a healthy self in me, she'd just been bound and gagged by my eating disorder self for so long I didn't even know she was in there. As my healthy self became stronger I was able to talk back to my eating disorder, open up, connect, and build relationships. Once I knew I had a healthy self it made it much harder to go back to my eating disorder, even in the times when I so desperately wanted to. When

my healthy self was in control I had much better relationships with others. The only way I was going to keep my relationships was not going back to the way things were."

—CR

Your Healthy Self Will Heal Your Eating Disorder Self

We don't put the emphasis on getting rid of your eating disorder self, but rather on strengthening your healthy self to do its job. Getting your healthy self stronger takes time, and working at it varies in degree and intensity from individual to individual. Of course, in order to recover you need to get rid of your eating disorder behaviors, but you will learn to view your eating disorder self as the part of you that alerts you about something you are feeling or that needs your attention. You need to learn how to listen to this part of yourself, determine what is going on, and figure out the best way to respond, other than by engaging in eating disorder behaviors. The fact that something is wrong is important, but the way your eating disorder self tells you to handle it is unnecessary and self-destructive: "Don't eat that," "Go buy your favorite binge food," "You must purge." Engaging in these behaviors does not solve things for you, make you happy, or bring you true peace of mind. Your eating disorder will continue and any underlying issues you may have (see Key 3) will be left unresolved. Learning how to not react to, but rather to pay attention to and deal with, the real feelings or needs underlying these thoughts and behaviors is the goal. When your healthy self is strong enough and can handle the various things that happen to you in life, there is no more reason for your eating disorder self to exist. Your eating disorder self will no longer be an "eating disorder self," it will just be the part of you that lets you know that something is wrong. Then it is the job of your healthy self to take care of it. When your healthy self is fully in charge, you will no longer feel powerless to your eating disorder thoughts and compelled to use your eating disorder behaviors. In fact, eventually you will no longer even have eating disorder thoughts. When this happens we say that your eating disorder self has been integrated back into your healthy self, which we will discuss in more detail further on.

Personal Reflections:

Gwen: Being able to recognize my "healthy self" apart from my "eating disorder self" was a major challenge in my recovery. At first I didn't understand the concept at all. I went through a phase of really believing I simply did not have a healthy self. I thought my eating disorder self had really become my *self*. I even tried to fake having a healthy self and imagine what I would say if I had one. Faking it turned out to be quite helpful for me. I realized that I did have a healthy self and knew what to say to others, but I just never used it for myself. Now as a therapist, I encourage clients to just try to imagine what their healthy self would say if they had one. This technique always seems to help. In my own process of working with this concept, I was often confused when I was acting from my eating disorder self and when I was not. Sometimes what sounded like a healthy part of me talking turned out to be my eating disorder self trying to get its way. For example, I often justified my desire to exercise as a need for some fresh air, and a tool to improve my mood, clear my head, and otherwise take good care of myself. I knew those were "healthy–sounding" statements, but in truth, those responses were really my eating disorder trying to find a way to burn off more calories. It took me awhile to unearth my real, authentic, healthy self. I had become quite adept at fooling others and even myself. Seeing how manipulative my eating disorder had made me was painful and scary sometimes. After so many years, I was afraid that nobody would be able to help me or stop my eating disorder self, but the assignments, gentle confrontations, and nonjudgmental questioning by Carolyn allowed me to slowly develop a clearer understanding of myself and the dynamics of my eating disorder. When I shared these feelings of fear and doubt with Carolyn and others I finally felt some connection with my authentic healthy voice. For example, if I wanted to, but was afraid of not being able to get well, it was obvious to me that the fear was coming from my healthy self, because my eating disorder self would not care if I didn't recover.

Carolyn: When Gwen came for treatment, she had been living with her eating disorder for many years without any prior attempts to seek recovery. She was also in denial about the seriousness of her situation. Gwen had a husband and children, and was able to function at a relatively high level in many areas of her life, which only validated her distorted belief that she was really "OK." In truth, Gwen was very ill at the time of her admission. Her anorexia was completely in charge. Gwen reluctantly presented for treatment only after suffering a seizure triggered by her eating disorder behaviors. (Seizures are one of the many health risks of eating disorders.) Avoiding another seizure was the only motivator she could summon for recovery. At the time, Gwen really believed her "eating disorder self" was just "who she was," and many of my attempts to connect to a healthy part of herself only served to increase her resistance. Gwen's love and protection for her three children were very evident in the things she did and said. I could hear her healthy self when she talked about the needs and lives of her kids. It was in Gwen's love for her children where I found my entrance to her healthy self.

Gwen and I talked about topics such as her weight, and her "addiction" to weighing herself, or denying herself certain foods. I often asked her to imagine what she would tell her young daughter about these same issues. She easily recognized the discrepancy between how she would respond to and what she would say to her daughter and what she said to herself. Here was the evidence I needed of Gwen's ability to access her healthy self. Similarly, I also observed how healthy, caring, and recovery-minded Gwen sounded when she offered feedback to other clients in group therapy sessions. I began to use that observation as another way into Gwen's healthy self. After all, if Gwen believed that what she was saying was true for others, why wouldn't it be true for her too? She initially attempted to explain this discrepancy away, but I could tell she was beginning to internalize my feedback and recognize her own healthy self. A primary focus in Gwen's treatment, as in most cases, was helping her to distinguish the behaviors driven by her eating disorder self from the behaviors truly motivated by her healthy self. This awareness took time to develop, but over time, she grew more adept at differentiating between the two.

Strengthening Your Healthy Self

To strengthen your healthy self, you have to practice talking back to your eating disorder self, even if at first you don't believe what you are saying. When we first ask clients how they generally respond to one of their eating disorder thoughts such as "Don't eat that or you will get fat," we usually get a blank stare in return. In the beginning, clients often tell us that they have no idea what to say back when they hear eating disorder thoughts like that. Challenging and talking back to your eating disorder self is usually hard. It takes practice to create a repertoire of responses so that you more readily are prepared to combat your eating disorder voice. You will need to be able to come up with statements from your healthy self that are unique to you and your situation, but reading examples written by others can help in eliciting ideas. Our clients have come up with several healthy self-statements to counteract the eating disorder voice.

Effective, Healthy "Self Statements"

- I want to be a role model for other girls and women by accepting my body.
- If I overeat, I know that I can get back on track without restricting or purging.
- What good is having this body if I don't have any fun in it?
- Being alone with my "desired" body doesn't work. Bigger jeans = bigger life!
- This feeling seems intolerable, but it is just a feeling and it will fade.
- I *know* that I have a distorted body image and do not see myself as others do.
- My best thinking got me here. Maybe it is time that I try something else.
- When it comes to weight, 300 calories of cheese and crackers is no different than 300 calories of fruit.
- There are no good foods or bad foods. No specific food can make me fat.
- I need to think about what I want to eat, instead of just what has the least calories.
- Restricting my food will just set me up for bingeing later.
- Full is not the same thing as fat.
- Right now I cannot be the judge of my own body.
- Other people I love and respect are recovered, so I can get there too.
- If I never learn to tolerate my natural body, I will never get well.
- I want to have relationships and fun and I can't have those *and* my eating disorder.
- Having weight loss as my goal keeps me sick and I am letting it go.
- There is never a "thin enough" I will get to; I need to start acceptance right now.
- Exercise is only healthy for me if it is a choice and not an obligation.

- It does not take any willpower for me to pass up a cookie. What is hard for me is to eat the cookie; that is how I will exercise my own free will.
- Balance is the key, not extreme thinking or acting.
- Any self-esteem I think I am gaining from my body is being cancelled out by what I am doing to myself to get it.

You are probably thinking what most of our clients are thinking at this point, which is *But what if I don't believe these statements? Even if I say them I won't mean it.* We have three important things to say: 1) you have to practice. For example, a baseball player has to practice in the batting cage to sharpen his skills and reflexes for when those skills and reflexes will be called upon in the game; 2) come up with something you do believe and would say to a young child or best friend in the same situation; 3) trust us, you have nothing to lose.

Contacting and Transforming Your Eating Disorder Self

We believe it is important to contact your eating disorder self and begin to learn from it, have discussions with it, and ultimately transform it.

One way to contact your eating disorder self is to journal prior to engaging in one of your eating disorder behaviors, such as a before bingeing or purging, or skipping a meal. It is important that you understand that we are not asking you to journal *instead of doing the behavior,* but rather, *before you do the behavior.* If simply journaling instead of engaging in a behavior was effective in stopping the behavior we would not have jobs and you would not have an eating disorder. Unfortunately, it does not work. If you would like to stop a behavior, but you persist in the behavior anyway, you will need to access and understand the part of you holding on to it. Journaling before engaging in the behavior helps you gain an understanding of why you might be doing it and what you fear might happen if you stop doing it. Journaling is an important step toward making more conscious choices and ultimately putting your healthy self back in control. Knowing what to say to yourself when faced with eating disorder thoughts and urges, and not backing down when your eating disorder self speaks up again, is the key to strengthening your healthy self. External controls such as punishments, coercion exerted by friends or family members, or even going to a treatment program may work to contain eating disorder behaviors in the beginning, but unless you internalize the ability to talk back to your eating disorder self, and get your healthy self in charge, the eating disorder self can easily take over again, and will do so when the external controls are removed. Having a repertoire of Healthy Self Statements available is useful, but taking it further to developing an effective internal dialogue where you can spontaneously respond to your eating disorder on your own is the goal.

Counteracting an Eating Disorder Thought

The following is a list of examples provided by our clients demonstrating how to challenge an eating disorder thought. These are short and to the point and will give you ideas to help you quickly and assertively challenge your eating disorder self.

1. **Eating Disorder (ED) Self**: The only way I can feel OK with myself and deal with my emotions is to restrict and exercise.
   Healthy Self: Even when you exercise and restrict you still don't feel OK with yourself. Yes, it numbs you from your emotions temporarily, but those feelings don't go away, they always come back. Exercising and restricting is only a quick fix.
2. **ED Self**: I had such a hard day. I deserve to eat whatever

I want, which is a *whole* chocolate cake. Nothing will make me feel as good as bingeing does.

Healthy Self: You did have a very hard day. You need to do something fun, or find something to help release all of your stress, like yoga or a nice bath, and have a piece of cake too. Eating the whole cake will feel good while you're eating, but afterwards you just feel ashamed and even more stressed out about your eating and weight.

3. **ED Self:** Even when I am at a healthy weight I will be miserable, so I might as well be thin and miserable, rather than fat and miserable.

   Healthy Self: You can't predict how you will feel at a healthy weight because you have never been there long enough. All you know for sure is that you are absolutely miserable and alone when you are sickly thin. That is a known fact, whereas you don't know how you will feel if you gain weight and become healthy.

4. **ED Self:** Even if I resist bingeing this one time, I am still fat, and what will one night of healthy eating matter anyway? Seems like a waste of time to try.

   Healthy Self: Every time you are able to eat in a balanced and healthy way instead of bingeing, you are strengthening your skills for the next time. It's never a waste to try.

5. **ED Self:** If I don't lose weight, I can't ever be happy.

   Healthy Self: Your mind is in control of your happiness, not your body. There are plenty of people who weigh as much or more than you who are happy. If you work on making your life happier in a variety of ways, you might focus less on food, and both your mind and body will improve.

Writing Assignment: Your Eating Disorder Thoughts

Get your journal and write down several of your recent eating disorder thoughts. Try writing back to each eating disorder thought from your healthy self, using the examples from our clients if you get stuck. It might help if you ask yourself how you would respond if someone else expressed the eating disorder thought to you. It is usually easier to come up with what you would say to someone else.

Challenging your eating disorder thoughts helps you gain awareness and increases your ability to counteract them, quiet them, and then be able to respond to them in a healthy way. If you practice and persist, you will eventually find yourself better able to come right back from your healthy self when your eating disorder self speaks out or begins to take over. Be patient with yourself. There will be times when you can't counteract the eating disorder thought or times when you get frustrated for even continuing to have eating disorder thoughts. A client illustrates this process in her own words below:

> *"I learned to practice and at the same time have patience and awareness when I am having a 'fat chat' in my head, instead of criticizing and scolding myself for not being able to always 'change the negative thought.' It is hard enough having these chronic negative thoughts. I can practice simply noticing that I am having them, name them, realize that they are the eating disorder thoughts, and have patience with myself that it's not something that can be flipped by a switch to turn off. The chatter will come and go—being aware of it is one step toward dealing with it and distinguishing that there is the eating disorder, and that I am also an individual and the eating disorder is not all of me."*
>
> —KB

Dialoguing With Your Eating Disorder Self and Your Healthy Self

At first, when you begin to challenge your eating disorder thoughts, you might say a sentence or a few sentences. Eventually, however, the idea is for you to engage in a lengthy back-and-forth dialogue between your eating disorder self and your healthy self. Usually writing things down from your eating disorder self is easy but writing back from your healthy self is more difficult, and you get tripped up, not knowing what to say, or believing in the words you are saying. With practice, and perhaps by even going over your journaling with your therapist or someone else you trust, the process will become easier and you will get better and better at it. Writing out full dialogues on paper helps you formulate counterarguments and responses to your eating disorder self. Eventually your healthy self will be prepared, and will know what to say and how to help you resist.

Through dialoguing you will be able to see more clearly how your eating disorder is influencing your thoughts and behaviors and also your life. The following is an example of a client's full dialogue. There are many ways to do a dialogue and this is just one example:

ED Self: "Today I have to be perfect. No extras, no salad dressing, not one calorie more than my allotment. I'm only allowing myself a small salad all day with no dressing, gym right after, and no extras. I have to make up for what I ate yesterday when I met my friends for lunch. I already feel fat from it. I have no excuse for eating as much as I did. I'm so weak when I am around other people. I should say no when people ask me out."

Healthy Self: "Do you really think it will make you happy to sit home alone just so you don't have to eat with people? That sounds like a sad life. Your lunch was fine. You can't just eat salad for the rest of your life and there is no need to. You have trained yourself to feel guilty for eating and have forgotten what is really important to you."

ED Self: "Maybe someday when I am thin I can splurge and eat out with others. I don't have enough self-control to do that now. If I want to look good I need to be strong and stop caving in to everything I want; no wonder I look like this. I'm embarrassed to be seen like this. This is what thin people have to do. They eat salad. This is what is important to me."

Healthy Self: "Do you really want to eat only salads? It does not seem to make you happy or bring you joy and you are not much fun to be around. What is the point of being thin if you can only eat salads, and are alone?"

ED Self: "I feel good when people tell me they wish they could eat like me and resist desserts. This makes me feel special and in control. Without that I don't think there is anything good about me. At least it is something people admire."

Healthy Self: "But even you know that if people saw what you ate later when they aren't around, they would think differently and be bothered and/or worried. Now you always wonder, *If people really knew me, what would they think?* You used to have fun, you went out dancing, had crushes, and many friends. Now you are obsessed with your diet and the gym and feel worse about everything in your life. Your whole life is about starving and feeling good temporarily, only to end up bingeing and feeling horrible about yourself. Does this make sense to you?"

ED Self: "Not really. I feel sad when I think about the fun I used to have. I forget how much I've changed, but I don't know what to do with myself right now."

Healthy Self: "OK, we will make a plan together for the next 24 hours and just try it and see how it goes."

ED Self: "OK, I will try."

Healthy Self: "That's a start!"

Writing Assignment: Dialoguing With Your Two Selves

Pick a time when you are having eating disorder thoughts, get your journal, and begin to write back. Let the dialogue flow between your two parts of self. We guarantee that this process will get easier. Remember that if you feel stuck, you can think of what you would say if someone else you cared about was saying the things your eating disorder self says to you. Be sure to end the dialogue with your healthy self getting the last word. We cannot emphasize enough how important dialoguing is in helping your healthy self get back in control.

Role Play: Dialoguing Out Loud

Talking back or role-playing with another person is another way to dialogue with your two selves. Think about whom you could ask to role-play with you, such as a relative, friend, mentor, or therapist. You can say your eating disorder thoughts out loud and let the other person counteract those thoughts. It is imperative to also let the other person play the role of your eating disorder self while you talk back from the healthy self position. With time and practice, you will begin to hear your healthy self or "healthy voice" becoming stronger. The stronger this voice becomes, the stronger your healthy self becomes. The degree of your recovery is the degree that your healthy self is in control.

> *"In therapy, I practiced saying my eating disordered thoughts out loud. I had been so ashamed of them before, but once I started saying them and having someone else counter them over and over again, it became clear to me that they were not true. Now I'm better able to counter those thoughts myself. Practicing with someone else helped me so much that now my healthy self can override my eating disorder thoughts once I'm aware of what's happening."*
>
> —MM

Integrating Your Eating Disorder Self and Healthy Self to Become Whole

As we have noted already, the final goal in the recovery process is to become a whole and integrated person, erasing the experience of two separate parts of self. If you continue to work at contacting your eating disorder self, challenging the way it tells you to behave, and working at finding alternatives, you will go through a series of stages to final recovery, or what we call "integration." Your eating disorder self will be out of a job once you discover how it serves you and then allow your healthy self to do that job instead. (Remember, even if you have not figured out the purpose it serves, your healthy self can still get back in control by not letting the eating disorder thoughts dictate what you do.) The process of integration is automatic and happens over time, as your eating disorder self is no longer necessary and your healthy self is in control. You will find yourself one day looking back and realizing you are no longer engaging in your eating disorder behaviors, and even further down the road you won't even be thinking those thoughts. From our own personal recovery and our professional experience, we have identified specific stages people go through in the process of integration.

Stages of Integration

1. **You engage in eating disorder behaviors with no real understanding of a separate eating disorder self.**

    This is when you are engaging in eating disorder thoughts and behaviors all the time and you feel like your behaviors are you. You may not have any idea that there is a part of you that is different or could be different. In fact, the idea that you have an eating disorder self or healthy self may seem stupid, frustrating, or belittling.

2. **You begin to recognize that you have two conflicting aspects of yourself, but still believe you need the eating disorder behaviors.**

    Here, you become aware that you have two opposing parts of self. There are many ways you may have come to this realization. You might want to go out with friends for lunch, but convince yourself you shouldn't or can't go after an inner battle between those two parts. You might notice your eating disorder self harassing you for wanting to make a different choice, or attempting to go against your first impulse with food. You might see how you talk to other people, but can't apply those same words and arguments to yourself. Someone else might point out to you that you seem or sound like two different people sometimes. At this stage, you might be beginning to develop awareness of a conflict inside of you, but you do not know what to do about it.

3. **You begin to use your healthy self to challenge your eating disorder self.**

    In this stage, you begin to see more clearly the part of you that does not want to engage in the eating disorder behaviors. You have glimpses into the possibility of getting well. You also begin to see there is a part of you that knows what to say to other people, but not to yourself. You might believe this healthy part of you has been repressed or overshadowed, and you would like to reinstate its control over your life. This stage can last a long time. You may make attempts to challenge your eating disorder, but then still engage in the behaviors. You may require outside help determining what is your healthy self verses your eating disorder self. You may doubt this "technique" or process will work for you and need a lot of encouragement in order to keep trying.

4. **Your healthy self is getting stronger, and you "get" the need to work hard and internalize fighting off your eating disorder self.**

    At this stage you see how your healthy self can help you recover, and that the real fight is inside of you. At this point, you are getting better at recognizing when your eating disorder self is talking and better at responding from your healthy self. You realize that it takes continued practice to fight off the eating disorder self.

5. **Your healthy self is increasingly in control, but your eating disorder self is still around, speaking up and taking over at times.**

    Over time, you will find your healthy self is increasingly winning out over your eating disorder self. Whereas in the beginning your healthy self might be in control very little, during this phase it begins to win close to 50 percent of the time and that increases to 60, 70, 80, or 90 percent as you keep working at recovery. Your eating disorder self still sneaks in and still takes over during times of stress or great difficulty. At some point your healthy self is mostly in control of symptoms, but your eating disorder thoughts are still present.

6. **Your healthy self is in charge, but old remnants of your eating disorder self are still around.**

    At this place in your recovery, the need for you to use eating disorder behaviors is gone, but you persist in having eating disorder thoughts. You are able to make decisions from your healthy self and the eating disorder self becomes a thing of the past, like an old friend. You believe your eating disorder might be gone, but you are careful because you are worried it might come back, since it has not been gone that long. You are definitely recovering but not sure or confident in saying it is all over and you are "recovered."

7. **Your eating disorder self and healthy self are integrated. You are recovered.**

You are not thinking in terms of healthy self or eating disorder self anymore. You are one person now with no feelings or thoughts of having two separate parts of self. You have no interest in or urge toward eating disorder behaviors, and no thoughts or pulls in that direction. You no longer experience staying well as a fight or feel like you have to be on guard in case your eating disorder self speaks up or comes back. You know how to turn to other people to get your needs met, or can handle things on your own. You are not thinking that this is your healthy self in control, but rather that this is who you are. Your healthy choices are automatic and come from an integrated whole self.

As we have already said in this book, you can't pinpoint the day when you got an eating disorder, and you will not all of a sudden one day be recovered. There is not a moment that marks the fully recovered point. It is more like if you were healing from a broken foot that required you to be in a wheelchair. You have to do exercises for mobility and strength until you are able to get out of the wheelchair and start using crutches. The crutches help you get around until you realize that a cane is all you really need. After awhile you realize you can walk without a cane or any assistance, but you have a slight limp. Your limping isn't so bad so you walk and walk and your limp vanishes. Eventually you can walk and run and dance and your foot continues to get stronger, until one day you realize your foot works just like it was never broken, maybe even better. You are "recovered" and there is no reason you will ever have to treat it delicately or feel broken again. You are the only one who can truly know if you are recovered from your eating disorder or not, and when you are there, don't let others tell you that you are just "recovering" and no one can be recovered. We know better, and you will too.

Final Thoughts

The severity of your eating disorder is the degree to which you continue to have an eating disorder self that is in control of your thoughts, feelings, and behaviors. We have shown you that recovery involves connecting with and strengthening your healthy self and getting it back in control of your life. Once you do this your eating disorder behaviors will subside and your eating disorder self will be integrated back into your core self to take its proper place. What used to be an eating disorder self becomes a part of your healthy self that serves as an alert system, signaling that something needs to be attended to. What this something might be is what we will turn our focus to now in Key 3, It's Not About The Food.

Additional Assignments

Writing Assignment: Creating Your Own Healthy Self Statements

Come up with a list of statements that you know would be helpful in talking back to your eating disorder self. Put your list somewhere so you can look over it a few times a day. Continue to add to the list periodically. You might even keep your list with you so you can refer to it when having a difficult time. Share this list with family and friends so they also learn effective ways to respond to your eating disorder self.

Writing Assignment: A Goodbye Letter to the Eating Disorder Self

Even if you do not yet feel ready to do so, it can be very useful and enlightening to write a goodbye letter to your eating disorder self. Use your healthy self to tell your eating disorder self what it has done for you but also the price you have had to pay. Let it know you will not be following its directives anymore.

At some later time—the next hour, day, or week—write back from your eating disorder self and let it defend itself for why it needs to stay around. This exercise will help you discover what your eating disorder self still believes it is doing to serve you. Finally, don't let your eating disorder self have the last word. Write back from your healthy self again explaining how you can take care of yourself in a healthier way and where else you will get help. (Tip: Don't be hostile or abusive toward your eating disorder self. A true healthy self does not do that.) Once again: talk to your eating disorder self like you would talk to a friend you are trying to help who has an eating disorder.

Key 3

IT'S NOT ABOUT THE FOOD

Just getting in control of my food and weight was not enough. I had been to programs and worked with professionals who got me to stop my behaviors but since I never dealt with any of the underlying issues, the behaviors kept coming back. Until I dealt with why I starved, or why I purged when I did eat, my behaviors continued to provide me with comfort and distraction. Until I learned to replace what my eating disorder gave me with healthier ways of getting the same thing, I stayed sick. Now I know that any desire I have to restrict or purge my food is related to some other issue and I need to stop and take a look inside.

—CR

A commonly held assumption about eating disorders is, "It's not about the food." What does this mean? If it's an *eating* disorder, how can it not be about the food? People started using the phrase, "It's not about the food," to help explain the complexity of an eating disorder, and to help debunk the notion that it is all just about dieting and weight. What the statement means is that, even though your relationship with food has taken over your life, and normalizing your eating is essential for recovery, food itself is not the problem. Simply creating a meal plan or gaining weight won't cure an eating disorder. Treatment programs that provide consistent monitoring and control of your behaviors can help you gain weight or stop the binge-and-purge cycle, and some may find recovery this way, but for most this is not enough to guarantee lasting results. There are many factors that can contribute to the development of an eating disorder. In this key we will explore how you can go about addressing those that are relevant to you.

Whether or not your eating disorder began as a way to get healthier or lose weight, it quickly became much more. Chances are, your eating disorder has become a way you cope with other problems. Like many of our clients you might find yourself resistant to looking, or unable to see beyond issues of food and weight:

> *"When I was completely caught up in my bulimic cycle, you could not have convinced me that it was not about the food. I had heard about concepts like 'managing your emotions with food' and 'numbing your feelings with food,' but I really believed that those things did not apply to me. My eating disorder worked so well at managing my emotions and numbing my feelings that I was incapable of understanding what was happening. I thought all I needed was someone to help me get in control so I could lose weight. When I got some distance from my behaviors, it started to become clear how much they had helped me cope with a variety of underlying issues."*
>
> —SW

You may need help figuring out what else, besides your relationship with food, is wrong, or you may already know what is wrong, but are unable to change it.

> *"When there's fear or behaviors about or around food, that's a huge sign that there's something else going on . . . something I haven't looked at, dealt with, or cried about in a while, because when I am using my eating disorder behaviors I don't have to look at, deal with, or cry about much of anything because I'm focused on one thing: how to avoid calories or get rid of them."*
>
> —KL

Why Eating Disorders Are Not "About the Food"

There are four main, overarching reasons for why we say that your eating disorder is not about the food. We will list them here first and then describe each category in detail:

- An eating disorder is not about any particular food and is not an addiction to food.
- An eating disorder is fueled by a cultural climate, which causes negative feelings about your body, your image of it, and your relationship with it.
- Although many people diet to control or lose weight, those with an eating disorder usually have some other underlying issues that push them harder and further.
- It's not about the biological makeup of food, but rather the biological makeup of you, that contributes to the development of an eating disorder.

An Eating Disorder is Not About Any Particular Food and is Not An Addiction to Food.

There is *no* proof that binge-eating disorder, bulimia, or anorexia, which is essentially food refusal, are illnesses caused by any certain foods or food addiction. The 12-step addiction model was originally applied to eating disorders when it was used to help compulsive overeaters—now referred to as binge eaters—abstain from their "binge" foods. Later, this 12-step approach was adapted for bulimia and anorexia. The 12-step approach has helped many people with eating disorders, particularly those who binge, but not because any certain food or type of food is addicting, or abstinence from the food the cure. 12-step programs provide a variety of services that can be very helpful. They offer free support from others who have been there; they provide a sense of community, and have sponsors who are available to help outside of the group meetings. We particularly like the idea of people in recovery helping others along the way. In giving back you not only help others, but you strengthen recovery in yourself as well. We also appreciate that 12-step groups are available in most cities and sponsors can be called in the middle of the night. However, there are some aspects of the 12-step philosophy that can hinder or impede recovery from an eating disorder or can even be detrimental to recovery if they are not adjusted or adapted.

Adapting The 12-Step Model For Those With An Eating Disorder

1. We suggest that you use the model to work on your specific behaviors such as bingeing, restricting your food, or taking laxatives, rather than trying to abstain from certain foods. If you binge or binge and purge, abstaining from certain foods, such as sugar and white flour, can elevate their status in your mind and make you want them even more, contributing to a later binge. If you already restrict your food, write out something that clearly defines what would constitute restricting, for example, anything less than a certain amount of calories or less than three meals and three snacks.
2. In 12-Step meetings, there is a customary introduction: "Hi, I'm (name) and I am an anorexic." We believe that using the term "anorexic," "bulimic," or "compulsive overeater" reinforces the notion that the eating disorder is part of one's identity. We prefer our clients to perceive themselves as "suffering from anorexia," rather than as being an anorexic. We prefer that the person say, "Hi, I am (name) and I suffer from 'compulsive overeating' or 'bulimia' or 'anorexia' or even better, 'I suffer from an eating disorder.'"
3. The 12-step abstinence model involves "black and white," "all or nothing" modes of thinking. Such dichotomous thinking is problematic for eating disorder cli-

ents and can interfere with honesty and recovery. Furthermore eating is different than drinking. In AA there is no acceptable amount of drinking but obviously one has to eat and deciding what amount is enough and what is too much lands in the area of gray rather than black and white. Recovery involves slipping up, making mistakes, and learning from your symptoms and behaviors. There is too much perfectionism and obsessive thinking in the temperaments and personalities of many with eating disorders, and one of our tasks is helping people to learn to live more in the gray areas of life.

4. It is important to know that you can be fully "recovered" where the eating disorder is gone, a thing of the past. The 12-step philosophy uses the term "recovering." In the 12-step model, people don't ever get over the eating disorder. If you are not engaging in behaviors, you are abstinent or in remission like a non-drinking alcoholic, but you still have the illness and have to deal with it one day at a time. We don't agree with this. There is no evidence indicating that once you have an eating disorder you have it for the rest of your life. We are recovered and know countless recovered people. Research also supports that you can be fully recovered. One final point: the word "recovery" or "recovering" is useful during the process of getting well, but can be misleading and confusing, because these terms can refer to someone who is still symptomatic or someone who has been without symptoms for 5 months, 5 years, or even 15 years.

An Eating Disorder is Fueled by a Cultural Climate, which Causes Negative Feelings About Your Body, Your Image of it, and Your Relationship With It.

We have never treated anyone with an eating disorder who did not have some problem with his or her body. Most clients are dissatisfied and many are also distorted regarding their appearance. Body image disturbance is part of the diagnostic criteria for anorexia, which is defined by the American Psychiatric Association (2000) as "Disturbance in the way in which one's body weight or shape is experienced, undue influence of body weight or shape on self evaluation" (pg. 589) and the criteria for bulimia includes: "Self evaluation unduly influenced by body shape and weight" (pg. 594). Body image disturbance is one of the hardest things to treat and is the last thing to go in the recovery process.

Living in this current cultural climate, where women are bombarded with the thin ideal, it's hard to imagine a female whose self-evaluation isn't unduly influenced by her shape and weight. If you have an eating disorder you have taken this to an extreme. You are most likely obsessed with losing weight or controlling your weight, and some of you do not see, or do not admit the seriousness of your already low body weight. Your relationship with food is based on your relationship with your body, how you perceive it, how you feel about it, and your acceptance of it. If you instantly found out that there was a pill that allowed you to eat whatever you wanted and not gain weight, how would this change your eating behavior? If you knew you could eat whatever you wanted when you were hungry and stop when you were full, and be the weight you wanted to be, how would this change your eating? If you have an eating disorder, what you weigh, what you eat, and how you look have become more important to you than who you are.

Body image disturbance is brought on and perpetuated by living in a cultural climate where being fat is abhorred and where achieving an impossibly extreme version of thinness is considered desirable and attractive. In the pursuit to reach the acceptable or desired level of thinness, many people begin with a diet. According to Keel (2006), those who go on a diet are seven to eight times more likely to develop an eating disorder than those who do not diet!

We are all inundated daily with hundreds or more messages with an emphasis on weight and shape. These messages make

IT'S NOT ABOUT THE FOOD

us all feel inadequate in terms of our appearance. We live in a culture that bombards us with these messages through magazines, billboards, ads, television shows, and commercials, and thus resisting those messages is extremely hard. We find that most females and all of our clients say they feel objectified, judged, scrutinized, measured, evaluated, and "in need of improvement." The use of extremely thin women, digitally enhanced and Photoshopped to perfection, fuels dissatisfaction and unhappiness and the need to improve ourselves to look more like they do, when in reality *they* don't really look that way, either. We tend to blame our "flaws" and ourselves for our unhappiness instead of the pervasive and constant messages that tell us we are not OK the way we are.

Every person in this culture is affected by these messages in one way or another, but people with eating disorders seem to be especially vulnerable, as we will continue to explore in this key. Since you cannot eliminate these messages, you need to find antidotes to combat them. Over the years, we have shared with our clients things that helped us not get trapped in body scrutiny or dissatisfaction. We suggest you avoid buying popular magazines that show only thin bodies, push diet tips or how to lose weight or get-in-shape-quick fads, which means most magazines. Don't watch television shows that feature and promote women with unhealthy bodies. Go even further and write the television station about it. Avoid, interrupt, or walk away from conversations about dieting or comparing bodies or saying negative things about your own, or anyone else's body. Write to advertisers, television producers, or networks who shamelessly use "anorexic-looking" models or actresses or make absurd advertising statements like, "You can never be too rich or too thin." Buy clothes paying no attention to the size and buy food without reading calorie labels. We both used all of these antidotes when recovering and we teach our clients to do the same. Like many women suffragettes who fought for the right to vote, we may not see great changes in the cultural messages happen anytime soon, but we can begin now in the hope of changing the world for our daughters and granddaughters. In the meantime, practicing the antidotes helps you to feel better and protect you from body image bombardment now.

Writing Assignment: Exploring Your Body Image

In order to get a better understanding of your body image, use your journal to answer the following questions.

1. Do you remember a time when you did not have a body image problem?
2. What do you think are the characteristics of a person who is OK with his or her body?
3. What family issues or personal challenges may have caused you to develop body dissatisfaction?
4. Has anyone ever helped you with your body image? If so, how?
5. Other than changing your weight, what would help you with your body image?
6. What things do you keep yourself from doing because of your body?
7. How would you help a young girl of 14 improve her body image or accept her body?
8. What steps can you take to protect yourself from harmful cultural messages?
9. What things can you begin to do to practice acceptance of where you are right now, even if you want to change?
10. What are some positive things you can say about your body?

It will be helpful for you to look at the various questions you answered and reflect on how you might like things to change.

Chances are that what you have been doing has not helped you, not just in terms of your body image, although that is important, but also in terms of how happy and loving or lovable you are. Most women in this culture have body image issues at least to some extent. However, for most people body image issues surface and are worked through without the person resorting to behaviors that are physically and mentally destructive in order to "fix" the problem. Most healthy people have a line that they will not cross in order to change their body, no matter how badly they feel about it. For various reasons explored in this key, that line, or limit, is something that people with eating disorders seem to be missing. Part of your recovery will be developing your own line or limits where you are no longer willing to betray yourself to "fix" or change your body. Throughout the keys we will provide information to help you with your body image.

Although Many People Diet to Control or Lose Weight, Those with an Eating Disorder Usually Have Some Other Underlying Issues that Push Them Harder and Further.

Not everyone exposed to popular culture hates their body or goes on a diet, and not everybody who diets takes it to the extreme and develops an eating disorder. Clearly, then, there are other contributing factors. Although the exact cause of eating disorders is unknown, there are a variety of *risk factors* that increase your vulnerability to developing one. Certain circumstances or experiences that have been identified as risk factors by researchers include but are not limited to: being overweight as a child; dieting as a child; having a mother who diets or has an eating disorder; early menstruation; being bullied or teased; engaging in certain sports with a focus on appearance or weight, like ballet, cheerleading, wrestling, and gymnastics; certain careers like modeling or acting; and a history of childhood abuse (Brewerton, 2004; Rorty & Yager,

1993). It is possible that many of these risk factors propel someone to a more serious or intense degree of body dissatisfaction, and push that individual into dieting and other behaviors as they try to "fix" themselves. There are many things that can contribute to the development of an eating disorder. The list gives an indication of what might make someone vulnerable to getting caught up in an unhealthy spiral of dieting or weight loss. But, none of these factors necessarily explain your personal situation. You have to look at your life and see what might have contributed to your eating disorder. To facilitate your understanding we will share some of our own stories.

Personal Reflections:

Carolyn: When I went on a diet with a few of my friends, why did I take it so seriously? Why was I was the only one who developed anorexia? Part of the answer involves going back to a time in my life before I ever started to diet. My dad always dieted, and as I entered my teens he began to make comments about my weight. I knew he loved me but his comments like "you'd be so much prettier if you lost a little weight," undermined my confidence and self-esteem. When I was a teenager my dad divorced my mom and married a very thin, beautiful fashion model, and I had to move to a new house and start a new school. I was enamored with my stepmother's beauty and her modeling career. There was a specific, telling incident that happened which I forgot about until years later in a therapy session. One day when alone, I secretly tried on one of my stepmother's dresses and it was too small! I was only 14 and she was smaller than me! I remember saying to myself, "Someday I will fit into this dress." I wanted to be like my stepmother. I wanted my dad to like me and not leave me. It was some time after this in the 9th grade that I tried out to be a cheerleader and lost to the thinner more attractive girls, and I subsequently began my first diet.

IT'S NOT ABOUT THE FOOD

All these events in my life—my dad choosing a model over my mother, moving to a new house, and attending a new school—left me feeling insecure. So when all my friends and I went on a diet, my feelings about my stepmother made me especially want to succeed. Sure enough, losing weight brought the approval and attention that I craved. I became proud of how little I could eat in a day and became obsessed with my weight and weight loss. I loved the praise I got for losing weight and "having such good willpower." I loved showing my friends, who also were dieting, that I had the "control" to stick to my diet and succeed. I started restricting desserts and snacks in between meals, then fats, then starches, then protein. Eventually nearly all foods seemed too high in calories except a few fruits and vegetables. The weight kept coming off and I felt good about it. However, the time came where I didn't want to lose any more weight but my fear of gaining weight and the taboo I had created in my head about eating so many foods had such a grip on me that the weight kept coming off and I couldn't stop it. I did not understand what had caused things to go awry, how I had gotten so out of control. You don't have to understand why you are where you are now either. I recovered from my eating disorder before I ever figured out all the things that had caused it. The important thing is to start turning it around.

Gwen: My mother was obsessed with her own weight, constantly talked about dieting, and was always on a diet. I was a very thin child, but as I entered puberty and started gaining some weight, she became very worried and determined to spare me the shame she felt about her body and the anxiety of weight problems. She rushed me off to Weight Watchers and signed me up at the local gym to get ahead of "the problem," but instead of helping me, which I know was her intention, she planted the seeds of body shame, diet mentality, and low self-worth. She taught me that if I wasn't thin, I would not be happy, or feel confident. It didn't matter what else I accomplished in life; being thin was what I needed to feel valuable and lovable. Eating soon became a source of guilt and shame, and something that made me feel like a complete failure. My self-esteem and body image continued to decline throughout high school. I withdrew from sports and other things I enjoyed because of self-consciousness and fear of judgment. When I arrived at college I was lonely, depressed, and hopeless. I called home in a desperate moment and my mom responded in the only way she knew how. She suggested I increase my confidence by finally losing that extra few pounds and she sent me the diet that she and my dad were on. My erroneous belief that weight loss would fix my self-esteem and end my depression created the perfect storm of factors to allow for my diet to become my disorder.

Abuse as a Risk Factor

We are often asked about, and there is a lot of misinformation about, abuse as a risk factor, so we want to say a few things about it. Being abused does not necessarily lead to an eating disorder, but research shows that if you were sexually, physically, or emotionally abused and you developed post-traumatic stress symptoms, you are at a higher risk for developing an eating disorder (Brewerton, 2004, 2007). We have treated many people who have been abused, sexually or otherwise, and use eating disorder symptoms as well as other self-destructive behaviors to manage their feelings and feel in control of their life. The behaviors often express something about the way those who were abused feel about themselves as a result of what happened to them. Often behaviors such as bingeing and purging become ways to try to numb out and forget and dull feelings and memories, and control the body. Clients also describe these self-destructive behaviors as ways to punish themselves or ways to create physical pain to match the pain they feel on the inside. The behaviors can provide a sense of relief, but only temporarily. An eating disorder never heals anything and only makes matters worse. If you have an eating disorder and have experienced sexual abuse or other trauma, it is important for you to seek help from a professional or program with expertise in both areas. We have listed further reading on this topic in the resource section.

It's Not the Biological Makeup of Food, but Rather the Biological Makeup of You, that Contributes to the Development of An Eating Disorder.

There are still other factors we have not yet discussed that contribute to why, given the same or similar circumstances, one person develops an eating disorder while another person does not. Why does one person who was teased as a child for being fat develop an eating disorder while another does not?

Carolyn: "After beginning a diet in high school, I developed an eating disorder, while my friends who also dieted did not. My sister, who grew up in relatively the same environment as I did, did not even diet."

Why are there such differences even with similar circumstances?

One emerging answer has to do with biology and genetics. Research has shown that there are certain genetic factors that raise your risk of developing an eating disorder. If you have a family member or relative who has an eating disorder it raises your risk of developing one. Of course this could be learned behavior—like mother like daughter, as in the case of Gwen and her mom. Some of it can be learned, but twin studies reveal the influence of genetics. If an identical twin has an eating disorder, the chances that the other identical twin will also develop an eating disorder are significantly higher than is the case with fraternal twins (Bulik, 2010; Wade, Bulik, Neale, & Kendler, 2000). This points to a genetic component to the disorder, in addition to environmental influences, but we have yet to fully understand the nature of this genetic predisposition. Ongoing research will continue to help our understanding. What is known is that having certain genetic temperament traits such as anxiety, perfectionism, obsessive-compulsive tendencies, harm or risk avoidance, sensitivity to rejection, or lack of impulse control, all seem to make people more susceptible to developing an eating disorder and can be considered risk factors of a biological or temperament nature (Strober & Peris, in press). The twin and trait studies point to a genetic contribution to the development of an eating disorder. Combine a genetic predisposition with other factors, such as a culture that reveres thinness and pushes dieting, a negative body image, a psychological stressor such as parental divorce, and you can see "the perfect storm" coming together. The current understanding of the development of an eating disorder is that "Genes load the gun and environment pulls the trigger." The term "environment" includes the culture you live in, the family you grew up with, and all the events and developments you experience in your life.

We listed several environmental risk factors earlier. We are not saying that if you have any of those risk factors, if you have the above temperament traits, or if you have a family member with an eating disorder, you will certainly develop an eating disorder. What we are saying is that these are all traits and tendencies that will make you more vulnerable to developing one. Also, it is important to note that absence of the risk factors doesn't guarantee that you won't get an eating disorder.

To help with your understanding we will discuss how our own temperaments contributed to our eating disorders.

Personal Reflections:

Carolyn: When looking at my own history, genetics might explain why I persevered in dieting when others did not, and why I developed an eating disorder and my sister did not. My sister and I both experienced the same difficult events described earlier (my dad leaving my mother for a fashion model and the transfer to a new school), and although she was younger than me, which makes a difference in our respective experience of the situation, we also have very different temperaments. My genetic makeup has given me a temperament that leans toward perfectionism, anxiety, and compulsive behavior. My temperament helps explain why, when I went on a diet with all of my friends, I took it very seriously, continued to lose more and more weight, and could not stop. I was the only one who wouldn't "cheat" on my diet. I was the only one who consistently attained my weight goals. I was the only one who developed anorexia. So, did "my genes make me do it?" Not solely, but they helped. My eating disorder was a combination of my genetic predisposition, the prevailing cultural climate of "Thin is In," and many environmental stressors in my life. The way I see it, my genes by themselves are not a problem. For example, my perfectionism can be an asset or a liability depending on how I channel it. It was important for me and will be important for you to understand how your traits can work for or against you.

I have the genetic predisposition classically described by researchers as typical of individuals with anorexia nervosa. I was a perfectionist, obsessive, anxious, harm avoidant, and a control junkie. If I was told to do something, I did it. I was too worried (anxious) about what might happen if I did not do my best at everything all the time. I followed the rules, did my homework, and pushed myself, even at a very young age. I was literal, a rule follower, and very controlling. In kindergarten, I was mad on Halloween because I was in a witch costume and all the other little girls were dressed up as fairies, princesses, or characters like Alice in Wonderland. I remember thinking they all just didn't get it! Halloween was supposed to be about monsters, goblins, and witches!

My temperament and genetic traits helped me earn straight A's, skip the sixth grade, graduate high school when I was 16, and earn two master's degrees by the time I was 21. However, when I applied these same traits to losing weight, I pursued dieting with the same vigor and tenacity I pursued everything and ended up with an eating disorder. Had I lived in a different culture where all body sizes were admired, where there was no emphasis on thinness or special status for those who are thin, and where all my friends were not on diets, I would not have dieted or developed anorexia, though I might have had other problems. If I had dieted but had a different temperament, I probably would not have developed anorexia. But take my genes, add in the cultural climate, and combine all this with my psychological stressors at the time and not only was dieting a reasonable endeavor on my part, but the tenacity with which I pursued it, and the eventual development of an eating disorder, were understandable outcomes.

I have been recovered from my eating disorder for over three decades, but I still have the kind of hard-wiring my genetics dictate. The good news is that I understand myself better and have learned tools that help me focus and direct my behavior in appropriate ways. I calm my anxious temperament through meditation, walking in nature, music, or yoga. I turn my drive and perfectionist tendencies toward things like my writing, lecturing, taking care of my clients, and running the best treatment center I can.

Gwen: My temperament is marked by the features of perfectionism, worry, obsessive-compulsive tendencies, people-pleasing urges, and occasional impulse control issues. I usually felt like a failed perfectionist, never quite measuring up to what I thought I should be or what I thought others expected of me. With my obsessive tendencies, I often could not stop, sleep, or think of anything until I completed or fixed something I was working on, and I worried constantly about what people thought about me. The most difficult times came when my temperamental tendencies all came to the surface at once. An example of the way my traits worked in service of my eating disorder was my split-second decision to join the United States Army. I wanted to "Be all I could be," get whipped into shape, become perfectly lean and disciplined, and be kept "in line." I thought I was becoming lazy and wasn't sure how I was going to keep up my rigid diet and exercise routine, which my mom had instilled in me from an early age. The army would provide me with a strict drill sergeant who would keep me from slacking. It seemed like the perfect solution. I didn't take the time to talk to anyone about this decision, or think about it for a day, or even ask any questions. The minute I saw the sign outside the recruiter's office, a light went on in my head, and I suddenly *knew* that this was answer to all of my worries. An hour later, I had signed on the dotted line and I was on my way home to make arrangements for boot camp. Four days later, I was on a plane to Fort Knox, Kentucky. As you can imagine, once I got there, things started to quickly unravel and fall apart. My "strict" drill sergeant seemed to feel sorry for me rather than try to keep me in line. I cried a lot, which isn't very army-like, and when asked about why I had joined, I did not possess the ability to explain my reasons. After several distressing incidents, the army decided I was "emotionally unstable" and after four weeks I was honorably discharged. For a long time, however, my traits continued to propel me deeper into eating disorder behaviors. My perfectionism and obsessive nature led me to calorie counting, food scrutiny, and compulsive weighing. Finding a way to understand my traits and myself in a more balanced way was essential for me. My perfectionist and obsessive tendencies help me stay organized, make me work hard, prevent me from procrastinating, and help me run a successful household and therapy practice. Even my impulsiveness, when controlled and channeled in the right direction, keeps my kids entertained and my marriage from being dull (that is what I tell my husband, anyway!).

Traits as Liability or Asset

Consider the following traits and see how they can be either an asset or liability. We tell our clients that they can take any trait of theirs (whether it is caused by genetics or not) to what we call the *darkness* (liability) or the *light* (asset). This concept will help you understand that you are not doomed by any genetic predisposition you came into the world with, or for that matter, by any personality trait you may have developed along the way.

Liability	**Asset**
Perfectionistic	Precise
Obsessive	Thorough
Anxious	High energy
Impulsive	Spontaneous
Critical	Discerning
Manipulative	Strategic
Stubborn	Determined
Controlling	Directive
Compulsive	Driven
Avoidant	Careful

It is helpful to see how traits that on the one hand can be negative can also be positive when you work on developing awareness of them, and learn skills to channel them in the right way.

Writing Assignment: Your Traits—Assets or Liabilities?

See if you can think of any traits you have that you feel get in your way or are a problem for you. Think about things other people have said about you that were hurtful or critical. It might help to think of things about you that drive your eating disorder or interfere with your ability to get better. Make a list of your traits and then figure out how they can be an asset. Knowing your traits and how you can turn them into assets, rather than liabilities, can help you better understand yourself as well as others. You will find that your traits play out in various arenas; for example, if you are controlling about your food, chances are you are controlling in your relationships as well. If you are impulsive in your dealings with food, you are probably impulsive with money and relationships.

Writing Assignment: How is Your Relationship to Food Like Your Relationship to People?

Your approaches to both food and relationships will have similarities because of your temperament and who you are. Think for a minute about how you are with food. Are you cautious? Are you bold? Do you try to be in control? Do you fear you will never get enough? Now ask yourself if this is similar to your relationship with food. When we asked one of our clients with bulimia this question, she said, "Oh, I binge and purge men!" A client with anorexia said, "I scrutinize everything I eat and everyone I meet." Since our traits play themselves out with people, food, and in other areas, it can be useful to explore this. Write out everything that you can think of regarding how this might be true for you. You will begin to see how your temperament guides your behavior in a variety of situations. The good news is you can work on changing your relationship with people, and your relationship with food will change as well, and vice versa. We suggest you come back to this assignment and do it again during the course of your recovery. This will help you see how your relationships with both food and people are changing.

From Risk Factor to Pieces of Your Puzzle

Knowing about cultural pressures, environmental risk factors, genetics, and temperament is useful in terms of understanding and perhaps even preventing eating disorders, but it falls short in explaining why you in particular developed your eating disorder, and how to successfully treat it. People who develop eating disorders may have things in common, but each person has his or her own unique factors that contribute to their disorder. Think of your eating disorder as a jigsaw puzzle with many different pieces making it up. Your jigsaw puzzle is unique to you. In trying to understand your eating disorder, it is useful to explore the various pieces that together make up the whole picture. Some pieces of your puzzle may be more important or critical than others in terms of getting better. You don't have to know all the pieces of the puzzle in order to get better, but knowing some of the pieces can help you understand, and even target, specific issues to work on.

Looking Further Into What Contributed to and Perpetuates Your Eating Disorder

Even with reading all the information so far, it may be hard to discern why you have an eating disorder and what it could be doing for you. In order to help you identify and work on your particular issues, we provide a list called "The Real Issues"

IT'S NOT ABOUT THE FOOD

adapted from the book *Your Dieting Daughter* (Costin, 1997). This list covers the most common issues that clients with eating disorders have identified as contributing to their illness. Read through this list and see if it helps you identify parts of your eating disorder puzzle.

Real Issues

1. **Poor Self-Esteem:**
   - I'm afraid of myself and of being out of control.
   - I'm not worthy.
   - People don't like me.
   - I can't trust my own judgments or make decisions.
2. **Need for Distraction:**
   - When I'm bingeing or throwing up, I don't think about anything else.
   - I need something that distracts me from my thoughts and feelings.
   - Worrying about my weight keeps me from worrying about other things.
3. **Fill Up Emptiness:**
   - Something is missing in my life and I try to fill it with my eating disorder.
   - I feel empty inside and bingeing takes me away from that temporarily.
   - Eating fills up my emptiness.
   - All my eating disorder rituals help me fill up a void in my life.
4. **Belief in a Myth:**
   - I will be happy and successful if I am thin.
   - Thinner people are happier.
   - I have to be thin to be attractive and desirable.
   - Losing weight will solve my problems.
5. **Drive for Perfection:**
   - I have to be the best at everything, whether it is taking a test or dieting.

- I have the willpower to do things others can't do.
- I'm either fat or thin.
- I'm either perfect or a failure.
- If I can't win or be the best, I won't try.

6. **High-Achievement Oriented:**
    - I feel constant internal pressure to work hard and achieve.
    - I can only achieve a good body through my eating disorder.
    - I am driven everywhere else and use my bulimia as a release.
    - Restricting is a real achievement, mind over matter, literally.

7. **Desire to be Special/Unique:**
    - I get a lot of attention for my willpower over food.
    - I don't know who I would be without my eating disorder.
    - My eating disorder causes others to worry about me and take care of me.
    - My eating disorder makes me stand out and be different.
    - My low weight is the only special thing I have.

8. **Need to be in Control:**
    - I have to be in control of my body, and what goes in and out of it.
    - My eating disorder helps me feel in control of my "out of control-ness."
    - My eating disorder behaviors keep my feelings under control.
    - My eating disorder is the one thing no one has control over but me.

9. **Desire for Power over Self, Others, Family, Life:**
    - My eating disorder gives me power over my body.
    - I feel powerless most of the time, except when it comes to my eating disorder.
    - My eating disorder gives me power over others.

IT'S NOT ABOUT THE FOOD

- It's powerful to be able to resist food, like a saint or monk.

10. **Desire for Respect and Admiration:**
    - I finally got respect from my peers when I lost weight.
    - I wanted to be admired and tried restricting to lose weight, but I couldn't do it, so I had to throw up.
    - When I binge I am rebelling because I know I will never get the respect and admiration that people get for being thin.
    - People respect my ability to resist food.

11. **Difficulty Expressing Feelings:**
    - I don't know how to express my anger, so I binge and purge.
    - I feel like I swallow my feelings when I binge.
    - I can't deal with conflict or confrontation so I resort to my eating disorder.
    - Restricting helps me shut down and deny my feelings.

12. **Need for "Safe Place to Go"/Lack of Coping Skills:**
    - My eating disorder is a "special world" created to keep all the "bad" out.
    - If I follow my own imposed rules, it helps me feel safe.
    - My eating disorder helps me get taken care of without asking for help.
    - My eating disorder has helped me avoid taking on adult responsibilities.

13. **Lack of Trust in Self and Others:**
    - I don't trust people so I isolate from them with my eating disorder.
    - I don't trust anybody; I use my eating disorder as my best friend.
    - I can never make a decision; bineging and purging provides procrastination.
    - It's easier just to follow my eating disorder rules than to trust myself or anyone else.

14. **Intense Fear of Not Measuring Up:**
    - I know I can't compete, so I let my eating disorder take me out of the running.
    - I won't have anything if I don't have my eating disorder.
    - I'm constantly comparing myself to everyone.
    - I am terrified of being fat.
    - I am terrified of being deprived.
    - I am terrified of being deprived and of being fat.

Writing Assignment: Identifying Your Real Issues

Go back through the Real Issues List and decide which of the 14 issues apply to you. Write those down along with the examples that fit. Add any other issues of your own that you can think of and give specific examples. Take some time to journal about each issue, giving examples of your thoughts, feelings, and behaviors related to the issue and how your eating disorder symptoms are involved. Once you have identified which issues you know are present in your life and how you use your eating disorder to help you deal with them, you can begin working on resolving them or finding healthier alternatives to cope. Once again, we suggest sharing this assignment in therapy or with significant others who can help you come up with ideas.

Personal Reflections:

Carolyn: I already described myself as a perfectionistic, driven kid (Real Issue #5). I felt compelled to achieve and be the best at everything (Real Issue #6). When I went on a diet and lost weight I got compliments from others who found it hard to do so and my need for admiration was reinforced.

IT'S NOT ABOUT THE FOOD

(Real Issue #10). I got praise and increased attention from both males and females at my high school for my weight loss but also for my strong willpower, that is, for my ability to resist eating. All of this made me feel unique and special (Real Issue #7), and drove me to diet even more. I ultimately had to learn to deal with my need to be the best, to achieve, and to be special. I had to learn to love myself for who I was and accept that I was worthy even if I was not "the best" or accomplishing something.

Gwen: Until I got treatment, it never even crossed my mind that there were underlying issues contributing to my obsession with my body and weight loss. I needed to be thin. I knew that from an early age. It was just the way it was supposed to be.

Carolyn: When Gwen came in for treatment, she had not explored the possible underlying issues that could be contributing to her self-starvation, her body dissatisfaction, and her inability to satisfy her body's real needs without guilt. Gwen was stuck in a familiar cycle: she wanted to be thin, feared being fat, and was unable to see what else was beyond the struggle being played out with food and her body. I decided to have a session with Gwen and her husband, Albert, and present the Real Issues List for both of them to look at and see what, if any, issues rang true.

Gwen: When Carolyn gave me the Real Issues List, it was my first introduction to what could be causing or contributing to my eating disorder. My husband, Albert, and I looked through the list and picked out which ones applied to me. All of the issues he and I selected that day surfaced throughout my treatment, and were worked on as part of my recovery over the next several years. These underlying issues take a lot of awareness, intention, and practice to change, because they are usually ingrained and connected to fundamental beliefs and fears. Going through the Real Issues List was the first time I could identify my underlying issues but I still could not understand how those issues were connected to my eating disorder. It may take time to see how certain underlying issues are related to your eating.

Carolyn: Gwen and her husband were able to identify several issues from the list. This made them both hopeful that there were things Gwen could work on to help her get better. What was interesting is that Albert picked out issues from the list that Gwen initially didn't think applied to her. After discussing it together, she came to realize that in fact they did.

Gwen: I remember when Albert first pointed out that I was a perfectionist and tried to reassure me that I didn't have to be perfect, I felt misunderstood. I kept saying, "Yes I do, you don't understand me." Even though at first I didn't think I was a perfectionist I came to realize how true it was. I started to explore the idea of lowering my expectations of myself in some areas, or as my good friend, Sam, liked to tell me, "Go for the silver." I had to learn that not being perfect did not mean failure and that no one expected me to be perfect. An important turning point for me was when I started to see that I was honest about my feelings without being critical or judgmental of others; I was less worried about being perfect, others experienced me as "real" and that made them feel more comfortable with me which meant they could be more authentic and real with me.

Carolyn: It turned out that using the Real Issues List as a starting point helped Gwen to see a myriad of issues that related to her eating disorder. Gwen continued to work on the issues throughout treatment and came to see how some of the issues were part of her personality and she would have to figure out how to best deal with them throughout her life.

Gwen: "Terrified of Not Measuring Up" seemed to be the deepest of all of the underlying issues for me. Feeling terrified of not measuring up is the one underlying issue which still continues to show up for me now and then. What used to be the eating disorder voice has become a critical voice I still hear from time to time. Fears of failure, judgment, criticism, or competition are very hard feelings for me to tolerate even today, but I no longer use any eating disorder behaviors to deal with those feelings; that is long gone. I now know that these feelings are my alert signal that something is wrong or needs to be looked into. I explore what might be going on and figure out the best way to deal with it.

From Eating Disorder Voice to Critical Voice

Even after the eating disorder symptoms are gone, you might hear what we often refer to as a "critical" voice inside your head in regards to areas where you have some insecurity. A strategy for dealing with this voice is being able to recognize that your own inner critic sounds strangely similar to your eating disorder voice (Key 2), except that it chimes in about all kinds of things, not just about what to eat and not to eat. You can use the same technique you learned in Key 2 and dialogue with your inner critic and your healthy self.

> **Gwen**: I had to learn how to consciously ignore my critical voice. Contrary to my thinking, Carolyn taught me that the critical voice was not my conscience helping me do the "right" thing. The voice was left over from old wounds and old messages I had internalized about myself. It was not useful, and it was not coming from any wise place, or higher place, inside me. It was an inner critic keeping me afraid. I ultimately learned the difference between this critical voice and my core self or healthy self, but in the beginning I just had to try the good old "fake it till you make it" strategy. In other words, I had to act my way into a new way of thinking, instead of waiting for my thinking to change my behavior. It was a paradigm shift for me, but possibly one of the most important ones. I realized that if I waited until I was less afraid of something before trying it, it might never happen, but if I tried something even if I was afraid, I would always become less afraid of it over time. Learning to talk to myself

less judgmentally was also very difficult, but not impossible. Even now if I notice that I am stuck in my head agonizing over something I did or said and I can feel myself getting more angry and critical, I stop myself. I now know that this type of self-deprecation will not help me at all. I try to use the concept of acceptance of the truth without any judgment, which you will learn about in Key 8. Basically, I accept the situation without judging myself. I might say something like, "I am disappointed in myself and I wish I had handled that differently, or better, but I will learn from this." This way of thinking keeps me focused on the situation and how I might be able to repair it, or at least do it differently the next time. In the past, I would have thought something more like, "I am so stupid. I ruined everything and I can't do anything right so I'm done trying." This way of thinking was more about judging myself than the situation I had handled poorly, and over time it chipped away at my self-esteem. Changing my way of talking to myself has helped me immensely and I don't think I could have recovered, or gotten very far in my life, if I hadn't learned how to do it. It is a skill and can be learned by anyone, but it takes dedicated thought, effort, and practice.

It is important to learn the difference between having an inner critic and healthy self-reflection. An inner critic is nasty and mean. An inner critic will cause you to doubt yourself and keep you unhappy, insecure, and stuck. Self-reflection can help keep you humble and help you continue to improve yourself and grow. When writing this book we realized that both of us still have a critical voice that chimes in with things like, "Who do you think you are?" "Don't get too full of yourself," and "What will people think and say?" These kinds of messages used to drive us to eating disorder behaviors, but now we realize there is something we need to look at and figure out what is causing our self-doubt.

There are many real issues and other factors that have to come together in just the right way to make up your eating disorder puzzle. To our clients we say, "We are experts in eating disorders but novices in regards to you." When you are trying to get better it is important to look at your own unique situation and all of the underlying issues that perhaps made it easier for eating disorder behaviors to take hold of your life.

Some Final Thoughts

We hope this key has helped you understand how various issues, aside from your desire to control your weight or shape, have contributed to the development of your eating disorder. You have begun to explore the many ways in which you have used your eating disorder to cope with various situations and the feelings associated with them. The next key, "Feel Your Feelings," is dedicated to helping you begin to develop new tools so that you can recognize your feelings, learn to tolerate them without resorting to eating disorder behaviors, and finally use them as a guide for living a more healthy and happy life, complete with the full range of emotions that come along with it.

Additional Assignment

Writing Assignment: Exploring Your ED Puzzle

We end this key with asking you to get your journal and write about what you have learned. Spend some time summarizing your thoughts and feelings about the information in this key. The following questions are designed to help you think further about the development of your eating disorder and how your behaviors might be helping you deal with some underlying issues.

- *Write about when you developed your eating disorder, or when you first started dieting.*
- *What else was going on in your life either before or around that time?*
- *What are some of the things that you felt/feel that dieting or your eating disorder behaviors or even having an eating disorder gave/gives you?*
- *What problems or feelings did/does your eating disorder help you deal with or distract you from?*
- *How well does the eating disorder work to help you deal with or cope with underlying issues?*
- *Even if the eating disorder behaviors "work," what price do you have to pay, in other words what negative consequences are there?*
- *What are you afraid will happen if you stop your eating disorder behaviors? (Although it is OK to list weight issues, be sure to include things other than gaining weight or getting fat).*

KEY 4:

FEEL YOUR FEELINGS, CHALLENGE YOUR THOUGHTS

You could say that the biggest key to my recovery was learning how to take care of myself in a real way, instead of starving and always trying to lose weight. I began to value always delving deeper, peeling the layers of the onion, and finding the "root" causes to my behaviors, and the feelings that had to come out.

—RL

Gwen: "What am I supposed to do with all these feelings?"
Carolyn: "Feel them."

Identifying your underlying issues can bring insight and awareness, but just understanding is not enough to make you well. It's not what happens to us, but what we do with what happens to us, that makes the difference. You will have to learn to deal with your thoughts and feelings in healthier ways in order to get better. You can never undo the past or change the fact that you were born with "anxious" genes or were teased in school, but you can work on managing or lessening your feelings of anxiety. You can learn to identify the thoughts you have, and the things you continue to tell yourself. You can learn to accept, tolerate, and *feel* your feelings. Learning how to identify, understand, and regulate your thoughts and feelings will help you figure out what you can and can't do about a situation, and help you make better choices in your life. Your eating disorder behaviors have been driven by your problematic thoughts and feelings, and possibly served to numb, distract, filter, express, or otherwise manage your feelings.

How Coping With Weight Turns Into Coping With Other Problems

Your eating disorder can be connected to your thoughts and feelings in numerous ways. Some people actually recognize that their problems with food began when they started using food as comfort for or distraction from painful *feelings*. Others will say the only *"feeling"* that drove their behavior initially was *"feeling* fat," and they are unsure if or how their behaviors help them deal with other feelings. Let's look at some examples.

Let's say that an eating disorder behavior, such as restricting all carbohydrates, starts as a way to lose or control your weight. If you are successful, other people compliment and praise you, you *feel* good about yourself and the behavior is reinforced. Initially, all of the attention and your *feelings* of accomplishment boost your self-esteem or *feelings* of self-worth. As you continue, you enjoy the *feelings* of success and accomplishment.

Let's look at another example. If you are trying to lose weight and *think* that eating desserts are bad and you are not "allowed" to eat them, what thoughts and feelings arise if you eat a piece of cake? You might *think* you are weak and undisciplined and you *feel* guilty, ashamed, or something similar. Then, let's suppose that to get rid of those calories you purge. If purging reduces your guilt or shame, then purging is being reinforced as a coping mechanism for whenever you break your dieting rules. If purging becomes the way you get rid of food you consider "bad," the next time you eat cake you might *think* that since you broke the dessert rule anyway and you are going to purge, you might as well eat several pieces of cake or even other things you don't "allow" yourself to eat. Depriving

FEEL YOUR FEELINGS, CHALLENGE YOUR THOUGHTS

yourself of certain foods usually causes feelings of rebellion and intensified desire. At some point, the behavior that started out as a way to "fix" or cope with anxiety, guilt, or shame about eating transfers to other areas. For example, if you fail a test and you feel guilty and ashamed, you may think, "I can get rid of these feelings by bingeing and purging." Now you have transferred your eating disorder behaviors from a way to deal with negative feelings about food and weight to dealing with negative feelings in general. Another example of this is that restricting what you eat may make you feel in control and powerful over food or your body, but over time, this tendency starts to be confused with feeling in control and empowered in other areas in your life. One last example is that clients who struggle with compulsive eating find themselves eating to numb or cover up the bad feelings they have about what they just ate, and eventually to numb out other bad feelings in general.

If your eating disorder goes on long enough, it can get to the point where you don't even need anything negative to happen to trigger or instigate an eating disorder behavior. Repeatedly engaging in eating disorder behaviors will cause them to become habitual, and you will find yourself engaging in them just because you "can" or just out of habit. The eating disorder becomes a way of maintaining homeostasis. Similar to an alcoholic who wakes up and drinks, the illness can get to the point where nothing particular is causing you to restrict or binge or purge, you just do it habitually. In fact, not doing it makes you uncomfortable. When an eating disorder is very entrenched it becomes a coping mechanism to just help you get through the day. You probably don't even realize all of the things you might be feeling if you weren't engaging in the behaviors. Eating disorder behaviors keep your feelings out of your awareness. Stopping the eating disorder behaviors is important and necessary to understand and feel your feelings. If you stop your automatic behaviors, we guarantee you that thoughts and feelings will come up.

Thought-Feeling-Urge-Action Chain

We have found a simple way to help our clients understand, dissect, and change how their thoughts and feelings lead to their eating disorder behaviors. If you are at the total habituation stage of your eating disorder, the following information will be harder to take in, but it is still possible to do. Whenever you have a strong, triggering feeling, you will have an urge to react and cope with it in the best way you know how. If you are like most of our clients, you are coping by using one or a combination of the following behaviors: restricting your food intake, which often serves as an illusion of strength and self-control; bingeing to escape, numb, or comfort yourself; or purging to get the feeling out of you, experience relief, or lower your anxiety. The chain reaction looks like this: Thought–Feeling-Urge-Action.

Thoughts

Your thoughts are the beginning of the chain reaction. Most people greatly underestimate the influence their thoughts or "cognitions" have on their feelings and behavior. If you have an eating disorder, you will find it is accompanied by disturbing, distorted, and unhealthy thoughts. These thoughts result in painful feelings and destructive behaviors. When working with clients we are always asking them, "What do you tell yourself about that?" This helps you uncover what you are thinking and telling yourself about the experience you had, or are having, or are afraid of having.

Feelings

Many people want to avoid or get rid of their feelings and get upset when they can't. The truth is that you can't control your feelings, but you can control how you perceive them, express them, or defuse them, and what you do about them. Getting down on yourself for having certain feelings is a waste of energy and will only make you feel worse. The goal is to accept, understand, and feel your feelings, discharge or separate them from your body, and move on.

Urges

Whether it is an urge to eat or not eat, binge or purge, urges are hard to control, but they can teach you a lot if you don't react immediately. Not reacting to the urge is sometimes called "surfing the urge," which is essentially just feeling your feelings and riding them out before reacting. You need a little time to become aware of what is underneath the feeling, and also time to figure out and separate any thoughts that might be fueling the feeling and making you feel worse. Initially your urges will be quite strong, but the good news is that your habitual urges will lessen and change considerably over time as you develop better ways of coping or reacting.

Actions

Using your eating disorder to cope with your feelings is, at best, a temporary way to make feelings go away. If your real underlying feelings are completely unattended to, they will keep resurfacing. Giving in to the urge and going to food, or away from food, to "fix" any feeling will ultimately fail you. You might be afraid to actually feel, express, and take appropriate action related to your feelings because you are afraid of hurting others, being judged, or harming a relationship. Maybe you have been labeled as "overly sensitive" and are purposely trying not to act on your feelings. As you learn to feel your feelings and express them in healthy and effective ways, they will begin to inform your actions rather than control them.

The Power of Thoughts

Your thoughts, which are based on perceptions or beliefs you have learned from outside sources or come up with yourself, often contain inaccurate information that can mislead you. Our goal is to help you learn to recognize and challenge your destructive thoughts that might be sabotaging or getting in the way of recovery or fueling your behaviors. Cognitive-behavioral therapy (CBT) is a well-known psychotherapeutic approach and has been shown to be the most useful approach for treating bulimia. We have found it extremely beneficial with all of our eating disorder clients. CBT is based on the idea that it is our thoughts that cause our feelings and behaviors. This means that if we want to change our feelings and behaviors, we need to look at and then work on changing the way we think. We have the power to change our thoughts even if we don't have the power to change the situation. We can't always control the first thought that pops into our head, but we can learn to control subsequent thoughts after that.

Unbalanced/Distorted Ways of Thinking

In his book *Feeling Good,* David Burns (1980) provides a helpful list of the most common distorted thoughts (cognitive distortions) and explains how they create huge problems by undermining self-confidence, increasing anxiety, fostering depression, and putting a strain on relationships. We have provided you with an adapted list reflecting examples related to eating disorders.

Cognitive Distortions

1. **All-or-nothing thinking:** This is also known as "black and white" thinking or perfectionist thinking. Intellectually, you know there are shades of gray, but in certain

FEEL YOUR FEELINGS, CHALLENGE YOUR THOUGHTS 99

circumstances, intellect and reason go out the window. "One extra cookie means I have to eat the whole box," and "I am either thin or fat" exemplify this type of extreme thinking.

2. **Over-generalization:** A negative event is seen as a pattern, or one mistake means you will not be able to do it right, so you say, for example, "I ate dessert and purged therefore I'll never get better" or "I overate at the party again. I'll never have any control."

3. **Discounting the positives:** Accomplishments or compliments are not taken in. Someone says something nice about you but you reject it by minimizing it, or feel undeserving and wave it off as if it is nothing to feel good about. You also might turn praise into expectation and therefore resist compliments.

4. **Emotional reasoning:** You believe your feelings make it true. "I feel fat" means, "I am fat." "I feel hopeless" means, "I am hopeless." It is hard to separate reality from feelings.

5. **Mind-reading:** Thinking you know what others think or will do or how things will turn out, or any number of things that are impossible for you to know. "People envy my ability to control my food" and "Nobody will find me attractive unless I lose weight" are examples of such thoughts.

6. **Personalizing and blaming:** Believing that things are always done to you intentionally, blaming rather than taking responsibility or trying to fix the situation. "My mother's dieting caused my eating disorder." "He didn't come to the party because he doesn't care about me or want to be seen with me."

7. **Magnification or minimization**: Things either matter too much or not enough. "No store has clothes that will fit me," or "My weight loss is not that bad" are typical thoughts.

8. **Mental filter:** You take in all the negative aspects of an

experience and filter out the positive. "I stopped bingeing and purging six days this week, but the one day I did binge and purge ruined everything."
9. **Should statements:** You criticize yourself (or others) with "shoulds" and "oughts", e.g., "I should be able to get better on my own."
10. **Labeling**: Taking on behavior as if it was your identity. "I ate too much," becomes "I am a failure." Slipping up on your meal plan becomes "I am a loser."

When you read through the list of cognitive distortions, do any of them seem familiar? Were you able to see yourself in some of them? It's helpful to think of your first thought as an "automatic thought" and while some will be healthy and balanced, in times of stress or emotional upset, your automatic thoughts tend to become distorted in often predictable and painful ways. It is important to learn which automatic thoughts you default to so you can begin to recognize when you are trapped in irrational or unhelpful thinking. A single distorted thought can have a cascading effect, intensifying distressing emotions, triggering unhealthy behaviors, and creating difficulties in relationships. The first step in changing or balancing your thinking is learning to recognize when it is distorted. Understanding how this distorted thinking harms you and finding more balanced ways to think will help you feel different and make better decisions in your life and your relationships.

Writing Assignment: Gaining Insight Into Your Distorted Thinking

Look at the list of cognitive distortions and see which ones might apply to you. Make a list of personal examples. Include

FEEL YOUR FEELINGS, CHALLENGE YOUR THOUGHTS

eating disorder and non-eating disorder examples. For each example, write about how your current way of thinking serves you. What does it protect you from? Does it really work? How does this thinking get in your way?

Personal Reflection:

Gwen: I always felt like I was either a success or a failure, indulgent or lazy, but it never occurred to me that I was a perfectionist. I didn't realize that never feeling good enough, thinking I wasn't trying hard enough, or always feeling inadequate were actually the signs of perfectionism. I thought they were indications that I was a failure. I also wasn't aware that being this way negatively affected my relationships, but it did. A personal experience taught me about my own perfectionism and gave me the impetus I needed to change.

A friend was listening to me criticize myself for getting a B on a paper. I was labeling myself as stupid and a terrible writer. At the same time I was going out of my way to reassure my friend that her B was just fine, good enough, and it definitely didn't mean anything negative about her. She seemed offended, annoyed, and eventually asked me why I was making this distinction between us. Did I think I was more capable, needed to do better, or should be held to a higher standard than she was? I had been unaware of this paradox in my thinking and didn't know how to answer her. I felt misunderstood and terribly guilty, but mostly confused. What she could not see, and what I didn't realize at the time, was that I *actually did* think I needed to do better than others. It was not because I thought I *was* better, but rather to make up for something defective deep inside of me that I could not name or explain. What I came to realize was that my belief that I had to be perfect or I was a failure was not only making those around me feel judged, it was also perpetuating my feelings of unworthiness and shame. Inside I had a belief that I was unworthy, so I tried to overcompensate by perfecting parts of myself that were visible to others, as an attempt to guard against others seeing the real me and what I feared was unacceptable. Through careful exploration of my thoughts, feelings, and behaviors I learned I hid behind my perfectionism to protect myself from judgment or rejection from others. The problem with this way of protecting myself was that it prevented me from getting what I truly wanted and desperately needed, which was for others to see and know the real me, flaws and all, and still accept and love me. If I never allowed that to happen, I would never feel truly loved. I had to learn to challenge my thoughts and take risks, one of which was being seen with my imperfections.

Cognitive distortions become entrenched and automatic, even when there is evidence to the contrary that challenges them. Changing your thoughts is a skill that takes effort, but isn't as hard as it might seem. Even if you have been thinking a certain way for a long time, your brain has the capacity to learn to think differently. New pathways are created each time you counteract a negative, distorted, or extreme thought with a more appropriate or reasonable one. We think of it as being fair and balanced in your thinking and seeing things as a total picture, instead of just seeing the worst of it. Learning how to counteract your cognitive distortions and balance your thinking will help you create a healthy inner life where mistakes are acceptable, failure is part of progress, and confidence grows with experience.

Challenging Your Thoughts and Distortions

Learning to challenge your distorted thoughts before they wreak havoc on your feelings is a crucial skill. In Key 2 we focused specifically on eating disorder thoughts, but most of our clients describe their "eating disorder voice" as becoming

FEEL YOUR FEELINGS, CHALLENGE YOUR THOUGHTS

a "critical voice" like we described in Key 3 and popping up in many other situations that are not food-related. The voice might be critical, negative, blaming, powerless, or something else entirely, depending on the situation. Using the dialoguing technique described in Key 2 for your distorted thoughts will help you find more balanced ways of thinking in any situation. It's important to realize that black and white thinking, personalizing, blaming, mind reading, or any of the common cognitive distortions can contribute to your eating disorder in a number of ways. The bad feelings that result from these distorted thoughts often lead to using eating disorder behaviors to cope, so learning to balance your thoughts is a very important skill for life and recovery.

> *"At some point I realized that my eating was fine, but I kept hearing a critical voice inside bugging me about other things, like I was lazy or not smart enough. I realized that I might always have an inner critic, but I could fight back with the same skills I learned to fight my eating disorder thoughts."*
>
> —AH

The following dialogue is an example of a client combating her automatic thoughts:

Situation: Kevin didn't call me this weekend.

Automatic Thought: He obviously doesn't want to be with me. His friends probably told him to blow me off.

Healthy Self: You have no idea why he didn't call and you are jumping to conclusions. You need to wait and find out the truth of the situation.

Distorted Thought: I am so afraid this means it's over between us. This has happened to me before. I am so anxious I can't think of other reasons.

Healthy Self: You have no evidence for that. Although it is possible there is no way you could know that now. You have to do something to calm yourself down and wait for more information.

Distorted Thought (beginning to fade): OK, I know I jump to conclusions; it's just really hard. I keep telling myself that it is probably the worst case and I know this is my pattern.

Healthy Self: So tell yourself that you no longer are going to jump to conclusions about things but will wait to find out and save your energy to deal with real problems whey they arise. Perhaps you can call Kevin and ask him what is going on.

Distorted Thought (transforming to healthy self): Yes, true. I don't want to assume things. It is difficult not to feel anxious but I will go for a bike ride and call Kevin later.

Writing Assignment: Dialoguing With Your Distorted Thoughts

Write down some of your automatic, critical, or distorted thoughts. You may already know some of your common ones but if not, a good time to see them clearly is right before or after an upsetting situation. After writing them down begin to challenge them using your healthy self. The goal is to have a full dialogue with your thoughts just as you learned to do in Key 2. Look out for the cognitive distortions and extreme words like "always," "never," "everyone," and "nobody"—they are red flags for distorted thoughts. Rarely are these extreme statements true and if you are honest, you will find a lot of contrary evidence. After writing down and then analyzing the evidence for and against the thought, it is very important to come up with a more bal-

anced way of thinking about the situation. This exercise might seem tedious at first, but our brains are very adaptable and in a short period of time, you will find yourself automatically noticing and challenging your distorted thoughts and dealing with things in a healthier and more balanced way. A client described the process of challenging her thought in this way: "Someone once told me that 'I am not responsible for my first thought, but I am responsible for my second thought.' Those few words are mighty powerful and helpful to me. Any time I'd look in the mirror, I'd automatically say something negative about myself. I made a vow that whenever I said anything negative about my looks, personality, or anything, I would—every single time—counter it and say the exact opposite of what I originally said to balance it out. After awhile, I really did start to think more positively, and others noticed this too."

Your Feelings

Ideally, our feelings are supposed to alert us when something in our life needs attention. Our feelings also give us vital information on how to proceed. If we can connect to our feelings, and understand and accept them, they can help us decide when to make one choice over another, or when to move toward something and when to move away. If you are disconnected from your feelings or are overly emotional, making good decisions is difficult at best, and even unlikely. Young children haven't fully developed rational thinking abilities yet, so they are good examples of what it looks like when decisions are made from a purely emotional place. A child may want a new puppy but has no idea of all the time, energy, and money that is necessary to care for it. A child may be afraid of monsters under the bed even though he or she is told over and over that there is no such thing as a monster. When you are taken over by your emotions you make choices that don't seem that rational later once the emotional charge has died down. If you feel angry or sad your feelings can interfere with your ability to make choices. Therefore it is important to recognize and feed your feelings and move past them in order to make good decisions. You feel too guilty or fearful to eat even a bite of ice cream, even though logically you know one bite of ice cream can't make you fat. Effective problem-solving and healthy decision-making occur when you are able to identify, feel, and then integrate your emotions or feelings with your rational mind or thoughts. When your emotions are high, tapping into that rational space can be challenging, but we are sure you will quickly realize that learning to be patient and allowing the rational thoughts in is a skill worth working on.

Exploring Your Emotions As Signals

Although your emotions serve as signals that something is going on that needs your attention, problems arise when you experience feelings of fear, shame, and anger, signaling that something is wrong, and you react before exploring further. Sometimes your feelings will be based on distorted thoughts: erroneous assumptions, faulty information, or irrational fear. For example, let's say you expected to receive an invitation to a wedding and everyone else has received their invitation, and yours isn't in the mailbox. It is understandable that you would feel hurt, sad, and angry if you were purposely excluded from such an occasion. If you immediately act on those feelings when your emotions are running very high, your anger might incite you into an outburst or aggressive action that you would regret and feel embarrassed about if you received your invitation the next day or found out that it was just lost in the mail. Instead of using your feelings as signals to react immediately, try to think of your feelings as signals to investigate further, communicate or reach out for support, and then react or respond in the most effective way.

Feel Your Feelings

As you progress in your recovery, your feelings will become more noticeable and seem more intense. Reconnecting with the myriad of feelings that have been covered up for so long is the reason why getting better often feels worse, at first. Recovery involves learning to feel your feelings associated with all the various stressors that surface in your life, without using your eating disorder or any other way of escaping or masking them. The notion that we are supposed to *feel our feelings* may sound obvious, but many people, not just those with eating disorders, do all kinds of things to avoid, suppress, or distract from their feelings. People get into trouble with addictions, eating disorders, stealing, self-harm, or a myriad of other behaviors because they have not learned to acknowledge, accept, and tolerate their feelings.

If you are worried about not knowing what you feel, simply stop yourself from engaging in an eating disorder behavior and notice all the feelings that come up. Whatever they are and wherever they came from, a good part of your work will be simply dealing with them.

Writing Assignment: What Feelings Are There

In order to start examining how your eating disorder is serving you, and what feelings are associated with it, make a list of the last few times you engaged in your eating disorder behaviors. List any feelings you were aware of at the time, or which, you now realize, you may have been trying to avoid, distract from, or manage. If you aren't sure, just list what else was going on at that time. Have you ever been interrupted from engaging in an eating disorder behavior? What were the feelings that came up when you did not get to go through with the behavior?

"Feeling Fat": Is It Really a Feeling?

Feeling fat is something that plagues people with eating disorders and soon becomes a trigger for all kinds of feelings and behaviors. "I feel fat" is a standard refrain of our clients. Many therapists will say, "Fat isn't a feeling," but having had eating disorders ourselves, we remember "feeling" fat and accept it when clients tell us that. Having said that though, we also understand that when therapists or others try to explain that fat is not a feeling, it is because they want you to look further into what other feelings (or thoughts) might *also* be there lurking under the surface. Sometimes "feeling fat" can be fueled by fear of judgment, moments of self-doubt, shame, or insecurity. We cannot say exactly what lies beneath "feeling fat" for you, but chances are it is a feeling you have a hard time tolerating. People with eating disorders complain of "feeling fat," regardless of what they weigh, thus corroborating that it can have little or nothing to do with actual weight or size, and more to do with a distorted perception mixed with feelings of anxiety, judgment, or discomfort. If you assume you will stop feeling fat when you lose more weight, or get to the "right" weight, we would argue that is not likely to happen for you if you have an eating disorder. Body dissatisfaction and distortion continues, fueled by the false belief that if you just lose a little more, you will finally feel thin enough, and therefore good enough, worthy, lovable, or whatever insecurity is lurking under your relentless pursuit of weight loss. Many clients report feeling happy, doing well with food, and feeling OK in their bodies, until they get on the scale and see they have gained a few pounds. All of a sudden they feel fat, depressed, unworthy, ashamed, and want to do something to "fix" that feeling. Think about that: why would a number on a scale, or a few pounds, be responsible for all those feelings? This is not how most people normally react, so if you react that way, something else is going on *inside* that you need to attend to. As long as you believe that changing something on your outside will solve the problem on the inside, these deeper issues will stay hidden and unresolved. We understand the statement, "I feel fat," but this means a variety of things to a variety of people, and you need to decipher what it means to you. Furthermore, transferring painful and uncomfortable feelings into "feeling fat" can become an automatic process. It feels safer to say, "I feel fat" than it does to say, "I feel lonely" or "I fear I will never find love."

Writing Assignment: "I Feel Fat"

Think back to the last time you "felt fat." Write about what was going on right before you had that feeling. What were you doing? Who were you with? What other feelings were you having that you can identify? To see what else might be there, try to replace the word "fat" with any other word such as "angry," "scared," or "overwhelmed."

Understanding and Regulating Feelings

"I realized that I would never achieve what I wanted in life if I continued down the path I had made. I had to learn acceptance and embracing instead of avoiding and pushing away—whether it's people, food, feelings, or life."

—SB

Whether you are disconnected from your feelings, or overwhelmed by the intensity when you do feel them, with very few, or possibly no, tools for managing or regulating them, it's understandable you would try to avoid them. You might react to your feelings in ways that initially seem helpful, but cause more problems in the long run. People with eating disorders will say that avoiding or escaping their feelings through behaviors such as purging or skipping a meal provides temporary relief from feelings that seem intolerable. Eventually, though, the feelings come back. To become a more balanced person and live a full life you need to challenge this thinking, face your issues, and feel your feelings. It can be hard, painful, and scary to actually feel your feelings. There may be many areas in your life where you have repressed your feelings for a long time, but emotional healing takes place when you are able recognize and confront your issues and not use your behaviors to avoid the feelings that arise.

You might not even realize you are using your eating disorder to manage or avoid your feelings on a day-to-day basis. The connection between your eating disorder behaviors and your feelings can be very difficult to detect at first, but will become clearer over time. As your recovery progresses, exploring, accepting, tolerating, and *feeling* your feelings becomes not only less overwhelming, but rewarding.

Personal Reflections:

Gwen: Feeling vulnerable was the first feeling I realized I couldn't tolerate, although I didn't want to admit it, because even thinking about admitting it triggered the very feeling of vulnerability I was afraid of. I did everything I could to keep myself from feeling vulnerable. I was guarded, untrusting, and went out of my way to appear easygoing, fine, and happy all the time. I'm not sure if I even knew what I was afraid would happen if I was vulnerable, but once in awhile when I

FEEL YOUR FEELINGS, CHALLENGE YOUR THOUGHTS

was not guarded or distracting myself, feelings of sadness, emptiness, and fear would creep in. I would get a glimpse of the lost person I had become in my eating disorder and how alone I felt, and it terrified me.

Instead of acknowledging my fears and vulnerability and reaching out for help, I went back to my eating disorder, which seemed to act as a buffer, a distraction, and a way to keep the focus on the outside, instead of inside, where the problem really was. On the outside, I tried to look like a person who had perfect control over her life. Even when I had some idea my outside appearance had crossed over from "thin and together" to "definitely ill," I still could not give up the rigid, almost cult-like belief that if I was just thinner, I would feel better. If I didn't feel good enough, it was because I wasn't thin enough. I felt so invested in my eating disorder and my belief system, it was hard admitting to myself that I had it all wrong this whole time.

Carolyn: In our therapeutic relationship, Gwen was highly sensitive about the possibility of making me angry, hurting me, or doing anything she thought would make me dislike her. Any strong feelings made her want to escape to avoid any confrontation or any expression of anger, which she feared would hurt people. Gwen needed help realizing that, in reality, it was not her strong feelings or her anger that was a problem, it was the hurt and fear underneath. It was important to help Gwen see that behind her anger was hurt and sadness, and although expressing it would make her feel vulnerable, denying her feelings was driving her to use her eating disorder to cope. I began working with Gwen to help her recognize that her biggest fear was feeling vulnerable in any way and the more intense the feeling, the more vulnerable she felt. I can even remember her cringing when I said she needed to learn how to be "vulnerable," so we jokingly referred to it as the "V word" from then on. I tried many approaches to help Gwen learn to tolerate vulnerability a little better. I encouraged her to take small risks in expressing herself and staying present, first with me, next her husband, and then her friends. Even though she was very resistant to all of these new experiences, her sense of humor and her drive to succeed proved to be very valuable traits that helped her through.

I also tried to model for Gwen that it is possible for a person to be vulnerable and even emotional, and still hold onto themselves and be strong. Gwen learned what I had learned so many years before her: that feeling her feelings was not only tolerable, but actually helped her be less overwhelmed. For both of us feeling our feelings helped us, both then and now, to live a more authentic and enjoyable life.

Gwen: Learning how to be more open was very difficult, but I tried to take some risks. The hardest part was admitting and talking about things I felt ashamed of. For many years I was not in touch with the shame I had developed about my body, and I forgot how bad it felt and how vulnerable it made me feel. Initially, my eating disorder seemed to be the antidote to my shame. The more weight I lost, the stronger and more confident I felt. As my dieting willpower strengthened, the shame I had been carrying around for so long initially seemed to melt away, along with the pounds. For the first time ever, I felt successful at "controlling myself," which was intoxicating and even redemptive after so many years of trying and failing to lose weight. Being thin was "evidence" that I was in control of my appetites and protected me from the perceived judgment of others, or so I thought. My shame was redirected into guilty feelings about eating "bad foods" then into eating in front of people, and finally I was unable to even admit when I experienced hunger. I didn't realize losing weight was just a temporary fix, and my shame was much deeper than my extra weight. Eventually, my eating disorder itself added to my shame. I knew I was living a double life and was terrified people would discover the truth and reject me. I acted confident and put-together, but inside I knew I was fooling everyone and worried that my weak, gluttonous self would be exposed at any moment. In my relentless quest to lose weight, I was chasing acceptableness and betraying myself in the pursuit. The relief of my eating disorder was never enough and never lasted. Eventually, it became impossible to deny reality, and I knew I needed to seek help if I wanted to live. My biggest fear had come to be. I was exposed, vulnerable, and everyone was going to know I had this problem. I could not think of anything that scared me more, and I wanted to run away. Little did I know that at the bottom of that dark center of my shame was the only path to freedom. Admitting I needed help and then accepting the help were both very scary and humbling experiences. I was told that I needed to be nicer to myself, which was a whole new concept to absorb, but how to go about doing it was even more baffling to me. The most helpful discovery I had was when I realized I could use my healthy self/voice to talk back to the critical and even shaming voice inside my head. I learned that when I had a critical thought, I could counter that thought with something kinder. Most of the time what I said back involved accepting I was *doing the best that I could*, that I was *good enough* as a mother, wife, and daughter. I started to allow myself to be less than perfect. Even though it took a lot of intention and practice, I could see it was working to reduce my shame in a lasting way. I realized that shame was the flip side of my perfectionism. As I started judging myself less harshly, I was also less afraid of the judgment of others. This came as quite a surprise to me, because I had spent my whole life protecting myself from the judgment of others by judging myself first and more harshly. Feeling my feelings, not judging them, expressing myself, and counteracting my negative thoughts started working, and more and more, I actually started to *feel* good enough.

Name It To Tame It

People with eating disorders are often confused about or out of touch with what they are feeling. You might have had a hard time identifying your feelings before you even developed an eating disorder, but after you have had an eating disorder for some time, this task is even harder. You might wonder why identifying and talking about your feelings is helpful. From our own personal experience, our work with clients, and from new brain research, we know that when you identify and talk about your feelings it helps you to better control, regulate, tolerate, and diffuse them. Using words to describe your feelings is useful for you if you have trouble knowing what you feel or if you are overwhelmed by your feelings. Very simply put it turns out that by describing your feelings you link and integrate your left (language mode) and right (emotional mode) brain hemispheres. This integration helps balance both emotional dullness and dysregulation creating emotional health and stability. This has been referred to as "Name It To Tame It" (Siegel 2010, pg. 116).

Writing Assignment: "Feelings Journal"

Keeping a feelings journal will help you immensely in identifying your feelings. There are different ways to keep a feelings journal. One way is to just keep a journal with you so you can jot down and describe various feelings you have during the day. Another idea is to get your journal out at night and write about the various feelings you had during the day. Take a moment now to write about a few feelings you have had today, including some that may have arisen from reading this book.

Don't Judge Your Feelings

It is important to accept your feelings and not judge them. Feelings arise and they are what they are. Feelings are not good or bad, right or wrong. You feel what you feel. Even if your reasons for feeling a certain way are faulty, the feeling is still there. If someone yells at you and you feel angry inside, but you tell yourself you should not feel angry because "anger is bad," you will end up dealing with your angry feelings in some other way.

If you label your feelings as being invalid, bad, or unimportant, chances are you will not express them or seek support. Express your feelings, even your feelings *about* your feelings. In other words, if you are angry but feel bad about it, say that. If you feel jealous, but guilty about feeling jealous, say that. The goal is to become the most transparent you can be. You are not responsible for your feelings, but for what you *do* with them.

Your Emotions Are Your Body's Response To Your Thoughts

If your boyfriend is mean to you and calls you a name and you feel angry, that anger is in your body. Your body is responding not just to what your boyfriend said but also to what you think about what he said. For example you might think, *What an idiot, I didn't deserve that*. Your body then takes on the energy of that thought and you *feel* anger. If you had a different thought such as, *Oh he was stressed today, I'll let him have some space and not take what he said personally*, then your body would have a different energy. Our body manifests our thoughts into feelings and the emotions that go with them.

It is useful to understand that your feelings and emotions are inside of your body. This knowledge can help you begin to gain separation from your emotions, which leads to being able to regulate them. One way we help our clients grasp this concept is by asking them to change the way they talk about feelings. For example, instead of thinking *I am angry*, it is more accurate and helpful to say, "I have anger in me." Saying this might sound awkward and we don't expect people to go out in the world and talk like that, but we use this phrasing to demonstrate a crucial truth; if you have anger *in* you, you can figure out how to get it *out* of you. There are many ways to get anger out of your body: taking time to let it slowly drain out, listening to calming music, going for a run. The important thing is that once you have gotten any intense emotion out of your body, it no longer can take over your ability to think clearly and communicate what you might need or want.

What exactly is your body feeling when you feel anger? Does the word "anger" *really* describe what is going on inside of you? No! Anger is just a convenient word we all use to label an emotion, but it is not a good description of what our body is really experiencing, or feeling. In fact, there are many feelings associated with anger. Think about when you feel angry. How does your body actually feel? Are your palms sweaty? Do your face and neck feel hot? Does your pulse become elevated? Just the act of noticing and describing the various sensations in your body can help dissipate the anger and calm you down. All the things we are describing will help you to separate yourself from your emotions by identifying the feelings you have in your body. Then you can come up with a way to counteract the feeling. For example, if you feel hot you might have to literally find a way of "cooling off." Focusing on deep and long breaths will help slow down a fast pulse, or you can do something to discharge the anger, for example one client we know releases anger from her body by practicing martial arts. The goal is learning how to separate from your feelings and emotions and get your body back to neutral. When you can do this, you will be able to resist being overwhelmed or taken over by your feelings. Once you are back to neutral it is easier to think clearly to figure out what you need to say or do. Learning how

FEEL YOUR FEELINGS, CHALLENGE YOUR THOUGHTS 117

to identify, describe, and separate yourself from your feelings helps free you from being controlled by or overreacting to them.

Getting the Feelings Out of Your Body: Opposite Action

A good way to reduce the intensity of a feeling and help you get it out of your body is to do the opposite of what your initial and usual urge is telling you to do. "Opposite action" is a term from dialectical behavior therapy (DBT), which is a type of therapy that successfully teaches core skills for regulating difficult emotions in effective ways (Astrachan-Fletcher & Maslar, 2009). It is hard to do opposite action when your emotions are telling you otherwise, but it works extremely well. Opposite actions don't work well if you are just going through the motions or faking it. You have to really do it with meaning if you want it to be effective. You might need a therapist or someone else to help you decide when to apply opposite action. For example, in a situation where you have a justifiable fear and need to run for your life, it would be foolish to do the opposite such as approaching the situation. Opposite action is meant to help you neutralize your feelings so they are not overwhelming or overshadowing your ability to think clearly.

Examples of Opposite Action

EMOTION	URGE	OPPOSITE ACTION
Anger	attack, yell, lash out to hurt	validate, speak quietly
Fear	avoid, run, scream	approach, do it over and over

EMOTION	URGE	OPPOSITE ACTION
Guilt	hide, avoid, isolate	admit, accept, move on
Sadness	shut down, withdraw, isolate	get active, set goals, socialize
Shame	hide, punish, keep secret	talk openly, express feelings

Somatic Therapy

Biologically based therapies, also known as somatic therapies, are based upon our understanding of the human nervous system, and how troubling or traumatic experiences disturb the body and the natural rhythm of internal states of well-being. Somatic therapies help you interrupt and reduce or eliminate unpleasant or disturbing emotions and sensations within the body. Somatic therapies focus on body sensations and help you recognize that there are other sensations in the body besides the disturbing ones and how to have more control over your body states. Because our fears are manifested in our body and are often not really about the current situation, or are illogical, trying to get rid of them by using traditional talk therapy is often limited. Imagine a woman who was assaulted or robbed in a parking lot after work. She might become highly anxious when she finds herself in a parking lot, in the dark, or even just alone. No matter how many times you reassure her she is not in danger, she can't get her body to calm down or believe it. The same is true for people who are reminded of other situations or feelings that were harmful or frightening. Somatic therapy is about teaching you how to tune into your body sensations, and learn how to regulate them. We help our clients develop mindful awareness of their body sensations. We help them notice when their body is out of balance as well as notice positive or neutral sensations that lead to reestablishing natural rhythms of well-being, like expanded, deeper breathing and release of muscle tension. We encourage you to explore this area further and refer you to books in the resource section.

Some Helpful Strategies for Dealing with Your Body Sensations

There are many body-oriented techniques, like body scanning, that can help systematically relax each part of your body. There are body stances you can take which are associated with the feelings you are trying to lessen. For example, if you are afraid, you might notice that your shoulders are very tense and hiked up towards your ears, your breath is short, and your stomach feels like it is in a tight knot. If your body was reacting this way, we might ask you to focus on your breathing and ask you if you want to experiment by changing your body stance. The idea is to put your body in the position it would be in if it was calm. Even if you feel afraid, you can physically lower your shoulders, take deeper and slower breaths, soften and relax your stomach and back muscles, and counteract anything else that your body does when afraid. What happens in the brain when you do this is pretty miraculous. Placing your body in a more relaxed stance kicks in your parasympathetic nervous system, changes your brain, and actually helps your body to calm down. Body therapies are often used when dealing with trauma, or traumatic stress symptoms, but they are useful for learning to tolerate and change sensations and feelings of all kinds.

Sometimes You Just Need Some Self Care

Even though we have devoted much of this book thus far to telling you to face, feel, and express your feelings, we also recognize that sometimes it is useful and kind to have positive self-care methods to help you comfort or distract yourself from the feelings you have. Sometimes you just need a break from things or something to make you *feel* better. The following are methods and skills we have found useful for our clients and ourselves.

Distraction

Distraction is a very useful coping skill when used appropriately. People often confuse distraction with avoidance, but when you use distraction skills your intention is to distract yourself only if there is nothing else to do about the situation or until you are in a calmer, more rational state of mind. Distraction helps to get your mind off of something that seems to be taking it over, like strong urges or something very upsetting. Urges are feelings and they come and go. For most people, urges tend to dissipate after twenty minutes or so, but it can be a useful experiment to see how long your urges last by timing one. Finding things that truly work to distract you can be a challenge and will take some experimentation. There are literally hundreds of activities that you could try in order to distract yourself, but we will list here only a few ideas.

- Call a friend.
- Dance around your living room.
- Organize or clean something.
- Volunteer or help someone else.
- Paint or do an art project.
- Go out for a meal with someone.
- Watch a movie or television.
- Play a video game.
- Knit.
- Go shopping.
- Journal or read.
- Go for a drive.

Self-Soothing

Self-soothing is another important way to help you cope. Self-soothing consists of finding a way to comfort yourself in times of distress or trouble. It may be easier to self-soothe after you have distracted yourself a bit, especially if your feelings are very intense. Some self-soothing methods can serve as distractions, but often, strong feelings require a distraction that matches the intensity of the emotion for it to be helpful. If you are angry it might be hard to take a bath and relax, but cleaning out the garage might work perfectly. Self-soothing is meant to help relax your body and mind. An effective way to do this is to engage your five senses. Everyone is different, so something that soothes our senses might aggravate yours. Just like with distraction, this takes experimentation and an open mind. As you read through this list of ways to self-soothe through the senses, think about what might work for you and consider trying new things as well.

- Sense of vision: look at nature or pictures that remind you of places or people you love; look at art; watch a fire in a fireplace.
- Sense of touch: take a hot bath or shower, get a massage; hug someone who is comforting; pet an animal; put on warm and comfortable pajamas and slippers.
- Sense of taste: have a cup of your favorite tea or coffee; eat your favorite meal; buy a new flavored lip balm.
- Sense of smell: burn a candle or incense; use a favorite perfume or buy a new one; put fresh flowers in your house.
- Sense of hearing: listen to soothing music; listen to a meditation CD; listen to a fountain or waterfall.

Creative Assignment:
Your Resource Box

Making a resource box is a great assignment to do with a friend or a few friends. Read the assignment over and see if you can find someone who will do this project with you. Get an empty box, for example a shoebox, and decorate it any way you like. You are going to turn this box into a resource box, which will contain items you will need at the moment you find yourself wanting distraction or comfort. Fill the box with things that would be hard for you to go get in the spur of the moment. You will be surprised how grateful you are to have the items readily available. Examples our clients have shared with us include: favorite CDs, a special brand of tea or coffee, a favorite perfume or aromatherapy essential oil, bath foam and great smelling soap, candles (and matches), pen and paper, pictures of loved ones or beautiful places, and special notes from people or favorite quotes.

Additional Assignment

Internet Assignment:
Awareness App

We recently learned about a new iPhone app called AWARENESS. For a few dollars, this app gives prompts throughout the day using a gentle "gong" sound, which serves to remind you to record a feeling and what you are doing. This app also leads you in a brief meditative exercise that can be done anywhere and finishes with an inspirational quote related to the feeling you recorded. You can get reports and graphs on your feelings, 20-minute meditations, and much more. Using AWARENESS could be a fun, interesting, and innovative way for you to learn more about your feelings.

Final Thoughts

Hopefully, this key has helped you understand your feelings better and be less afraid of them. We hope you have gained insight into some of your triggers, urges, and subsequent actions, and how your eating disorder helps you and hurts you at the same time. The feelings underneath your symptoms, whether they are part of the cause or what is perpetuating your eating disorder, might not have been obvious or may still not be obvious to you, especially since feelings change and expand over time. Don't be discouraged if your head is spinning and you are finding all of this overwhelming. Some things need to be read over, talked about, and worked on many times in order for you to fully grasp how it is that you have come to use food or behaviors like bingeing and purging in order to deal with underlying issues and the feelings associated with them. Healing involves learning to cope with your feelings without your eating disorder behaviors, as well as learning to accept your natural healthy body weight and putting food and weight back into their proper perspective in your life. You will not be able to do this without directly dealing with food and weight issues in your day-to-day life. Even though we explained in Key 3 that eating disorders are not about the food, we know we didn't fool you and you know that on some level they are absolutely about food, and eating, and weight. In the next key we will address your relationship with food and hopefully inspire you to take some risks, begin the process of change, and begin to build not only a better relationship with food, but also with yourself and others.

KEY 5:
IT *IS* ABOUT THE FOOD

I remember standing in the hospital cafeteria and thinking, *There is nothing here for me. I can't eat any of this*, and then I looked around and—it hit me. Everyone runs on food. Every hug, every kiss, every page ever written is because of food. Without food there is no life. Everyone has to eat! I was so disconnected from the real purpose of food as nutrition and so focused on the emotional uses of food that I forgot that we all run on food. This was an important realization in my recovery and still strikes me as important.

—TA

Many people come to us for help and tell us they want to "get better," but they don't want to change the way they eat, gain any weight, or accept their ideal or natural weight. They want to gain insight into family dynamics, talk about their feelings, and discuss underlying issues, but they are very resistant and sometimes even unwilling to deal with or change their problematic food behaviors. We understand this. We both initially felt resistant to changing our eating behaviors in the beginning of recovery.

In Key 3 we explained that eating disorders are not about food because: a) food itself does not cause the problem; and b) there are many other aspects, other than issues of food and weight, that are involved in an eating disorder. The reality, however, is that it *is* possible to recover without ever gaining insight or dealing with underlying issues that caused your eating disorder, but if you don't change your relationship with food, you cannot recover. Key 5 is devoted to understanding and changing your relationship with food.

Are You Too Rigid, Too Chaotic, or Both?

Most people with eating disorders struggle with issues of control around food and are either too rigid, too chaotic, or both. Those who restrict are too rigid, those who binge (whether they purge or not) are too chaotic, and if you do both, you vacillate between rigidity and chaos. Finding balance in your relationship with food is the goal and challenge. Rigid control over your food and weight actually leads to being out of control of your life. Your rigid rules and fears are actually controlling *you*, rather than the other way around. If you binge, you most likely feel chaotic and long for some degree of control. You may find that you do not easily fit in one category, or stay on one end of the spectrum, but rather vacillate between rigidity and chaos. People often slide between the diagnostic categories from one type of eating disorder to another. Regardless of what kind of eating disorder you have, you are not eating or living in balance. Your life has become driven by thoughts and beliefs regarding what you think you should look like and what you think you should do to make that happen.

> **Carolyn:** At some point early on in my work as a therapist I realized that all my clients had tenets related to food and weight that they were trying to live by, even though they had never formally written them out or told anybody. After hearing these over and over I compiled a list called "The Thin Commandments" of these rules or beliefs clients had reported to me over the years and published it in my book, *Your Dieting Daughter* (1997). Look over the list and see which ones seem familiar.

The Thin Commandments

- If you aren't thin, you aren't attractive.
- Being thin is more important than being healthy, more important than anything.
- You must buy clothes, cut your hair, take laxatives, starve yourself, and do anything to make yourself look thinner.
- Thou shall "earn" all food and shall not eat without feeling guilty.
- Thou shall not eat fattening food without punishing oneself afterwards.
- Thou shall count calories and fat and restrict intake accordingly.
- What the scale says is the most important thing.
- Losing weight is good, and gaining weight is bad.
- You can't trust what other people say about your weight.
- Being thin and not eating are signs of true willpower and success. (pg. 13)

Food Rules

Aside from beliefs like The Thin Commandments, most people with eating disorders have developed what we refer to as "food rules." Even if you have not written them down, spoken them out loud, or formally considered them rules, you likely hold certain beliefs about what you should or should not do with food. Some of our clients immediately recognize what we mean when we ask about their food rules, but others need examples and time to think about what rules they are actually following. For example, you might have a rule about not eating anything after 9:00 p.m., not eating dessert, or that you must purge if you eat something "fattening."

The reason you have developed food rules or other rules regarding your weight is to provide you with a way of "keeping yourself in line." Rules can give you a sense of control and assurance that nothing bad or unexpected will happen. Food rules are objective, measurable, and they limit choice, making you feel "safer" when you are tempted or anxious around food. It is easy to believe that these rules will alleviate the mistrust you feel about your own appetite, desires, and decisions. If you believe you cannot trust yourself or your body, it makes sense that you would develop rules, whether consciously or not, to keep you in line.

Writing Assignment: What Are Your Food Rules?

Take a moment to write out your food rules in your journal. Write down as many as possible, the reason for each rule, and what you think it does for you. Write the rules as well as your beliefs, if you know them.

Next, it is important to evaluate your rules. Look over your rules one by one. For each rule ask yourself, how did I come up with this rule? Do I plan on following this rule forever? What happens if I break the rule? The following questions will help you evaluate and reconsider your rules.

- *Is this rule based on facts or fears?*
- *How does this rule inhibit relationships? How does this rule enhance them?*
- *Do other people have to follow this rule to be OK, and if not, why do I?*
- *Does this rule allow for any flexibility, for unusual situations like being sick, or having an especially active week?*
- *Does this rule allow for special occasions or holidays?*
- *Would I tell anyone else to follow this rule? Why or why not?*

IT *IS* ABOUT THE FOOD

- *What am I giving up by following this rule? What am I gaining?*
- *What would it take for me to give up this rule?*

It's important to see your food rules for what they are, how they limit your life, and how they make you feel. To work at getting well you need to begin to challenge your rules, let go of them, perhaps even adopt healthier ones, and develop a more satisfying relationship with food.

Changing Your Relationship with Food

Following food rules or engaging in eating disorder behaviors can temporarily feel empowering and seem helpful. The problem is that this does not work in the long run, because even if you gain a sense of control, it is only an illusion and temporary at best. You probably feel afraid to let go of your rules and your behaviors, or change your weight, because you fear what would happen. Change can feel scary. You don't know what will happen, and you aren't sure if changing will be worth it. The fact that we and countless others stay recovered is a testament to just how much better it really is on the other side of an eating disorder. If this was not the case, we would have returned to our eating disorders and would not be trying to help you.

Letting go of eating disorder behaviors and finding balance with your food takes awareness, practice, and of course, patience. Even if you feel attached to your behaviors and resistant to changing them, we encourage you to be as open as possible to what we have to say. Nobody except for you can decide whether you want to change or not.

In order to begin changing your relationship with food, it is important to look at your current behaviors, so you can be honest with yourself about what you are doing and what you need to work on and change. Even though you might not be sure that you want to let go of a specific rule, belief, or behavior, the fact that you are reading this book suggests you want something to be different, or at least you are thinking about it. The following writing assignment will help you start looking at goals you have and thus changes you might like to make.

Writing Assignment: What Are Your Food Goals?

Whether or not you feel ready or able to achieve your goals, it is helpful to have them written down so you are clear about them and are able to revisit them regularly. Take some time, try to be honest, and set aside your fears for now. Answer the following questions as if you are not afraid of losing control or gaining too much weight or being deprived, or any other fears that might come up for you.

- *What would you like to do with food that you currently can't do (e.g. eat a variety of foods, eat without feeling anxious or guilty, eat with friends, go to restaurants, eat things you really like)?*
- *What behaviors would you like to stop doing with food, but currently can't stop (e.g., counting calories, eating all night, cutting up food into bits, only buying fat free food, bingeing)?*
- *Describe what you think a healthy relationship with food looks like. How would you would like your relationship with food to look if you did not have to worry about your weight?*
- *Compare your two answers. Referring to your journal will help you stay connected with your intentions and goals as you explore the ideas in this key and begin to work toward change.*

You may have so many goals that it seems overwhelming, or you don't know where to start. We suggest you pick a few to start with and focus on those until you make progress, and then you can move on to other ones. Even if you are willing to choose one goal to start with you are on the right path.

It might take a while to unravel the issues involved in both the development and deconstruction of some strongly held beliefs and ingrained behavior patterns. You developed your behaviors over time to help yourself in ways you might just be starting to understand, or maybe do not yet understand at all. To break your patterns you will need to start challenging your food rules. A good place to start is by looking at your rules about "good" foods and "bad" foods.

Letting Go of "Good" and "Bad" Food Labels

Writing Assignment: Good and Bad Foods

Many people follow some kind of rule about what are considered "bad" or forbidden foods and what are "good" or allowed foods. The list of good and bad foods can change based on the latest and most popular diet being promoted. If you have an eating disorder, you most likely have this list in your mind. Make a written list of the foods you consider good and bad and add any reason or information that makes you think this. Examine your own evidence or lack of evidence that supports your beliefs.

We have very important news for you: as far as your weight is concerned, there is no such thing as a "good" or "bad" food. If you label a food "bad," it usually means you think it has too many calories, not the right kind of calories, or is a food that makes you feel out of control, all of which will supposedly lead to weight gain. If you label a food "good," it most likely means the food is low calorie, and/or you hope it will help you lose weight or prevent weight gain. The list of what is considered good food and bad food can change based on the latest popular diet being promoted in the media. One year, fat is bad and the next year, carbohydrates are bad. We are well aware that different foods contain different nutrients. Some foods are more nutrient-dense than others, and some foods, such as certain kinds of fats, are better for your health than others, but as far as your weight is concerned, a calorie is a calorie. Weight is determined by calories consumed versus calories burned. No food is bad or should be forbidden. Your body does not gain weight from 300 calories of yogurt and fruit any more or less than it does from 300 calories of pasta and meatballs. This is a very hard belief to break down, so you may need to read that last sentence over and over. After you read this key, we hope you will be able to fight against your eating disorder self more effectively when it tells you certain foods are bad or will make you gain weight. We are also going to introduce you to a philosophy of eating that is simple really, but at first you will find it difficult to do, because it will be far from what you are doing now and you may not trust it. You may initially have to follow a meal plan or a more specific structure than the one we are going to present you with now (more to come on this) but we will start by teaching you the end goal so you can have it in your mind.

Conscious Eating

Conscious eating is the ultimate goal for you and your relationship with food. When we use the term "conscious," we mean *using knowledge and awareness.* When you practice conscious eating you place an emphasis on awareness of your body signals, incorporate general education about nutrition, take into account any relevant health information, and eat the foods you truly enjoy. Some of our clients have misused nutrition information or "health food" doctrines as a way to justify restricted eating. Eating only raw foods or organic foods or vegan foods might have some health benefits for a person without an eating disorder, but if you have an eating disorder you cannot afford to hide behind these kinds of nutritional dictates. Until you recover from your eating disorder, such rigid extremes have no place in your life and will continue to keep you in an unhealthy, good food versus bad food mindset. As long as you have an eating disorder, there is no way to justify that you are doing this kind of eating for health reasons. The health consequences of your eating disorder far outweigh those of eating cooked food or non-organic produce. Even well after recovery we do not recommend such rigid eating standards that would undermine conscious eating. Eating consciously is a powerful alternative to restrictive food rules and chaotic eating disorder behaviors. Eating consciously helps you decide when, what, and how much to eat, and ultimately allows for a healthier relationship with food and your body. Conscious eating is a shift in thinking and takes attention and patience to learn, but eventually becomes second nature and takes no effort. Feeling doubtful? We don't blame you a bit. We know it might be hard to believe that there is a way of eating that will help you heal your eating disorder and allow you to feel safe around food and maintain an appropriate weight.

Becoming A Conscious Eater

Since it takes knowledge and awareness to be a conscious eater, we provide guidelines that explain what kind of knowledge and awareness we mean. We trust and follow these guidelines and we have seen them work with our clients. At first some of the guidelines or how you can follow them may be confusing, but as you read through the key you will gain a more thorough understanding. We recommend discussing the following concepts with a dietitian who has experience treating eating disorders for more information, or to enhance our conscious eating philosophy and help you with this process.

Conscious Eating Guidelines

1. Be conscious of your hunger. Eat when moderately hungry; don't wait until you are famished.
2. Eat regularly. Do not skip meals, and if possible, don't go over four hours without eating.
3. Allow yourself to eat all foods (unless you are allergic or have some other serious health issue).
4. Eat what you want, while also being conscious of how foods make you feel, what you have already eaten, and relevant health issues (for example, candy may not be a good conscious choice if you have diabetes or if you haven't eaten any protein all day).
5. All calories are equivalent when it comes to weight (that is, a calorie is a calorie).
6. For meals, eat a balance of protein, fat, and carbohydrates. Your body needs all of these to function properly and efficiently. Deprivation of foods or nutrients leads to physical and psychological problems and can actually trigger eating disorder behaviors.
7. Stay conscious of your fullness and your satisfaction. You can eat a lot and not be satisfied. Texture and taste of food is important for satisfaction and eating enough is important so your body registers the experience of being comfortably full. The goal is to feel full and satisfied, but not physically uncomfortable in any way.
8. If you do overeat (which is normal to do sometimes), reassure yourself that your body can handle the excess food if you simply get back on track. It is OK to wait until you are hungry before eating again, but don't wait too long.
9. Enjoy food and the pleasure of eating. At times, enhance your eating to dining, using candles, nice dishes and flowers on the table.

IT *IS* ABOUT THE FOOD

10. Make conscious choices to avoid foods that make you physically feel bad after eating them.

As you can see, all of the guidelines are specific ways to help you be conscious and present when eating, knowledgeable about your choices, and aware of how your body feels. Developing a healthy, balanced relationship with food (not too restrictive or permissive) is an empowering and life-altering experience. The Conscious Eating Guidelines will help you find balance in your relationship with food. Even if this is not your first step in terms of changing your relationship to food, know that you can get there and commit to yourself that you will give it a try.

Putting the New Guidelines into Practice

When you are ready you can begin to put our new eating guidelines into practice. The "conscious" part is the core and will make all the other parts possible to follow. Some people resist the idea of adopting what they think of as even more guidelines. Many clients tell us they are already too conscious about everything they eat, eliminating every food they believe to be "bad" or "unhealthy." Others are very self-conscious and worry about what people will think or say about their food choices. Many clients who are overweight feel self-conscious about eating certain foods in front of others. They fear judgment or comments like "how could she be eating that?" We understand how hard it is to ignore or not care about what others think, but it is really important that you give yourself permission to eat all foods. There are also those who are unconscious when eating and lose touch with body signals, hardly taste the food they consume, and have little awareness of how much they are eating. The goal of conscious eating is to be conscious enough to stay connected to your bodily sensations of hunger and fullness, conscious enough to be aware of other people and the conversation around you, and conscious enough of health and nutrition information to make appropriate choices without depriving yourself.

When the brain is hijacked by an eating disorder your ability to eat consciously is impaired. If you have an eating disorder, you are probably no longer eating according to your hunger and fullness, and may not even recognize these cues. Most likely, you have been ignoring or overriding your body signals for a long time. Neglecting your hunger signals can alter your sensitivity to them and eventually make them difficult to detect. For example, if hunger is something you have tried to control, it might now trigger stress or anxiety rather than simply cueing you to eat. If you generally restrict your food you might experience hunger as a "good" feeling, because you feel powerful or successful when you deny yourself. If you overcome or resist your hunger it might feel like confirmation that you are "in control" or perhaps losing weight. If you are someone who binge eats, hunger may trigger fears of deprivation, or may have come to represent a variety of feelings, even shame. Responding to hunger by eating often makes people think they are weak or failing somehow. If this is true for you, you have forgotten that by responding to hunger you are taking care of your body and your energy level and optimizing the functioning in your brain and what we know is important to you—your metabolism. Feeling full can also be problematic and can signal feelings of panic, irritability, and remorse instead of satisfaction and contentment.

Having an eating disorder transforms normal, healthy body signals into stressful, anxiety-provoking feelings. Most people with an eating disorder end up abandoning body signals altogether and begin relying on external cues like dieting guidelines, food rules, or calorie counting. In fact, *your* decisions about when, what, and how much to eat are probably based on the kind of beliefs expressed in The Thin Commandments rather than from your body. Luckily, you can rebuild trust in your body as you practice conscious eating and start listening and responding to your body again. The great thing about conscious eating is that the body is quite adept at knowing and letting you know when, what, and how much you need to eat without risk of any mental or physical harm.

There are going to be obstacles at first, but if you don't give up and keep working at it, you will get there. If you are underweight or very restrictive, you might find yourself full very quickly due to slowed digestion, and because your stomach is not used to the sensation of having a normal amount of food in it. Also, if you are highly anxious about eating, you might feel hunger or experience a sensation of fullness after eating only a small amount. If you have been bingeing, you might not be able to feel fullness after eating a normal amount of food. All of these conditions will resolve themselves and return to normal as you begin to normalize your eating. You may have to initially use a specific meal plan to help normalize your body and retrain yourself to feel hunger and fullness. The thermostat that tells us the endpoints, hungry or full, is broken and it is reset in the process we label recovery. Following a meal plan retrains your mind and body to think about and experience food differently. A meal plan helps you reestablish patterns by actually rewiring your brain and body signals establishing healthy habit patterns that then shape your future decisions regarding what and when to eat. Awareness is achieved by mindfulness practices. Meal plans are an effective first step for many clients and will be discussed in more depth later in this key.

If you are still feeling skeptical about conscious eating, you may need to gather your own evidence before you trust that these new guidelines work. We often ask our clients to agree to try this approach for just one day, to see how it feels. You can also take the guidelines to a dietitian to discuss your doubts, fears, and any questions you may have. The more you are able to follow conscious eating, the more trust you will develop in yourself and your body.

Keeping Food Journals

A food journal is a way to gather data on what you are currently doing with your food. As you begin to make changes, your food journal will help you to see how things are going for you. After only a couple of days of keeping a food journal, it is easier to recognize the areas where you need more work. Many clients resist the idea of keeping a food journal. Some report feeling more anxious when having to write down their food or see the foods they listed. Others admit they don't want to face the truth about what they are doing with food. Still others feel overly controlled and then rebellious just writing things down. Whatever your reasons may be for not keeping a food journal, there are better reasons for working through your resistance and trying it out. To change a behavior you need to be clear about the behavior you want to change and be able to track your progress in some way that is measurable. Your food journal should consist of a series of five categories where you will be recording information.

Each entry in your food journal should include:

- The time you ate.
- The type of food you ate.
- The approximate amount you ate.
- Your hunger level before the meal.
- Your fullness level after the meal.
- Any feelings or thoughts you had about eating or anything else.
- Whether or not you felt the urge to purge after eating, and whether or not you gave in to that urge.

Please see the appendix at the end of the book for a sample of a food journal.

The Hunger Scale

Reconnecting with your own hunger and fullness is an important part of a food journal and an important step toward conscious eating. In each entry of your food journal, you record the amounts and types of foods you have eaten and rate how hungry you felt when you started eating and how full you felt when you finished. The hunger scale is a continuum which starts at 1 for extremely hungry and ends at 10 for extremely full. The following is a brief description of each number:

Hunger				Neutral				Fullness	
1	2	3	4	5	6	7	8	9	10

1. Extremely hungry, lightheaded, headache, no energy.
2. Still overly hungry, irritable, stomach growling, constant thoughts of food.
3. Hungry for a meal, sensing hunger, thinking about food and what would be good to eat. *This is the ideal hunger level for eating a meal.*
4. A little bit hungry, a snack would do, or making plans for eating pretty soon.
5. Neutral: don't feel hungry or full.
6. A little bit full, not quite satisfied, have not eaten enough.
7. Satisfied and comfortably full, could get up and take a walk. *This is the ideal target for conscious eaters to stop.*
8. A little too full, happens sometimes, wait until hungry again to eat, but not too long.
9. Overly full, uncomfortable, like what happens on holidays, try to learn from this.
10. Extremely full, painful, likely after an episode of emotional eating or binge eating. Very physically and emotionally distressing.

Over time, you will find using a food journal helps you become aware of how it feels in your body when you are satisfied, as well as when you are a little hungry, too hungry, a bit too full, or overly stuffed. You will be able to see how much time lapses between your meals, which can help increase your understanding about why you may have become too hungry and when you might need to add a snack. As time goes on, you will see patterns emerging. For example, most people notice that if they allow themselves to get to a 1 or 2 on the hunger scale, they are more likely to eat to an 8 or above later. It is harder to stop eating at the appropriate level of fullness when you start off overly hungry. Many of our clients tell us they hardly eat during the day if they have a social event to attend at night. They believe not eating all day will help them feel less anxious about eating normally when out socially. Other clients undereat during the day to "balance" the overeating they are afraid of engaging in at night. What both groups don't realize is that being overly hungry at a meal is a big set-up for overeating, and anxiety around food is increased rather than decreased. People with eating disorders tend to find themselves at the extreme ends of the hunger scale more often than not. The goal is to find the balance, and not let yourself get too hungry or too full.

It is important to note that some people have a very difficult time with the hunger and fullness scale. Some report that they just cannot seem to get in touch with the "feeling" of hunger, much less a certain level of hunger. Others report that their hunger is erratic with no pattern or explanation or it varies wildly according to their mood or menstrual cycle or the weather. Still others get caught up in the subjectivity of it all, trying obsessively to figure out the exact number that fits them before and after each meal. Knowing your hunger level on a scale from 1 to 10 is not critical. What is critical is to not let yourself get too hungry or too full. As dietitian Ralph Carson says, "When talking about hunger and fullness I like to use the analogy of filling our car with gas. The important thing is, don't let your car run out of gas and don't overfill the tank once it's already full."

IT *IS* ABOUT THE FOOD

Food journals can help increase your overall awareness and help you set goals in specific areas. Eventually you will learn to use your knowledge and awareness to develop new habits and patterns of eating that will help you normalize your weight and facilitate recovery.

Writing Assignment: Tuning into Your Hunger and Fullness

Tune in for a moment right now and see if you can determine, using the scale from 1 to 10, how hungry or full you are right now. You may not be sure, but do the best you can to estimate. When you start keeping a food journal you will be tuning in several times a day, and you will get better and better at gauging your hunger and fullness.

Take one day to fill out a food journal and record your hunger and fullness every time you eat. Don't worry if this is difficult at first. It takes practice. Try talking it over with someone or ask a friend to try to do a hunger and fullness scale also. It might be fun to do it together with someone.

We tell our clients to continue to use the hunger and fullness scale until they feel they can easily tune in to their hunger and fullness. Knowing your hunger and fullness is an important step toward becoming a conscious eater. We recommend using a food journal for as long as you find it helpful. You will need to see if using the food journal and the hunger scale is a method that works for you.

Meal Plans

Some people who come to see us are so lost, afraid, or out of control with their food that they want or need a specific meal plan. A meal plan can be a useful first step toward beginning to eat more or regain control over behaviors such as bingeing and purging. A meal plan is a structured way of determining, ahead of time, what and how much you are going to eat each day. Meal plans can be set up and adapted in a variety of ways. Many of our clients resist having a meal plan, while others are desperate for one in order to feel "safe" and make sure that their eating habits are accounted for and not slipping out of control.

If you need to gain weight, a meal plan will most likely be necessary because: a) you aren't in touch with hunger and fullness signals or they are inaccurate; b) eating according to hunger and fullness does not facilitate weight gain; c) you are probably too afraid to eat what you really want or what you need in order to gain weight; and d) you probably have lost track of what is an appropriate serving or what a real meal looks like. For all of these reasons you may need more structure. You might also need a meal plan because you are too afraid and entrenched in your current eating behaviors to try anything new and make any solid changes without specific structure and support. A meal plan will provide guidance and a sense of control around your eating and help get you started.

Since there is no way for us to know the foods you like, how much *you* should be eating or what foods to include in *your* meal plan, or many other individual considerations, help from a dietitian or other professional who specializes in the treatment of eating disorders is recommended. What we can do is introduce you to the basic principles of a meal plan and offer some helpful suggestions.

IT *IS* ABOUT THE FOOD

Making a Meal Plan

To make a meal plan, you come up with a written list of what you plan to eat for breakfast, lunch, dinner, and snacks. Meal plans can vary and range from being very general, such as listing how many calories you have to consume a day, to stating how many servings of protein, carbohydrates, and fat you need for each meal and then filling it in with your choices each day, to a very specific plan with the foods and portion sizes. (For example, Breakfast: 3 scrambled eggs, ¾ cup melon, and a bagel with 2 tsp of butter and 2 tablespoons of jam.) We don't usually advocate these kind of exact portion sizes. We prefer using hand estimates such as 1 cup = a fist, 3 ounces = palm of hand, and a tablespoon = a large thumb. The idea is to get in the ballpark of portion size estimates because *exact amounts do not matter*. Whatever your meal plan looks like, it should be a step toward lifelong eating and recovery, not a "diet." When working with meal plans, start where you can and then gradually increase or decrease the variety and frequency of your eating according to your own goals and needs. The idea is to create a balanced meal plan with the appropriate amount of calories to help you move toward recovery. Both of us started with meal plans. Our own personal experience and that of our clients has shown us that meal plans can provide the structure, containment, and safety needed to make difficult changes and let go of eating disorder behaviors. If you decide to try a meal plan and find yourself feeling overly controlled and rebellious as a result, you might need the freedom and flexibility offered by following the Conscious Eating Guidelines. If you are not yet ready or willing to go to a dietitian or eating disorder professional, find someone else in your life who can offer you the necessary support and accountability. Voicing your commitments or intentions to another person increases the likelihood that you will follow through. Meal plans are often a helpful first step in the recovery process and a bridge to the ultimate goal of conscious eating. If you would like to read more about the concepts we have outlined in this key, refer to the Resources section at the end of the book.

Personal Reflections:

Gwen: Early in my recovery, I needed to follow a meal plan. I was out of touch with my body, my hunger and fullness, and what was the appropriate amount to eat. I needed specific guidance and structure. Although I was initially afraid and resistant, it was actually easier to have a meal plan and not have the stress of making decisions in the moment. The meal plan helped me gain weight in a way that didn't feel out of control, get back to a regular schedule of eating, and incorporate a variety of foods back into my life. As I continued to get better I was able to follow my meal plan easily without any anxiety. Over time, I started to feel like my meal plan was another "diet" to follow, and I found myself feeling too confined and limited by it. I was afraid to branch out, but I wanted to eat more freely, and I had good role models encouraging me to do so. Fortunately, following the meal plan and eating regularly had helped me reconnect with my hunger and fullness and prepared me to begin using these signals to guide my eating. Navigating this next step in my recovery was still very challenging. Sometimes I was still hungry or not satisfied by what I had eaten, but I was afraid to eat more, or eat something different. I found a dietitian who explained a concept called "Intuitive Eating," which she said I was ready for. I could feel my anxiety and anger begin to surface as I listened to her explaining what sounded like a description of how to eat "normally," as if it was so simple. She sensed my resistance and suggested I try it for just one day. Trying it one day sounded reasonable to me so I agreed. It felt very strange and I didn't trust myself much, but at the end of just one day, I felt better both physically and emotionally, and was thus encouraged to continue working with this approach. After a few more days of

IT *IS* ABOUT THE FOOD

using my knowledge, the experience I had gained on my meal plan and my awareness of hunger and fullness to make decisions about eating, I knew I had discovered the tool for the final step in healing my relationship with food. This new way of eating gave me the freedom with food I wanted but feared, and the guidelines made sense and provided the sense of safety I needed. I slowly started to trust myself more and believe it was OK for me to eat all foods. There were times when I ate more than usual or ate when I wasn't hungry. The process took some time, but eventually, for the first time ever, I was eating freely, enjoying foods I had been avoiding for years, and maintaining my weight. It felt amazing.

Learning to eat in this way helped me to turn an important corner in my recovery. For the first time in many years, I trusted myself to know what to do with food without using outside information for guidance.

Carolyn: When I had anorexia there were no dietitians around, no books on eating disorders, and no places to find guidance on what to do about my eating and weight. The first professional I went to for help had never even seen anyone with an eating disorder, much less worked with anyone with the illness. He asked me to drink a soft drink in front of him so he could see what I would do. I did not go back. So the second person I saw, a female therapist, who had also never seen or heard about eating disorders told me I should eat by myself, if eating made me feel guilty. I knew if I did that, I would eat even less. After a lot of stops and starts, fear and resistance, I knew I had to find a way to stop my weight loss. I ultimately had to come up with ways to help myself begin to eat more normally again. I offer readers a few tips that helped me along the way.

I started saying to myself that "Full is not the same thing as fat." I would say it over and over again to calm myself when I would eat and begin to think I was fat. I stopped looking in the mirror when I got dressed, because I would see myself as too fat and want to not eat what I had planned. I bought loose, baggy, but nice clothes so I wouldn't notice the weight gain as much or the feeling of my stomach after meals. When I would want to try a new scary food I would start by having a very small portion of it, like half a piece of pizza or even less, and then eat other safe food to make up the calories. I did this to reassure myself that nothing bad would happen and I would not be fat the next day. Over time I would get to the point of having a whole piece of pizza and eventually two pieces, slowly replacing my safe foods with this new one I really liked but had been afraid of. I did this many times with many new foods. I stopped looking up the calories in food. It was hard and numbers remained in my head for a while, but over time the automatic counting happened less and less, and eventually I stopped it completely. I went out with friends to help me be accountable for eating. I bought food I really liked and kept it in my house (I used to buy food I didn't like because it helped me not eat much). If I wanted to eat a favorite food I had to also eat something that was important nutritionally. I did this because there were times when I would eat a cookie or ice cream and then be afraid to eat anything else. I wrote down what I ate and at the end of the day if I did not have enough food, I would make myself add more to get the total I had committed to. It took a long time for me to get to the amount of food where I gained weight, but doing it this way did help me eventually get there. I started having one day a week where I would go to a restaurant and order whatever I wanted. Again, this increased over time, to the point where I could always do it. And, finally, I stopped weighing myself. This was one of the most helpful things I did to recover, and it changed everything.

Accepting Your Natural Body Weight and Not Weighing Yourself

In order to repair your relationship with food and become a conscious eater, you will have to end your relationship with the scale. You will need to stop weighing yourself, stop making weight loss a life focus, and stop using a number to measure your self-esteem or gauge your self-worth. After all, the number on a scale is simply measuring "the force with which your body is attracted to Earth." Remember, our definition of being "recovered" includes *when you can accept your natural body size and shape and no longer have a self-destructive relationship with food or exercise. When you are recovered, food and weight take a proper position in your life, and what you weigh is not more important than who you are; in fact, actual numbers are of little or no importance at all.*

Letting go of your emphasis on weight and weighing is so important to your success in changing your relationship to food that we put it in this key. We are fully aware that an eating disorder is the result of a variety of issues and that wanting to lose weight or change your shape does not cause an eating disorder. We also know that if you keep your weight goal as the driving force in your life, you will not be able to discontinue behaviors that interfere with your recovery.

Learning to Accept Your Natural Body Weight

A discussion about ideal, natural, or healthy body weight often generates a lot of anxiety, resistance, and confusion. Just as you are learning that your body can be trusted to give you accurate signals about hunger and fullness, you must also learn to trust that your natural weight is predetermined by your genetics and not by your desire. Many of our clients have a hard time accepting their natural body weight, not because they are overweight, but because they are not the weight they would like to be. If you are engaging in eating disorder behaviors to maintain your weight, you really can't know your natural weight. Your body will send you signals (which are detailed below) when you are underweight. When you are at your natural weight, these signs will disappear. Many people have an idea what their natural body weight is and feels like, but we have listed some indicators below in case you are not sure.

Natural Weight Range, Physical Indicators

- Weight range is maintained without engaging in eating disordered behaviors (for example, restricting, bingeing, purging, or compulsive exercise).
- Having regular menstruation every month and normal hormone levels (as age appropriate).
- Normal blood pressure, heart rate, and body temperature.
- Normal blood chemistry values such as electrolytes, white and red blood counts, etc.
- Normal bone density for age.
- Normal levels of energy (not exhausted, shaky, or agitated all day).
- Normal, or at least some, sex drive.

Natural Weight Range, Psychological and Social Indicators

- Ability to concentrate and focus (reading, movies, work, school).
- Normal social life with authentic, in-person relationships (not just online).
- Decrease in or cessation of obsessive thoughts or food cravings or urges to binge.
- Ability to choose freely what to eat both when alone and with others.
- Ability to eat at restaurants, at friends' houses, at parties, and on vacations.
- Absence of food rituals dictating eating patterns and behaviors.
- No erratic mood swings.

Our bodies react negatively to being under or over our natural weight in spite of what we want or how we feel about it. It might be hard to believe, but even a few pounds below normal can cause abnormal physical and psychological changes. Starvation is a threat to survival and our bodies let us know when we are threatened. Even though the consequences are not as immediate, our bodies also give us signs when we are overweight in the areas of abnormal findings in blood pressure, lab values, hormones, energy, difficulty doing normal daily tasks, and many more.

Letting Go of Weight Loss as a Goal

One of the most difficult, yet important, shifts in your thinking will need to be letting go of weight loss as a goal. Orienting your focus toward making peace with food and your body instead of losing weight can seem impossible and feel disorienting. Many people with eating disorders have spent too much time, energy, and other resources struggling to lose weight, only to stay trapped in eating disorder behaviors. Here is a very simple explanation. If you have anorexia, weight loss is clearly inappropriate. In fact, your already low weight and your inability to acknowledge that or stop your drive to remain underweight is part of the diagnostic criteria of your condition. You have to let go of weight loss as a goal, or even maintenance of your low weight as a goal. If you have bulimia, then you will by definition be engaging in bingeing and then in some way compensating for it. Think about it—if you want to recover from bulimia, but you also have weight loss or not gaining weight as a goal, then what do you do the next time you overeat, or even just eat and feel bad about it? Your two goals (a) lose weight or avoid weight gain and (b) stop my bulimia, conflict with each other. If you keep weight loss or avoiding weight gain as a goal you will try to get rid of your food (purge) to avoid any weight gain. Here is one client's reflection on giving up her goal of losing weight:

> *"The goal of losing weight has been the goal that I have worked the hardest at. That alone makes it hard to give up on. I don't remember when it wasn't the first thing on my mind and often the only thing. To let go of it feels like cutting off a part of me. I constantly have to remind myself that I don't need to order the salad because weight loss is not my goal anymore. It is so ingrained that I keep forgetting. At first it felt disorienting. I realized that without weight loss as my goal, I felt really lost and empty. I began to see that life was passing me by. How did I get so self-absorbed and dull? I finally am at a place where I can truly say I want a better life more than I want to lose weight."*
>
> —JR

If you place too much emphasis on your body or weight, you lose sight of the more important things in life. Even if you have gained excess weight or a physician has told you that you need to lose weight for health reasons, you are still better off putting the emphasis on your health and happiness instead of a number. The bottom line is this: if you are trying to lose weight, you cannot progress in recovery from an eating disorder, no matter what you weigh or what kind of eating disorder you have. We are not saying that it is never OK for anyone to lose weight—we cannot know if that would be appropriate for you or not. We are saying that for recovery from an eating disorder, your focus has to be on getting over any eating disorder behaviors and developing a healthy relationship with food. Some people may gain weight in doing this and some people may lose weight. In either case, it is your body returning to its proper natural state.

IT *IS* ABOUT THE FOOD

Writing Assignment: Letting Go of Your Focus on Losing Weight

What would happen if you just decided to stop trying to lose weight? What did your eating disorder promise you if you reach this perfect weight? Do you think it is true, or have you noticed this to be true? How else has the desire to lose weight interfered with recovery? Write about what it might be like to focus first on recovery and then deal with any leftover issues regarding your weight.

Weighing

Weighing yourself is detrimental for the recovery process of any eating disorder. In surveys of recovered clients, they report that not weighing was one of the most important aspects to their success.

> *"Not weighing was instrumental in maintaining my recovery. I was a scale addict before treatment and would consistently return to my eating disorder behaviors, trying to manipulate the number on the scale. It is almost hard to believe that I do not weigh myself anymore and numbers never cross my mind. The scale no longer matters. It never helped me and for years interfered with my recovery. I will never ever weigh myself again for that reason. It is so freeing to not know. My identity is no longer based on a number. The number never got me anywhere; it only trapped me into not paying attention to my hunger or my body, which is all I really need to do to know what and when to eat. A scale never did and never can never give me that."*
>
> —JD

Weighing yourself will impede your progress in a number of ways. We recommend that you *stop weighing yourself and get rid of your scale.* The three most important reasons are:

1. If you are underweight, seeing the numbers going up can be very stressful and compound your anxiety. Sometimes clients are on the right track and feeling positive about recovery until they weigh themselves and see the number. Weighing yourself can delay, prolong, and even halt recovery. We have never seen it help anyone. If it is necessary that your weight be monitored, have a dietitian, therapist, doctor, or someone else you trust weigh you without telling you the number.
2. If you binge and purge you might find that your weight goes up when you stop these behaviors. If this happens you might conclude that you need to keep purging or you will keep gaining weight, which is not true. Your body needs to adjust to having food inside of it and this adjustment period takes a little time. You may also retain fluid temporarily, which will resolve with normalized eating, or your weight gain might be due to necessary rehydration. Imagine a simple garden hose. Now image the hose is filled with water. It weighs more, but it has not gotten bigger. It does not look any different on the outside. Sometimes, when clients stop bingeing and purging they gain a little bit of weight during the first few weeks, but often lose it again when their bodies adjust to consistent eating. If you need to have your weight monitored, because you are at a dangerously low weight or are too afraid to simply stop weighing and need a first step, let someone else weigh you (more on this later).
3. If you are a binge eater or for some other reason are above your natural weight, weighing yourself can be detrimental to your recovery. For real recovery, healing your relationship with food is the goal, rather than losing a certain amount of weight each week. Using the scale

as a measure of progress can backfire for a number of reasons. If you are successful with your goal of not bingeing after dinner or not turning to food when angry, but the scale doesn't reflect back what you think it should, it is very easy to get discouraged and return to the behavior. Not seeing the numbers on the scale go down fast enough can make you give up. It often takes a while for the results of healthy behavior changes to show up on the scale, so weighing can be very misleading.

Regardless of the behaviors you are working on, or how much you weigh, get rid of your scale. If you need to check your weight for any reason, such as you need to know if you are gaining weight or you need reassurance that your weight is not going out of control, get someone else to do it. Consult with a dietitian, therapist, doctor, or someone else you trust who is willing to weigh you and tell you only whether you are on track or not. Have an agreed-upon goal and weight range and come up with the terms or conditions that indicate the need for giving you information. We recommend that you set a goal to reach and then be told when you get there, or if you are going in the opposite direction. If maintaining your weight is the goal, whoever is weighing you should tell you if you are maintaining or not. You are maintaining if you are within 2–3 pounds of your maintenance weight. We know it is hard giving up the scale and letting go of weighing yourself, but it is one of the most important behaviors to change if you want recovery. We no longer weigh ourselves, we teach our clients not to weigh, and you will see that it works for you too.

The following is just a sample of what clients have to say about weighing:

"Prior to treatment, I would weigh myself several times a day, and the quality of my day would depend on the numbers I saw. I felt that the numbers on the scale defined me. When I was fixated on a number I could not focus on anything else, includ-

ing recovery. I would be upset if it was not what I wanted it to be, and it never was. I always thought I could lose more or had to not eat to keep it low. There was nothing good that ever came from weighing. It took time and trust to stop. I first let my dietitian weigh me for reassurance because I was afraid, but eventually I did not even need that. All I needed was to stop my eating disorder behaviors and follow my meal plan long enough to realize I would be OK and did not need a number on a scale to tell me anything."

—JW

"Not knowing my weight the entire time I was at Monte Nido was incredibly helpful in weaning me off the scale. Once I left treatment there were a few incidents where I thought I had to know my weight and I thought I could handle it. Every time I stepped on a scale, whether the number was the same, higher, or lower than I expected, I became consumed with the number. I would go over and over it in my mind, wondering how to change it, why it was what it was, and how I could make it stay that way or get better. Weighing was always a mind trap and immediately affected my eating and my mood. I finally got it that I was fine without weighing and it was unnecessary and even disruptive to my recovery and my life. I continue to not weigh myself today and it feels good to know the number has nothing to do with who I am."

—KM

Personal Reflections: Weighing

Gwen: At the height of my eating disorder, I was weighing myself several times a day. It felt like a compulsion that I had no control over. There were times I felt so desperate to know my weight that I would go to a drugstore and unwrap every scale and stand on it, pretending that I was a responsible consumer wanting to buy the best scale rather than the obsessed and desperate woman I really was. Making sure that I hadn't gained any weight was the only way I could lessen my anxiety. It reassured me that I was still the same, still OK, and still in control of things. But the reassurance I got never lasted and within a very short time, I would feel the familiar urge to get on the scale again.

My morning weight would determine what kind of a day I would have, how I felt about myself, what I would eat, and what I would wear. If I gained even one half of a pound, my mood would spiral downward and I would isolate myself in self-reproach and become more restrictive. If I stayed the same weight, I was usually disappointed, but not devastated, depending on what I had done the day before. If I lost weight, I felt a warm jolt of joy, satisfaction, and calm. I felt more confident to go out into the world. I thought that if I lost weight, I would feel safe and free to eat what I wanted, but that day of relaxed eating never came. Instead, the more weight I lost the more anxious and insecure I became. If the number I saw didn't reflect my hard work I would implode with anger, and sulk for days in a depressed funk, isolating from everyone while raging a private war against my body.

Carolyn and Gwen In Session

Carolyn: When I told Gwen that I did not tell clients their weight she was upset. Gwen was extremely anxious and untrusting. I wasn't sure she would stay in treatment. I felt strongly that she needed to know that I understood her fears. I also felt that she needed to know that my philosophy of weighing was important to her healing and not just a rule I used to control my clients. I needed to work cooperatively with her and let her know I would not just blindly enforce a rule, but would try to help her understand and agree.

Carolyn: "I don't tell people what they weigh because I have found that it does not help and, in fact, is information that they use against themselves."

Gwen: "But that doesn't seem right and I don't understand how I use it against myself. I think I should have the right to know my weight."

Carolyn: "Gwen, I am going to explain why I don't tell people their weight and why I think it is harmful for you. I don't weigh myself and my goal would be that you would ultimately decide not to weigh yourself, either. After this conversation, though, if I have not convinced you then I will tell you what you weighed today." (I rarely say I will reveal someone's weight. I did this because I was concerned about losing Gwen's trust and after saying this, I could see Gwen's body relax, as she realized I was really listening to her.)

Gwen: "OK."

Carolyn: "First of all, I don't think we should measure ourselves with a number on a scale. It never worked for me when I had my eating disorder or when I was trying to get better."

Gwen: "But if I don't know my weight I will be more anxious. Knowing my weight just helps me to reassure myself."

Carolyn: "Really, can you tell me how it helped to reassure you before you came here? It does not seem like it was really helping at all."

Gwen: "If I don't see my weight I will be too afraid that I am gaining and will probably want to restrict even more."

Carolyn: "You restricted your food the whole time you were weighing yourself. Let me guess, if you weighed more you restricted in order to lose it; if you weighed the same you restricted because you wanted to lose more or were afraid you might gain; and if you lost weight you restricted because a) it was working, or b) you were afraid to gain it back."

Gwen: (smiling) "Actually, that is pretty true."

Carolyn: "I won't keep you in the dark. I am not saying you should just gain weight. We will set specific weight goals. For example, let's start with a five-pound weight gain goal and I will tell you when you reach it. This is how I can protect you from sabotaging yourself. If you see the numbers you will want to interfere with the progress."

Gwen: "Yeah, I have to admit what you are saying is true and no one has really explained it to me that way. But I think I am afraid I will gain too much."

Carolyn: "But I already said that I would tell you when you made your first weight goal. You will know when you have gained five pounds."

Gwen: "I don't know. I just can't get myself to say I don't want to know the number; somehow I feel like I need to know."

Carolyn: "Of course you want to know it. It is kind of like a smoker who quits but wants a cigarette. I wouldn't expect you to say you want to gain weight, either. To get better you will have to do things that feel scary and that go against what makes you feel comfortable and "safe." If you keep doing the same things you will not get better. Does that make sense?"

Gwen: "Yes, but it really stresses me out. It's been 15 years of doing this and knowing my weight."

Carolyn: "OK, how about this. I want you to take 24 hours to think over all I have said. Let's talk tomorrow and see if you can come up with a good reason why you still want to know your weight, and how it will help you. If you can come up with even one good reason, I will tell you your weight."

Gwen: "OK."

Carolyn: The next day Gwen admitted that for the first time she felt truly understood. She felt hopeful that I might even be able to help her. She admitted that she had been unable to think of a reason why a specific number would help her and so I did not reveal her weight to her that day, or on any other occasion during the course of her treatment.

Final Thoughts

We hope you are on your way to taking steps toward becoming a conscious eater. Whether you are trying to listen to your hunger and fullness, make or follow a meal plan, give yourself permission to eat challenging foods, or find ways to cope other than turning to food, this will facilitate your recovery and free up your life. There are many overt eating disorder behaviors we have yet to address that are related to food and engaging in them will sabotage your recovery efforts and undermine the process completely if you are not able to stop engaging in them. There are also numerous behaviors such as exercising that might seem harmless to some people, but if you have an eating disorder you will need to explore these, as they could very well be sabotaging your recovery. Learning to change or let go of problematic behaviors is very difficult, but continuing them is not an option if you want to recover. Helping you change specific behaviors is the topic of our next key.

KEY 6:
CHANGING YOUR BEHAVIORS

> I don't think many people come into recovery thinking about how much they really have to change. I was overwhelmed by the uncertainty I felt, the challenge of trusting the unknown. I concluded that whatever I would find in the future would serve me better than what I had in the past or present. Letting go of a disordered life that compromised two-thirds of the time I have spent on earth was huge, but I just started changing my behaviors one at a time.
>
> —KM

People with eating disorders engage in a wide variety of behaviors that interfere with well-being and recovery. There are the obvious behaviors directly related to the consumption and elimination of food that substantiate the diagnosis of an eating disorder. There are also many other behaviors that sabotage recovery but are less overtly recognized as eating disorder behaviors, because people without eating disorders also engage in them. We address both categories in this key.

Changing Your "Overt" Eating Disorder Behaviors

Restricting, bingeing, and vomiting are what we refer to as "overt" behaviors because they are used in the diagnosis of an eating disorder. Without these behaviors, you would not have an eating disorder, so it may seem obvious to you that these are behaviors you need to stop. The truth is, many of our clients try to follow a meal plan or become conscious eaters without challenging or letting go of these behaviors, but without giving them up there is no way to become a conscious eater or recover. Other people want to stop their overt behaviors and have no idea how to do so. We realize that stopping these behaviors is very difficult and if you could just stop them you probably wouldn't be reading this book. The information provided in this key will help. Take small steps and use the tools you have already learned in the other keys along with the information that follows.

Overt Food Related Behaviors: Restricting

Usually when you first begin restricting your food intake, your body is still functioning properly with a regular metabolism, so losing weight can seem easy. When you take in fewer calories than you need, your body will begin to compensate by slowing down your metabolic rate. In response to restricting your intake (by not eating or getting rid of food), your body conserves energy by decreasing most bodily functions, such as digestion and heat production, and turns to storing as much energy as possible. People often tell us that learning about this on the Internet or in magazines makes them even more afraid to start eating again, thinking they have ruined their metabolism for life. The good news is you can restore your metabolism by starting to eat and taking in enough calories regularly throughout the day. This is one reason we encourage all our clients to eat three meals and three snacks, giving your metabolism continued boosts throughout the day. According to a study which researched the effects of starvation during World War II, all of the participants who, through a decreased caloric intake had lowered their metabolic rate by up to 40 percent, were totally recovered by one year, some sooner (Keys et al., 1950). Normalizing your eating behavior will help your body start to trust that you will be feeding it regularly. When your body is fed regularly it will return to its normal metabolic rate. You can't talk your body into it, or exercise to force your metabolism to normalize. The only way to communicate to your body that it is OK to ramp your metabolism back up is through regular healthy eating behavior. If you continue to restrict your food and you do not work to reverse the natural conservation process, your body will become resistant to repairing your metabolism and *over time, it will become harder and harder to maintain a healthy body weight.* Furthermore, if you continue to restrict calories, your body will lose muscle mass, which is a huge aspect of a healthy metabolism. Instead, your body will try to store fat, which is the preferred mechanism to store energy when the body perceives it is starving. Therefore, restricting to control your weight will actually change your body composition to include more fat and decrease your metabolism, which means you will not be able to consume as many calories as before without gaining weight.

Over time chronic dieters and people with eating disorders who consume too few calories cannot lose weight or have a hard time maintaining weight. The bottom line is that regular and frequent eating is the best way to have a healthy, efficient metabolism. Fasting or restricting is the best way to slow it down. When you get up each morning and eat "breakfast" you are "breaking the fast" and revving up your metabolism. To keep your body efficiently burning calories you need to keep giving it fuel. Imagine a fire that has been left in the fireplace to burn down over night. In the morning there are just a few embers left, barely burning. When you throw some twigs and a log on the fire, the flames shoot up and the fire burns bigger and hotter. If you do not put any new wood on the fire it dies down even more and might even go out. Your metabolism works like that fire, in fact; that is why we call it "burning calories." Putting food in your body is like throwing twigs or a log on the fire, increasing the rate of burn or your metabolism.

Writing Assignment: Permission to Eat

How do you feel about giving yourself permission to eat the foods you want or the amount you need? What are your fears? See if you can think of a certain food you can begin to add back to your diet. What might you need to begin making changes? If you think restricting has led to a binge, write about that experience and what you might be able to do next time to prevent that from happening. Many people with anorexia also end up bingeing, some to the point of developing bulimia. Depriving your body of anything can create a compulsion for it. We tell our clients, "Imagine you are underwater depriving yourself of breathing. You are desperate for one thing, air, and when you come up, you gasp for it."

Bingeing—Exploring the Causes and Strategies for Change

Binge eating is something that many people say they do occasionally, like at Thanksgiving or on a special celebration. This kind of overeating is occasional and will not cause weight gain or an eating disorder. The bingeing behavior that we are referring to is when you consume large quantities of food in a short period of time, paying no attention to hunger and fullness and in such a manner that feels out of your control. The binge is followed by feelings of guilt, shame, and intense discomfort from being overly full.

Binge eating is involved, at least somewhat, or at some point, in the course of most eating disorders except those with restrictor anorexia. If you binge, you have to discontinue this behavior if you want to overcome your eating disorder. As with any behavior you want to change, gaining insight into what is

CHANGING YOUR BEHAVIORS

causing the behavior can help. Binge eating is not due to laziness or a weakness in character, as is often supposed. The reasons you binge will become clearer as you work through the book, and you will find ways to change as you explore your lifestyle, belief system, and ability to listen and respond to your body and your emotional needs.

What Leads to Bingeing?

Exploring various categories might help when trying to understand what leads to your bingeing. The reasons people binge can be categorized into three main areas:

1. *Bingeing due to deprivation or restriction of food.*
   When you are overly hungry, you will find it almost impossible to listen to body signals, pay attention to healthy choices, stop eating when you are satisfied, or care about how you will feel afterwards. The physical drive to eat is so strong it usually overrides everything else. The same is true when you avoid or hold yourself back from eating certain foods. For example, if you think of chips as a "bad food" and don't allow yourself to eat them, when you do eat some, you may feel like you "opened the door" to chips and before closing that door again you find yourself eating way more than is normal or even satisfying. Many chronic dieters they tell us that sometimes even the thought of going on a diet or never being allowed to eat a certain type of food can trigger a binge. Planning to go on a diet on Monday, for example, often results in a weekend of bingeing. Incorporating "binge foods" back into your life will help to reduce the dieting mentality responsible for triggering the urge to binge. It is helpful to remind yourself that you can eat whatever you consider a binge food whenever you are hungry and you are not going to restrict or deprive yourself of this food later. Some people with eating disorders do not restrict calories, but

hold rigid beliefs regarding what types and quantities of certain foods are acceptable. If the person then happens to eat those foods, it can flip a mental switch that triggers a binge. It may be hard to accept the fact that restricting food is a set-up for a binge, but we have seen this pattern play out over and over again with our clients. It might be helpful to think of the part of you that binges as rebelling against restriction, rigidity, and rules. In fact, review "Dialoging with Your Eating Disorder Self" in Key 2. This technique might work in this situation and help you figure out how to get past your drive to binge.

2. *Bingeing as a result of emotions or strong feelings.*

Emotional eating is common for everyone once in a while, but for some people, especially if they do not find other ways to deal with feelings, emotional eating can turn into binge eating disorder or bulimia. If you immediately go to food after a fight with a friend, loved one, or after other upsetting situations, that is emotional eating. Certain refined carbohydrates like candy, cookies, and chips are often chosen for emotional eating because they: 1) contain fat and sugar and are highly palatable and rewarding to your taste buds and your brain chemistry; and 2) are commonly considered forbidden foods when on a diet. Bingeing on highly palatable food changes the brain chemistry, so that it reinforces more bingeing. Having said all that, it is important to recognize that a binge can involve any food. Many individuals who binge will binge on anything and everything. Bingeing is a compulsive behavior that feels out of control. When people binge emotionally they are trying to eat as much as possible to distract from feelings or fill up emptiness, cover feelings of sadness, soothe loneliness, stuff down rage, or drown out fear. In other words, bingeing helps you distance from your feelings as quickly as possible. Hopefully you learned some healthier tools in Key 4 to help you tolerate and cope with your feelings.

3. *Mindless, unconscious, avoidant, or habitual bingeing.*
The third type of bingeing is often used as a way to escape, or numb out. It is very common when you are trying to avoid something like making a difficult phone call or some other unpleasant task. You might be completely unaware you are even eating, or you might be aware you are compulsively eating, but have no idea why. We call this mindless or unconscious eating because often you do not know what is causing you to eat or what feelings you may be suppressing with food. There are many ways you can begin to raise your awareness about your unconscious bingeing so you can learn to interrupt this behavior. One of the first steps you can take is to avoid places or situations that encourage mindless eating—for example, many people eat mindlessly while watching television. Try to not engage in other distracting activities when you eat. If you are bingeing as a way to procrastinate, learning to set small achievable tasks, rather than avoiding an overwhelming goal, can greatly help you reduce bingeing episodes. Bingeing to avoid something fearful does not make it go away. At the end of a binge, whatever you are trying to avoid will still be there, and you will likely feel worse as a result of the bingeing. Sometimes people habitually binge because they have been doing it so long it becomes automatic, and is not triggered by anything in particular.

Writing Assignment:
Exploring Your Feelings Before a Binge

The next time you have an urge to binge, try "surfing the urge" for five or ten minutes and journal. Ask yourself, "What am I feeling?" and "What happened right before I had the urge?"

and "What might I be trying to avoid?" It could be a feeling or a task. You might also ask yourself, "What do I really need?" If you are not hungry, you don't need food, but you might be able to identify something else you need. The answer might be simple; perhaps you need a break from the kids, from studying, or from worrying. Your need could also be more complex, like needing to have a difficult conversation or find a new job.

Use the following to help you resist the urge to binge. Refer to the assignments in Key 4 regarding dealing with difficult thoughts and feelings, and refer to Key 7 for how to reach out to others for help.

Many people binge and do not go to any extreme to compensate for bingeing. Others will resort to some kind of compensatory behavior. The most common compensatory behavior is "purging," which we turn to now.

Purging

Most people think that purging means vomiting, however, in the clinical eating disorder world, purging is any method used to rid the body of unwanted calories or fluids. The four behaviors that are considered purging behaviors are vomiting, laxative abuse, use of diuretics, and use of enemas. All of these behaviors decrease your metabolism, and are harmful and potentially dangerous. All forms of purging eventually become ineffective, as the body learns to compensate. Let's look at each one separately.

Vomiting

If you engage in self-induced vomiting, or have in the past, you know it is a very difficult behavior to stop. The behavior may begin as a way to compensate for overeating, but can become a coping mechanism for other things and easily turns

CHANGING YOUR BEHAVIORS

into habitual behavior. Most clients who purge by vomiting want to stop, but it is difficult for them to accept that the behavior is usually part in a chain of problematic eating. Although this is not true for everyone, the chain often looks like this: restricting, bingeing, vomiting. It makes sense that a good way to stop vomiting is to stop bingeing, and a good way to stop bingeing is to stop restricting. Even though this is true and information on stopping those behaviors is provided earlier in this key, we often will try to focus on stopping the vomiting as the first intervention for many reasons.

If you focus on bingeing as the behavior to stop the chain, but then fail to stop a binge, you can find yourself saying, "I have to purge because I binged." Of course it's best not to binge but if you do, our response is, "Don't allow yourself to purge." In this way vomiting is the real target. No matter what, don't vomit.

Another reason we start with targeting purging is that to target restricting or bingeing as the first step puts you in vague territory because both are a bit difficult to define. There is a wide range of what people consider an appropriate amount of food. Restricting for one person can feel like bingeing to another. Vomiting, on the other hand, is easy to define, and a very specific behavior to target. There is no appropriate amount of "vomiting." It is a very specific and easy behavior to measure: you vomited or you did not.

Finally, not all vomiting happens as a result of bingeing. Sometimes a normal amount of food or eating a "forbidden" food, like dessert, will cause someone to vomit. Sometimes people vomit to "get rid of feelings." Therefore, for all the reasons stated, we often encourage clients to work on reducing or stopping their vomiting behavior first.

Exploring some of the negative consequences of vomiting might also help you stop. Your body reacts to vomiting by lowering your metabolism because by purging your food, you are restricting the calories your body actually digests. Vomiting is also harmful on the rest of your body. The most common effects include: dehydration, tooth enamel decay, cavities, gum disease and eventual loss of teeth, swollen parotid glands resulting in swelling of the face, and negative changes to skin, hair, nails, and even your bones. More seriously, vomiting can cause rupture of the esophagus (Barrett's esophagus), where the lining of the esophagus is damaged by stomach acid, and tears in the mucosal lining called Mallory Weiss Syndrome, all of which can be serious and even fatal. Other serious side effects are electrolyte and mineral disturbances, which can damage the heart and cause heart failure and death. If you are reading this and thinking these things won't happen to you, you are very wrong. These serious side effects are real possibilities, and the longer you continue the behavior, the greater the risk. There is no way to predict when these symptoms will occur. In our experience, most people seem fine—until one day they aren't. Doris and Tom Smeltzer's daughter Andrea died in her bed only one year after she was diagnosed with bulimia. In their powerful book, *Andrea's Voice* (2006) they share Andrea's journals, and help bring home the message that you can be OK one day and then, with no warning, your eating disorder can take your life.

Laxative Abuse

Many people with eating disorders take laxatives as an alternative form of purging. Laxatives are hard on your bowels and your body and you can easily become physically dependent on them. If you are taking laxatives to "lose weight" or avoid weight gain, you are putting yourself at risk and doing something that will never work out for you in the long run. Once you know the facts, you will see that taking laxatives for weight control makes no sense. The food you eat enters your stomach where it is broken down, and then goes into the small intestine where carbohydrates, fat, protein, vitamins, and minerals are absorbed. Whatever is left, usually bulk fiber or other waste, then enters into the large intestine as fecal matter. The main purpose of the large intestine is to reabsorb the water from the waste to make it more solid. The purpose of taking a laxative is

CHANGING YOUR BEHAVIORS

to stimulate the large intestine to empty, therefore since most of the calories have already been absorbed in the small intestine the "weight loss" you experience, after spending all day on the toilet, is mostly water, not real body mass weight loss. Therefore, taking laxatives will cause your body to lose fluid, but will be followed by periods of water retention and cause bloating, making you feel even worse, perhaps causing you to take more laxatives, and thus creating a vicious cycle.

Sometimes knowing the long-term ineffectiveness and dangerous consequences of laxative abuse is enough to help people stop. Here are the problems you will encounter if you use laxatives:

- Chronic constipation (due to dependency on laxatives)
- Severe abdominal pain: cramping, bloating, and gas
- Dehydration
- Nausea
- Loss of rectal function: losing control of bowels (unplanned and pretty awful)
- Electrolyte disturbance: causes heart arrhythmia and heart attack
- Complete loss of bowel function
- Partial or full colectomy

Many of our clients still have a hard time stopping laxative abuse even when they know the potential dangers and their ineffectiveness. Like them, you might still like feeling thinner after using laxatives. You may also be afraid of, or have previously experienced, constipation, rebound edema, and "weight gain" when trying to stop. These are temporary side effects but they can be managed and eventually will subside. It is important to note that medical risks associated with chronic laxative use get worse over time, so if you don't stop soon enough some of the damage could be permanent. We have seen clients who lost all bowel function and would soil their clothes and their beds spontaneously, and others who had to get partial or total colostomies and live with a surgically attached bag to collect all bowel evacuation. All of this was due to laxative abuse.

If you have used laxatives regularly, expect to experience a "withdrawal" period that is very uncomfortable until your body relearns how to function on its own. Try to begin to taper off of laxatives, reducing the amount you take gradually. Our clients have found that it helps to put your feet up during the day to reduce edema. Taking a warm bath can also help with edema, and eating high-protein foods may be helpful as well. In some instances, supplementing with non-laxative stool softeners, mineral oil, or fiber can help, but expect an initial period of physical and psychological discomfort. We highly recommend you seek help from a physician if you are trying to wean off of laxatives. Costin (2007a) discusses laxative abuse in more detail in her chapter on "Medical Assessment and Management."

Diuretics

Diuretics are another illogical and ineffective method of controlling weight. The purpose of diuretics is to reduce water retention in the body. Taking diuretics when your body does not need them causes dehydration and electrolyte imbalances, and can result in hospitalization and death. Persisting in the use of diuretics actually creates fluid retention, which can last even after the diuretics are discontinued.

Enemas

Occasionally we have had clients who have used enemas to lose weight. Let us be clear, the only use for an enema is to clean the colon of fecal matter. Any weight loss is due to getting rid of waste matter and you are better off getting rid of it the natural way! You might lose the ability to do so, if you use enemas. If you have severe constipation or a medical condition that you think might require an enema, see a doctor.

Recovery-Sabotaging Behaviors

There are several other behaviors that you may be engaging in that contribute to your eating disorder that are not as obvious or overt as the ones we just described. If you have an eating disorder, you need to look at all of your "recovery-sabotaging behaviors." In this section we explore a few of the sabotaging behaviors that we see most often. Hopefully, this information will help you think differently about what you are doing, offer useful ideas from others who have changed these behaviors, or help you discover a new idea or two about how to make a change. A three-step guide for changing behaviors is provided, along with some examples, to help you see what it looks like to work on a behavior change. See if the following list includes some familiar behaviors:

- Compulsive exercise
- Counting calories, reading food labels, measuring or weighing your food
- Food rituals (cutting food into bits, chewing excessively, spitting out food, eating on small dishes, etc.)
- Comparing yourself to others either in real life or in magazines and on television
- Body checking and measuring
- Keeping clothes that fit only when you are underweight to inspire you to eat less
- Fasting, cleanses, detox diets, diet pills

There are many recovery-sabotaging behaviors that might be part of your eating disorder but aren't on our list. It is important for you to identify, explore, and work on any behaviors that keep you in an eating disorder mindset or interfere with your progress. You might find yourself justifying some of your behaviors because people without eating disorders engage in them. Don't fool yourself. If you have an eating disorder, *all* of the behaviors on our list, plus any others you have, need to be honestly evaluated. You will have to let go of or change these behaviors in order to truly get well and stay well.

Compulsive Exercise

One of the most commonly "justified" behaviors is compulsive exercise. It is easy to defend a behavior that we are all told is good for us and even critical for optimum health, but too much of a good thing is bad. Carolyn once coined the statement, "Give a person with an eating disorder anything and they figure out how to abuse themselves with it." This statement is certainly true for those who compulsively exercise.

Many people think that compulsive exercising to get rid of calories is a form of purging, but technically, compulsive exercise is considered a non-purging "compensatory behavior." In eating disorder terminology, a compensatory behavior is a behavior used to try to "compensate" for bingeing. Other than purging, the two main ways people with bulimia try to compensate for bingeing is fasting and compulsive exercise. Bulimia is not the only eating disorder where compulsive exercise shows up. Even those who do not binge may use excessive exercise to avoid weight gain or enhance weight loss. In fact some people develop an exercise addiction without having other eating disorder features. The question is when does this good thing go bad? If you are a compulsive exerciser, you are over-involved in exercise to the point where, instead of choosing to participate in an exercise activity, you feel obligated to do it and can't stop. Essentially you have become "addicted" to exercise and continue your activity level even despite adverse consequences. Pinning down what is a healthy amount of exercise and what is compulsive or extreme isn't always easy or agreed upon. Basically you are a compulsive exerciser if you engage in excessive and purposeless physical activity that goes beyond any usual training regimen and ends up being a detriment rather than an asset to your health and well-being. Maine (2000, pg. 253) provided a list of behaviors that can help you identify whether or not exercise is a problem for you:

Signs of Compulsive Exercise*

- You judge a day as "good" or "bad" based on how much you exercised.
- You base your self-worth on how much you exercise.
- You never take a break from exercise, no matter how you feel or how inconvenient it is.
- You exercise even though you are injured.
- You arrange work and social obligations around exercise.
- You cancel family or social engagements to exercise.
- You become angry, anxious, or agitated when something interferes with your exercise.
- You sometimes wish you could stop but are unable to.
- You know that others are worried about how much you exercise, but you don't listen to them.
- You always have to do more (laps, miles, weights) and are rarely feel satisfied with what you have done.
- You exercise to compensate for overeating (or just eating).

Writing Assignment: Assessing Your Exercise

Read through the list, "Signs of a Compulsive Exerciser," and write down in your journal any item on the list that relates to you. If you experience any of the things on this list then exercise is a problem for you and will get in the way of your recovery. Do others tell you that you have a problem with exercise? Do you agree you have a problem with exercise? What, if anything, have you tried to do about this problem? Are you aware of any negative consequences of your exercise behavior?

---

* Reprinted with permission.

Problems With Too Much Exercise

Over-exercising is always bad for your body. Not giving your body enough rest and not giving it time to repair itself from exercise is damaging. Restricting your food and exercising too much is a very bad combination. If your body does not have energy to exercise based on food intake, it must create blood glucose for the brain and working muscles by breaking down protein from your muscles to use as energy. Less muscle means a lower metabolism. Spending all of your body's energy (calories) for exercise when some of it needs to go to supporting other systems, like organ and brain function, or hair growth and healthy bone development, is dangerous. In a healthy person, bones are constantly being broken down and rebuilt as part of a dynamic process, but when there is not enough energy coming in, the bones will become weak and break down under the stress of impact, causing stress fractures, broken bones, and other injuries. Your hormone levels may also play an important part in the process. Low hormone levels are associated with bone density problems. Too much exercise and too little food results in low hormone levels. Many compulsive exercisers stop menstruating even if at a normal body weight. The body shuts down functions when it perceives it is not getting the amount of fuel necessary to sustain the amount of exercise being undertaken. If you are not menstruating, it is a clear sign your body is not in balance and is experiencing stress. It most likely means you are not taking in enough calories or do not have enough body fat, and if you are exercising this is contributing to the problem. It is important to note that even though hormone replacement has been shown to help postmenopausal females with bone density problems, taking hormones in order to menstruate and try to alleviate or prevent osteoporosis or bone loss has not been effective for people with eating disorders. Furthermore, clients mistake the artificial period caused by hormone replacement (birth control pills) as a sign they are healthy and menstruating normally when this is not the case. While you are taking birth control pills your hormone levels are kept up artificially and then drop when you switch to the "spacer" or sugar pills, causing your uterus to bleed. If you are taking hormones you have no way of knowing whether or not your body is capable of doing this on its own. We recommend our clients get a bone density test. Even if your eating and/or exercise problems have not been going on for very long, a baseline bone density test is important for comparison at a later date.

We are unable to predict who will become addicted to exercise to the point of being out of control, but studies have shown that if you are not eating enough, exercising can become quickly addictive. The combination of restricted eating and running is particularly problematic. Rats eating a normal diet will periodically exercise if running wheels are provided in their cage. Deprive these same rats of food and they will become addicted to running, and even run themselves to death! We also know that running is a common precursor to relapse. We advise our eating disorder clients who run to find an alternative exercise, at least in the beginning of recovery and for a period after weight restoration or other stabilization. Some compulsive exercisers may have to stop running forever and find a new exercise. Other clients may have to stop all exercising, at least for a period of time.

Helping You Normalize Your Exercise

If you are a compulsive exerciser, you may have some unknown biological predisposition that made you more prone to this, but you are also likely to have psychological reasons as well. If you examine yourself closely you will probably find that you use exercise to deal with feelings, to soothe yourself to feeling in control, and maintain your self-esteem. You are most likely a task-oriented, high-achieving individual with a tendency to be dissatisfied with yourself unless you are consistently setting and achieving new goals. You also probably pride yourself on being able to push yourself and use mind over matter. You most likely value self-discipline and self-sacrifice. You will need to learn that true willpower and self-discipline means cutting back on, or cutting out, exercise! Think about it, what is harder for you, to exercise or take a day of rest?

You will also find that your emotional investment in exercise becomes more intense and significant than work, family, and relationships. In fact, we have discovered that compulsive exercise seems to be associated with issues of intimacy. Do you turn to exercise when troubled or under stress, rather than seeking help from others? Do people who love you complain about your exercise interfering with the relationship? If you are a compulsive exerciser, look closely at the issue of intimacy and your relationships. Many of our clients who exercise compulsively use it as a defense against a fear of getting close to others. They have a hard time being vulnerable with or depending on people. What will help is to work on your relationships. The next key will discuss turning to others for support.

Just as it is important to develop a healthy and balanced food plan, it is also important to have a healthy, balanced and fun exercise plan. Think about exercise as a way to be active and enjoy yourself, instead of as a way to "burn calories." Find things you love to do like dancing, hiking, or riding a bike. Find friends to be active with; together you can shoot hoops, play volleyball, rollerblade, or walk on the beach. Some people find they need to stop certain forms of exercise which seem to trigger eating disorder thoughts and compulsive behaviors (like running or spinning), but can healthfully continue with activities such as yoga, Pilates, or walking with friends. The process is just as important as the goal.

> **Carolyn:** I went to my first yoga class during my recovery from anorexia and exercise addiction. I had sustained several stress fractures from compulsively running and was forced to look for a different form of exercise. I decided to try yoga and I cried during the first class. At that point my exercise addiction was

CHANGING YOUR BEHAVIORS 177

very strong and I thought, "This is not exercise. This is too easy and will never keep me in shape." I decided to keep going and give yoga a chance since I did not like to swim, I did not have a bike, and spinning just did not seem interesting to me. Yoga not only kept me and keeps me fit, it changed my life in other important ways, which will be discussed in Key 8.

There are things you can do to begin the process of letting go of your compulsion to exercise. The following list of possible exercise goals is adapted from a chapter in Costin (2007a).

- Decrease the length of time spent exercising (you may need to do this gradually, in increments of time).
- Instead of running, which has no official start and stop time, go to a class that lasts for a set amount of time.
- Change the type of exercise you do for example, if you run, substitute a day of yoga or weight training.
- Decrease the number of days you exercise.
- Set a weight goal that is necessary in order to continue exercise or increase exercise.
- Possibly stop exercise altogether for a period of time (sometimes this is necessary for health reasons or to break the addictive cycle). (pg. 57)**

Writing Assignment: Fit or Fanatic?

Make a list of any possible signs that you might have a problem with exercise. Include things that other people have said about your exercise, and your moods and behavior when you can't exercise. Ask someone close to you what they truly feel about

---

** Reproduced with permission of the McGraw-Hill Companies.

your exercise behaviors, letting them know you will just listen to what they say without getting defensive. Refer to the list of possible new exercise goals. Come up with a goal for yourself that involves stopping, reducing, or changing an exercise habit. You will learn more about how to do this later.

If you compulsively exercise and cannot reduce your level of activity, or your health is already an issue, you might need to stop exercising altogether until you are healthier mentally and physically. Most people in this category have to be told by a physician to stop, be kicked off a sports team, or even admitted to a treatment program to get their exercise under control. It is advisable to seek the assistance of a professional in navigating this process. Please refer to the Resources section if you suspect or know compulsive exercise is a big issue for you, and you need more help and information than is provided here.

Counting Calories, Fat Grams, Carbohydrates, Etc.

Counting calories, fat grams, or anything else may start out making you feel safe or in control, but over time it becomes an obsession that you can't stop. The behavior takes on a life of its own, with a habitual quality that overrides any rational intent that may have been present initially. When we present the idea of stopping the counting, most people admit that they wish they could, but they think it is impossible. How can you get information out of your head? How can you stop adding up the calories, when it seems to just happen automatically? We both remember having those same concerns, yet neither of us count calories or anything else today, automatically or otherwise. The first step is to *stop looking* at labels and stop looking up the calories or fat grams in the foods you are eating. And, do not write any numbers down! In the beginning this might not seem like much, because you may continue to add the numbers up in your head, but over time as you add new foods to your diet and don't know the calories, you will not have enough information to add everything up. If you eat even one new food and don't know how many calories are in it, you won't know your total daily calories, and the system that is holding your brain hostage will start to break down. Of course there will be foods for which you already know the calorie count, but there are always new foods to try that give you the opportunity to free yourself from this mind trap. Trust us, this works. If you follow the conscious eating guidelines, you do not need to count calories.

Food Rituals

Food rituals differ from food rules, but they are just as resistant to change and will keep you stuck. Food rituals are behaviors you engage in routinely that make you "feel safer" about eating or while eating food. Examples of common food rituals include: eating the exact same food prepared the same way, eating at the same time every day, cutting up food into tiny bites, eating food only in a certain order, or always eating in the same or a certain size dish. You may not think these behaviors are a problem as long as you are eating your food, but the truth is that they keep you stuck in a life dependent on these rituals. Your brain will be resistant to changing, but as soon as you start to break the ritual, it will start to loosen up slightly, and each subsequent mealtime or snack will be easier. Imagine a big hill of dirt with a marble on the top. It could roll down the hill on any side, but if you push the marble down the same path many days in a row, a deep groove will develop, and soon the marble will easily go down that path. The brain works in a similar way; therefore, when you break a food ritual, it is like pushing the marble down the new path. Each time you do that, you will be making a different choice and giving yourself more freedom. While working on letting go of food rituals, make the commitment to not create new ones. It is very hard to break rituals once they have been established, so preventing any new ones from taking root is a great way to help yourself.

Comparing

Comparing yourself to others or people in magazines or on television is problematic, and a set-up for feeling bad about yourself. As with most sabotaging behaviors, clients tell us they compare to try to reassure themselves that they are OK—that is, thin enough—or to get inspired to "do better." There are several reasons why this method of reassurance or inspiration will never work out well for you. Aside from the fact that you have a distorted body image (even if you think you are the one person who has an eating disorder who doesn't), you also probably aren't comparing yourself to *all* people you come across. Instead, you only compare yourself to people who seem thinner, prettier, or in better shape than you. When at the movies, do you compare yourself to everyone you see in the lobby or theater (the real people) or do you compare yourself to the stars in the movie? When at the gym, do you compare yourself to the personal trainers, or the other gym members? You will always be able to find someone who is thinner, prettier, richer, or smarter, and you will always be able to find someone who has less of everything than you do, too. It's sad when we hear clients judging and ranking themselves and others as less than, or better than. Comparing body size with such a narrow range of what is considered attractive is a learned cultural behavior and you need to work hard to "unlearn" it. We guarantee you will be so much happier if you stop comparing yourself to others and learn to accept and value yourself for who you are inside. However, if you are going to compare yourself to others, at least be fair. Don't compare yourself to Photoshopped models in a magazine, or your yoga teacher. Compare yourself to all the people at the grocery store, or every third person you see on the street. This little rhyme might help you: *If you compare, you will despair, so at least be fair.*

Writing Assignment: Your Recovery-Sabotaging Behaviors

Review the list of recovery-sabotaging behaviors. Write down any behaviors you engage in from the list and add anything else you can think of. The goal is to know exactly which sabotaging behaviors are keeping you focused on your weight or appearance, or otherwise keeping you stuck in your eating disorder.

Making Things Manageable

It can be overwhelming to even think about all the goals you have to set and things you have to accomplish to get better. It helps to break this process down into small manageable steps. You might find it helpful to use our "Weekly Contract" form (see the Appendix) where you set specific goals for each week under several categories. Using the form will guide you into setting short-term manageable goals in the area of nutrition, behaviors, exercise, and relationships. Clients have found that the weekly contract form helps them to get specific about what they will be working on each week in these different areas and it keeps tasks manageable. You may find it helps keep you accountable for following through on your goals for behavior change. If you are in therapy you can take this to your therapist and work on setting goals together.

Resistance to Change is Normal

Letting go of or changing your behaviors is difficult, because most likely you have convinced yourself that they are keeping you in line, sane, or safe. Don't be surprised if you have an immediate and strong reaction to the very idea of letting go of your behaviors—many clients do. We often hear things like, "Oh, I have to do that," "I've always been this way," "That won't work for me," and "I'll freak out if I stop." These statements are built on false beliefs regarding what will happen if you change, or a belief that you do not have it in you to change. You may think that you do not have the qualities or skills that change will require, such as tolerance and patience. You might believe that people either have these qualities or they don't—which is a classic example of "black and white" thinking. The truth is that nobody is born with these skills. Behavior change skills increase with practice. People who have these skills have developed them. You can develop them, too.

A Three-Step Guide for Changing a Behavior

Hopefully, by now you have a sense of what behaviors you need to work on and what distorted thoughts and perceptions might be in the way of your making a change. We provide a three-step process you can use to change any behaviors you decide to work on.

Step 1: Raising awareness by tracking the behavior

The first thing you need to do in order to change is to raise your awareness about the behavior. For a week, notice and keep track of the behavior and how often, when, where, how, and why you feel a certain way when you engage in the behavior. The following is an example of the process of modifying body checking behavior by a client whom we will call Gina. Gina uses body-checking behavior in an attempt to control and manage her feelings, and to make decisions about food. Gina was asked to keep a journal of all of her body checking behaviors in order to increase her awareness of how often she did this behavior and how she felt before and after. Sometimes just an increase in awareness is enough to facilitate change,

CHANGING YOUR BEHAVIORS

but awareness is always the first step and a crucial one. The following is an excerpt from Gina's journal.

Monday
- 7:00   body checked in full-length mirror, checked to see if I could see bones (relieved).
- 8:00   after getting dressed, made sure that belt fit on last hole (relieved).
- 8:15   body checked in mirror to see if clothes made me look fat; changed clothes three times (anxious, confused).
- 8:45   body checked in window near bus stop while waiting for bus. Didn't like how I looked like in these pants (self-conscious, angry).
- 9:15   body checked in bathroom at work. Felt better about this mirror (relieved).
- 12:00   body checked in window to see if stomach is flat but it did not look flat (anxious), don't want to eat lunch now that I saw that. Walked around instead and stomach feels flatter now (relieved).
- 5:00   body checked in the bank window after work (frustrated).
- 6:00   changed clothes at home and checked but everything made me look fat, put on jeans and tight belt to help me not eat too much (cried).
- 7:00   ate very little, noticed that last belt hole seems tighter than last time (anxious, distracted, irritable).
- 8:00   watching TV, I feel my hip bones and make sure my clavicle is sticking out (somewhat relieved).
- 10:00   body checked, especially stomach in mirror before going to bed. (sad, frustrated). It still was not flat so I decided to do better tomorrow.

Notice how Gina's feelings go from relieved and comforted to anxious, irritable, and angry based on *perceived* changes in her body. Logically, Gina's body does not change that much in one day, but her "body image" obviously does. Initially Gina was very resistant to stopping her body checking. She thought her behaviors were helping her feel less anxious because they were meant to reassure her that her body is OK and she wasn't changing. In reality, her body checking often made her feel bad. Even when she was momentarily comforted by the checking behavior, she was still driven to check again and again to be sure. If anxious and distressed by what she saw, she was driven to continue checking in hopes of finding something to relieve her anxiety; or she was driven to alter her food intake to ensure a better experience next time she checked. Gina's behaviors around body checking will make it nearly impossible for her to make any changes in her relationship to food. Her body image is distorted and is taking up an enormous amount of time and energy and getting in the way of her recovery. Although Gina was at first convinced that her body checking was helping her, once she kept a log and gained awareness about the behavior, and her feelings around it she saw that it was problematic.

Step 2: Making a plan and taking small steps

When someone is willing to work on changing a behavior, we begin by setting some guidelines or parameters aimed at decreasing the situations that trigger or provoke the uncomfortable feelings and behaviors. In Gina's case, she was asked to cover the full-length mirror in her bedroom, leaving only a small mirror available so she could see her face and neck. Instead of body checking anytime she has the urge, she made agreements regarding how many times she would body check in a day—for example, once in the morning after getting dressed, once around noon, and once again at night before going to bed. She also came up with alternative things she would do instead of body checking, such as call a friend or listen to a song. She maintained a log to keep track of, and gradually reduce, the amount of times she did body checks until she was able to stop the behavior. Gina was also asked to get rid of

CHANGING YOUR BEHAVIORS

her belt she used for body checking. Gina agreed to consciously avoid looking into store windows as much as possible and find a way to reward herself for not looking. All of these suggestions helped Gina reduce and then eliminate body checking.

Behaviors like body checking become habits that are hard to break. Stopping any habitual behavior takes a lot of intention and conscious effort. It won't be perfect. For a while Gina caught herself looking in store windows, and that was OK, because she began to build self-awareness and perspective to notice and analyze how the behavior was affecting her. Over time, she saw that on days when she resisted her body checking behaviors, she was less moody, and more present with people. She also found that nothing drastic happened with her body when she was not checking it. After the initial anxiety and distress that is part of changing these self-sabotaging behaviors, everyone feels relieved to be free from them. The following are some examples of steps others have taken to help them with body checking or body image:

- I will get rid of my "skinny" jeans.
- I will not buy magazines that contain pictures that I know are triggering to me.
- I will remove that huge mirror that makes me feel bad and makes it harder to eat.
- I will buy some loose clothes like yoga pants that don't have a fixed size.
- I will no longer write down my calories.
- I will journal or call someone before carrying out any food rituals.

"I used to think body checking helped me stay thin. Although it took a while, once I stopped, I realized that it was the constant checking that actually made me so miserable—way more miserable than accepting my body."

—CR

> *"Cleaning my closet was a more invasive task than just getting rid of clothing. My clothes represented a lifetime of armor used to create a perfect and beautiful exterior to cover a dark, empty, twisted interior of lies, torture, and sadness. Each piece of clothing held a story related to weight, an event where I had to please people in my life, a time when bulimia had wreaked havoc on my system. I knew I needed to get rid of these clothes to protect myself and to begin my new life. I boxed the items and dropped them off at the nearest Goodwill hoping they would serve someone else in need of a fresh start."*
>
> —KM

Writing Assignment: Taking a Small Step

What small steps can you take to cut down on or avoid a behavior that is interfering with your recovery? Try to list things that you can measure: for example, cover one mirror, or give away clothes that you use to check weight or shape, only cut your food into half of the pieces you do now. Choose at least one action to begin with, and make a commitment to taking that step.

Step 3: Noticing the difference

The final step is analyzing how things are different now that you have made a change. Many people are surprised that just a small difference in thought and behavior can produce a big change in feeling. Remember that at first, most change feels worse before it gets better. The following writing assignment will help you analyze any changes. Gina felt sure her behaviors were decreasing her anxiety, and when she first stopped them, her anxiety did increase. It was only after some time away from the behaviors that she could see that her anxiety actually decreased.

Writing Assignment: Analyzing Your Experience

Write about how you feel when you are engaging in the behavior you are working on trying to stop, and how you feel when you are able to stop yourself. If you are able to stop your behavior for a few days, do your feelings change? Notice again in a week. You might even be able to write about what it feels like in your life to be letting go of the behavior altogether. Remember that at first you will feel very anxious not following through on your urges to do the behavior. If you give it time, you will start to see that the urges, and therefore the anxiety, both decrease, which make stopping the behavior easier.

Rewards and Consequences

Sometimes we ask clients to come up with incentives for making behavior changes. We often have clients make a list of the advantages and disadvantages of changing the behavior. Another technique is to come up with rewards or consequences that work for you. For example, if you don't weigh yourself for a week, treat yourself to a pedicure, or something else that feels rewarding. Devising consequences can help too but also be risky if you aren't creative about it, or if you are too punitive. Consider using this unusual consequences system some of our clients have found helpful. Think of something that you really do not want to do or that would go against your beliefs. Some good examples are: donating money to a cause you do NOT believe in, agreeing to wash your spouse's car, or cleaning your parent's house or garage. One favorite method came from a client who was a professional surfer who gave up her surfboards until she was abstinent from purging for three days in a row. This was the most motivation she had shown. Only you can decide what works best, but we have found that as long as you are the one coming up with them, rewards and consequences are useful in helping with behavioral change.

Progress, not Perfection

If you are like us and most of our clients, the process of change can seem quite slow, frustrating, or out of reach. You may think you are not getting anywhere, it's not worth it, or you just can't do it. Be careful not to criticize or berate yourself for lack of progress. Just imagine if you used this technique with someone else who was trying to change. Besides, if criticizing yourself worked, you would surely be well by now. One way to think about the process is to say that you are *working toward* something. You are learning to accept yourself where you are at this moment, are doing the best that you can, and will continue working toward change. This will involve having compassion for yourself.

Compassion and Change

In order to let go of your obsessive, destructive, or sabotaging behaviors, you will need to have compassion for yourself. The idea of having compassion may feel wrong and unacceptable. You might think compassion is self-indulgent, or believe that compassion for yourself or from others is permission not to change. What you might not be realizing is that nurturing behaviors—acceptance, compassion, forgiveness, and empathy—need to be in balance with rules, expectations, and limits. If either side is too dominant, unhappiness follows, and success remains out of reach. Learning the skills of self-compassion are just as important as learning how to set goal or limits and follow rules.

Compassion Involves Acceptance

Many people believe that they don't deserve compassion, or that allowing self-compassion means they are powerless, indulgent, or pitiful. When we challenge our clients saying that this belief seems a bit harsh, most reply that it feels "realistic"—which shows they don't understand the nature of compassion. This demonstrates how critical and negative their thinking has become. Self-compassion means *accepting* where you currently are and *understanding* how you came to this place in your life. Compassion is about learning to see the problems that you have in the context of your whole life. What we mean is taking into consideration where you came from, your understanding of the world, and the resources you had available, and accepting that *you have done the best that you could*. The best evidence for this way of thinking is simply that if you could have done better, you would have. You weren't able to take care of yourself any better than you did, but that does not mean you can't change now.

Some Final Thoughts

Changing the myriad of behaviors that contribute to your eating disorder or interfere with your recovery can feel insurmountable. In fact, you are most likely thinking, "If I could do that, I would be recovered." That is exactly what we are talking about here. We did it, thousands of others have done it, and you can do it too! Leaving behind your eating disorder behaviors can feel unsettling and unsafe, but fear is never a good reason to stay with something harmful and oppressive. The change will feel uncomfortable at first—we always remind our clients that it gets worse before it gets better—but going through the discomfort is the only way it will become more comfortable eventually.

Letting go of habits that you worked hard to establish, such as counting calories or exercising, can feel like all of your hard work and sacrifice was a waste of time. It is hard to admit that many good years were wasted on things that didn't really deliver what seemed promised. You might be tempted to hang on and just try a little harder or maybe a little longer to reach those old goals, but at some point you have to come to terms with the truth about what the behaviors are doing for you versus what they are taking from you. Your eating disorder will never really make you more lovable, a better person, or invulnerable to pain. As difficult as this realization is, it opens the door for creating a better life. Once you know the truth, you can never go back to denial or the belief that what you were doing was going to work. The great thing is that on the other side of *letting go* of your eating disorder is *creating and holding onto* that which can actually provide you with the love, self-worth, and connection you were seeking all along. We are talking about relationships and we turn our attention to that in our next key.

Key 7:

REACH OUT TO PEOPLE RATHER THAN YOUR EATING DISORDER

You need to turn to someone who offers a better relationship than the one you have with your eating disorder.

—Carolyn to Gwen during treatment

At first I would binge and purge when I wanted to eat something I thought was fattening. Over time I began to think about bingeing and purging when someone made me mad or hurt my feelings or when I was anxious. Eventually I would wake up and plan how I was going to binge and purge during the day. If I did not do it, I would feel mad or hurt or anxious. Learning how to reach out to people, tell them how I felt, simply talk to them when I was upset, or just have them be more a part of my life, was key in helping me recover.

—JN

Good family and social relationships are protective factors in terms of eating disorder prevention. The truth is, if you can turn to people for help in dealing with the problems life brings, you may never have to starve, binge, or purge your way to an eating disorder. Research indicates that supportive relationships, whether with friends, family, helping professionals, or mentors, are key to helping you recover (Strober & Peris, in press). Telling a friend or family member you have an eating disorder, going to therapy, joining a support group, or finding a mentor are all ways of reaching out to others for help. Reaching out to people can help you break old patterns, feel your feelings, heal underlying issues, and ultimately find more joy in your life. Eventually your relationships with people replace your relationship with your eating disorder.

You may or may not recognize how you use your eating disorder, rather than relationships, to obtain comfort, deal with feelings, or just get through the day. In order to recover and leave your eating disorder behaviors behind, you will need to learn to reach out to people instead. This key explores why relying on others to deal with difficult feelings and daily problems is a crucial part of recovery, and essential for creating meaningful and authentic relationships.

> *"I remember when I realized that I'd rather go shopping for new clothes with my friend and have fun just being with her than have my old anorexic jeans fit again. The less I got from my eating disorder and the more I started to get out of relationships, the more I wanted those relationships. It became increasingly clear that I got a much better response from people the less into my eating disorder I was. It was a big turning point in recovery to 'get it' that people did way more for me than my eating disorder ever did."*
>
> — RL

Getting Better Feels Bad. You Need Support.

Feeling your feelings, challenging your thoughts, and changing your behaviors are all hard work. You are bound to feel uncomfortable and overwhelmed. Getting over an eating disorder does not feel good—at least not at first. Hopefully you have tried some (or many) of the assignments in this book. If so, you know that interrupting a behavior, trying a new food, or getting rid of your scale can all feel bad, uncomfortable—and you may wonder if it is even worth it!

Writing Assignment: Why Does Getting Better Feel so Bad?

Get out your journal and take a moment to write about the various ways in which trying to stop your eating disorder behaviors has felt bad. How do you feel (or think you will feel) when you stop yourself from engaging in an eating disorder behavior or take a small step forward? How have your uncomfortable thoughts or feelings gotten in the way of your progress? What advice would you give someone else in your situation? Who do you turn to for help?

Most of the time when people recover from illnesses, they feel better. Depressed people are relieved when their mood starts to lift; insomniacs are grateful to get more sleep. When you start improving (restoring weight, stopping a binge, eliminating laxatives, or resisting an urge to purge), chances are you will feel a lot worse before you start to feel better. When getting better makes you feel bad, it is hard to keep going, and many people stop trying altogether. The best support for helping you through this difficult process will come from your relationships.

> *"My eating disorder was my best friend. I would turn to my eating disorder to help me out when I was suffering or needed something. It was a very difficult task, but I began to call first my therapist and then my friends when I felt upset or insecure, instead of resorting to my eating disorder behaviors. I was skeptical at first that this would make a difference, but in the end it changed everything."*
>
> —KT

Your first step in reaching out might be with a professional, counselor, or mentor. It may feel less risky to talk to someone who you know is there specifically for the purpose of helping you, and who understands the illness. In the beginning this will involve setting up therapy sessions or attending groups where you can talk and learn more about your eating disorder and explore your feelings, but eventually you will want and need more support than is available during sessions. You will need to reach out to someone when you are feeling lonely, afraid, or frustrated *and* at the times when you most want to engage in your eating disorder behavior. If you are seeing a therapist, dietitian, or other professional, you should find out the policy for contact between sessions. Ask if you can call, leave a voice mail, e-mail, or send a text message during the week if you need to. Just simply reaching out to someone can help you become more conscious of your behavior, bring your healthy self forward, and help you feel a connection to someone for support. Your therapist may not accept texts or e-mails for a variety of reasons, but some do and you don't know until you ask. You can also find other support people to text or e-mail, like people in a therapy group or 12-step meeting, or just a good friend. Eventually, you will need to find people who you can turn to for support, accountability, and help.

> *"It took me a long time to reach out to people rather than my eating disorder. I got to a point where looking my therapist in the face after bingeing and purging felt worse than not doing the behavior. I started to realize that when I let other people in they could talk to me, cry with me, or kick my butt in a good way, none of which the food or my other behaviors could do. What made it so hard to do, though, was that the behaviors and the food are quick fixes; they're a lot easier than getting someone on the phone or asking for help. I felt bad, I binged. I wanted it taken care of right then and there. I didn't want to wait. But once I started reaching out to people, it changed my life. Now I see that having those people in my life is more valuable than any quick fix I could've come up with."*
>
> —CR

Using Relationships to Put the Eating Disorder Out of a Job

Even if you are practicing the skills you have learned in the other keys, there are times when everything might feel too hard, or nothing seems to be working to help you. Your healthy self may not be strong enough to stop you from engaging in the behaviors, but it might be strong enough to at least call, text, e-mail, or even grab someone to talk with. The moment you want to go to the store and get all your binge foods, take laxatives, head to a bathroom to purge, or skip lunch, *ignore your eating disorder voice* and *reach out* to somebody for help. Whatever it is you think your eating disorder is going to do for you, you need to let someone else take over that function.

Resistance to Reaching Out

You may have already had several thoughts regarding why it is hard for you to reach out to others for help. Over the years we have heard countless reasons why our clients resist reaching out for support:

1. I don't want people to know how much I need help.
2. I am ashamed.
3. By the time I realize I am in trouble, it is too late.
4. I would not know what to say.
5. I don't see how talking helps.
6. I don't have anyone to call.
7. People won't know what to say.
8. People have not been there for me in the past.
9. I don't want to burden people.
10. I am afraid to rely on others because they will not always be around.
11. I am not sure I want to be stopped.
12. I will feel worse if I try and it does not help.

13. I tried it and it did not work.
14. I should be able to handle things on my own.

Writing Assignment: Exploring Your Reasons for Not Reaching Out

Using the list provided above as a guide, write down in your journal all the reasons you resist or have trouble with reaching out. We will come back to your list later.

Countering the Common Reasons for Not Reaching Out

We understand that reaching out can be hard, and yet it is essential. We have spent many years helping our clients combat whatever reasons they have for not allowing others to help them recover. Read through the counterarguments for each of the reasons listed above for not reaching out.

1. **I don't want people to know how much help I need.** Why don't you want people to know you need help? Is it because you feel weak and are afraid of being judged, or is it because you are not ready for help? Is it simply because you have not had the experience of letting others in? Try to get to the root of the reason and then see if you can back it up with evidence. If there is evidence, see if you can counteract it or if it is possible that things could be different. Whether there is evidence or not you are going to have to accept your fear and reach out anyway! More often than not, the people whom you are hiding things from for fear that they might judge you, already know you have a problem but don't

know how to help. Think about what your healthy self would say to someone else who needed help, but was afraid to ask for it. Remember how you feel when someone trusts you enough to reach out to you for help. People usually like being helpful and feeling needed.
2. **I am ashamed of my behaviors.** Shame is often a deterrent when trying to reach out for help, or disclose that you have an eating disorder. It is important to know that shame actually dissipates as you share your struggles and your true self with others. Being ashamed of your behaviors will not go away because you keep them private. In fact, not sharing them will only reinforce your negative feelings about yourself. The only way to get past your shame is to begin to share yourself and see that most other people still accept you afterwards. When our clients are able to do this, they usually find that honesty brings people closer together, not further apart. There are people in the world who are not kind. There are others who, for whatever reason, will not be able to support you, but the goal is to find those who can.
3. **By the time I realize I am in trouble it is too late to call someone.** The "too late" excuse is a cop out. It is never too late to call. Even if you call someone after you binge, purge, throw away your dinner, run when you shouldn't, or take laxatives, calling anytime is a step in the right direction. You can talk about what happened, get help understanding what may have triggered you, if anything, and discuss what you might do differently next time. Calling someone after you engage in the behavior may be the first step you take on the way to being able to call before engaging in the behavior. Remember, progress, not perfection.
4. **I would not know what to say.** You don't have to know what to say. Simply saying "I need to talk" or "I'm having a rough time" is enough. You don't have to think of anything profound or deep. You don't have to know why

you feel the way you do. You can talk about how you are feeling, or even something completely different. Sometimes just talking to a friend or even listening to them talk helps. The urge to engage in a behavior may pass, and you may sort out and dissipate difficult feelings. It can be helpful to tell a few good friends or support people ahead of time that you might be calling them when you are trying to refrain from eating disorder behaviors, or just having a rough time. You can let them know that you may not be able to say exactly what you are feeling or what is going on, but that just talking to them can help. Just the act of calling someone means your healthy self is getting stronger.

5. **I don't see how talking helps.** Many people are confused as to how talking can help. Talking can serve as a distraction long enough for your feelings or urges to pass. Talking things out can give you more clarity. Talking to others can offer you a different perspective. What is fascinating and important to know is that talking about your problems and how you feel about things actually helps your brain process and tolerate your feelings and regulate your emotional reactions. In fact, people who can talk about and process traumatic events or problems are less likely to continually suffer from them. We have found it helpful to remind clients of the simple phrase, "Name it to tame it," derived from brain research in interpersonal neurobiology and discussed in Key 4. Refer to our Resources section if you are interested in reading more about how talking helps us process our feelings and traumatic events.

6. **I don't have anyone I can call.** When people say they don't have anyone to call, what they often mean is they don't have anyone they feel comfortable calling. You may not have anyone right now you feel you can call, but you will have the best chance at getting well if you begin trying to find someone. If you truly have no sup-

port at all, it is evidence that you are too isolated. You can start by talking to a clergyman of your faith, attending a support group, or finding online support sites. There are a number of resources out there, but they won't come to you. You will need to call, write, e-mail, or otherwise connect with them. The longer you wait, the harder it will be. For more suggestions regarding online support, such as Mentor Connect, refer to the Resources section.

7. **I don't think people will know what to say to me.** The most important thing about reaching out is the fact that you reached out, not what the other person says or does. The act of reaching out will help you get stronger and not fall into automatic-pilot mode when you are struggling. Every call, e-mail, or text will not result in a perfect or even helpful response, but you will find out who is responsive or willing to be supportive and that is a good start. People might not know what to say, but if someone wants to be supportive they are usually willing to learn the best way to help. Sometimes giving others books or other material to read about eating disorders is useful. You might even need to tell people what is or isn't helpful for you. Sometimes knowing what helps comes from trial and error. Share the things that seem the most helpful as you discover what they are. It can be helpful to let a friend know when you just need to talk, or that you don't expect or need them to give advice or play a therapist role. Sometimes just having your feelings validated or having a distracting conversation is enough. You might also find that people sometimes have quite good and helpful things to say and these are the people you will find yourself wanting to call on more often. Lastly, if you are in therapy, you can bring someone in for a session and let your therapist help you work out the best type of support. Learning to communicate your needs is a skill you will need to develop as you recover.

8. **People have not been there for me in the past.** The fact that others may have disappointed you in the past does not mean this has to be your life-long experience and you should just accept it. In fact, this is exactly why you need to do your best to make the necessary changes to find people in your life who *are* there for you. You can start out with someone safe like a therapist, sponsor or mentor, but eventually you will need to branch out and begin having faith that not everyone will let you down, even if others have done so in one way or another. There are people who can't be relied on, or who don't want to support you, but that is OK. You need to let them go and move on to others who can. Chances are you will come across people who want to support you but aren't able to do so and then others who are supportive, but can't be there all the time. It is important that you don't interpret people's inability or unavailability as evidence that they don't care about you. It's important that you have reasonable expectations for your family and friends so they don't feel they have to always be available and say or do the right thing. No one can be there for you or do the right thing all the time and to try would be too draining on any relationship. You need to have reasonable expectations. It usually helps to look beyond the person's action to their intentions.

9. **I don't want to burden my friends.** Most people like to feel helpful and needed. Friends often feel bad if they find out that you don't trust them or feel you can't count on them. It helps to have a few people you can contact so you don't rely too much on any one person. It is also important that you let people know when they actually do help or are helping. Send a card or note of appreciation or thank people in person. Let them know how much their help and support means to you. If you reach out to people but they never feel they are helpful, they will start to feel burdened. It will be hard for others to keep trying to help if nothing they do seems to matter.

Be sensitive to the feelings of others as well as your own, and you will have better success at both getting the support you need and keeping the relationship healthy.

10. **I am afraid to rely on others because they will not always be around.** It is true that people cannot always be counted on to stick around forever, but to be in any relationship you take that risk. People move across the country, fall out of love, and even die. People would not get married or have children if they let the fear of losing someone get in their way. Relationships are impermanent and risky; there are no guarantees and no way to get around that.

    Furthermore not all relationships are meant to last, but we learn and grow from each one. Think of therapeutic relationships or teacher–student and coach–athlete relationships. There are many types of relationships that are not meant to be forever, but that doesn't mean they aren't important or you can't rely on the person when he or she is there. Every relationship is practice for you to learn how to support and be supported, love and be loved. Each time you are in a relationship you will learn and grow and develop your skills of being a colleague, friend, or loved one.

11. **I am not sure I want to be stopped.** Ambivalence is part of the recovery process. If you are not sure you want to stop a behavior, reach out to talk about that. Talking about your ambivalence can help you think about the pros and cons. Reaching out to someone doesn't mean the person will or even can make you stop, but he or she might be able to help you want to stop. No one has the power to make you give up your eating disorder. Slowly, step-by-step, you will start giving your eating disorder up as you start replacing it with something else and relationships are a part of this formula.

12. **I will feel worse if I reach out and it does not help.** Reaching out to others is moving toward people

and away from your behaviors. You might find this hard to believe, but simply reaching out means you are getting better, even if at first it does not stop your behaviors. You will learn more about yourself and what will be helpful. You might become less afraid of asking for help, less automatic in your reactions, and also better at knowing what you need. Don't expect that reaching out during a specific moment when you need help will stop your behavior right away. Reaching out for help to stop a behavior is not the sole answer to recovery, but it does provide a way to practice turning to relationships to get your needs met. Reaching out can also involve telling the truth about how you feel, communicating what you are thinking, and having an authentic relationship with someone else. You will not know all the ways that reaching out can benefit you until you have tried it many times with different people.

13. **I tried reaching out and it did not work.** Think about a child learning to walk. Imagine that child giving up after the first initial attempt. Learning something new takes practice. There are so many reasons why reaching out initially might not work. You might not be ready to let go of your behaviors, let anyone help you, or let yourself establish more meaningful relationships. You might need to find different people to reach out to and better ways to communicate what you need. Whatever the problems you've had reaching out to people, the only two choices you have now are to work at overcoming those problems or to continue dealing with everything yourself. Even though it feels impossible, we know you can do it because not only did we have to learn how to do it, we have helped countless others do it as well.

14. **I should be able to handle things on my own.** Most often people say they can handle things on their own because of one of the other reasons listed here. The truth is, if you could handle things on your own, you

would not have an eating disorder. Another reason you might want to do things on your own is pride. Letting others help you is not a "bad" thing and does not even imply that you can't do things on your own. Sometimes it is nice to get help even if you could have done it by yourself. Reaching out to others for help does not prevent, and can even enhance, your ability to reach in to yourself. Reaching in to yourself is covered later in this key.

Writing Assignment: Counteracting Personal Reasons for Not Reaching Out

Look at the list of reasons you came up with earlier for not reaching out to others. Take some time now to write counterarguments for every reason you have come up with. Hopefully, reading our counterarguments will have helped prepare you to respond. Remember, even writing about the reasons to reach out helps reinforce your healthy self, and will make it easier to reach out when the time comes, even if it seems too hard now.

> *"Acknowledging some hard truths is step one. Yes, people are unpredictable. They can be disappointing. They might judge you. So, yes, there are risks to reaching out to others. HOWEVER, more often than not, relationships are fulfilling and will help you get better. If you let someone in, you realize that all the things you thought were terrible really aren't that bad. Being private and secretive breeds shame, leading to more isolation. Food is a certainty. Controlling it, manipulating it, and so on, does give an illusion of safety. But, it's just an illusion. With little experiments in reaching out to others, it becomes clear that people trump food."*
>
> —TR

Suggestions and Ideas for Utilizing Your Relationships

There are many ways to reach out to someone. Much of the time, reaching out to people does not require an immediate response. You will reach out to stay connected, discuss problems, get opinions, and feel cared for. When you need help in the moment, you need to figure out what is the best way to get support. If the person is physically close by you can ask to meet up. If no one is around, you can pick up the phone and call, or send an e-mail. If you need help in the moment, getting an e-mail response might take too long, therefore in today's world, texting is often the most efficient and expedient way of communicating with someone.

Text to Connect

We use texting with clients as a way of providing ongoing support between sessions. We also teach clients to text others and ask others to text them for support. Research has shown that texting actually assists people in changing behavior. A recent study examined the effect that texting had on helping people stop smoking. Participants who used the text support system were twice as likely to be smoke free 6.5 months later than those who didn't. (Free et al., 2011). Many clients use texting as a way to reach out when they need help or as a way to get reminders from others to stay on track. Here are a few suggestions from our clients on how to use texting to help your recovery.

- Text before, after, or even while engaging in an eating disorder behavior.
- Text when having a difficult time.
- Text to be accountable for following through with a meal plan.

REACH OUT TO PEOPLE RATHER THAN YOUR E.D.

- Text to get support for a meal challenge.
- Text after an accomplishment to get validation and acknowledgement.
- Text for support before trying something new or difficult.
- Text to set up a time to meet or call.

Texting someone to help prevent an eating disorder behavior, or reinforce progress in recovery, brings out your healthy self. Texting provides connection, helps with accountability, can serve as a distraction, and may elicit a helpful idea or response. The person receiving your text doesn't always even have to respond. Sometimes just sending the text is enough to get you through a hard time. There may be times, though, when a quick response is the very thing that helps the most. Over time you will discover how best to use texting as a method of support.

Transitional Objects

We have found that, because people cannot always be around 100 percent of the time, it helps to have a transitional object that reminds you of someone you find supportive. Think of a transitional object as a "stand-in" for the person. For example, a baby blanket is used as a transitional object to help soothe and comfort babies, reminding them of their mother when she is not there. We use various transitional objects with our clients such as rocks, sea glass, or inspirational quotes to give them something to remind them of our work together when we can't be with them. The transitional object helps them stay in touch with what they are working on, what was said in a particular session, or commitments they made. You can use transitional objects in the same way. A best friend might give you her bracelet, a therapist or dietitian might give you an inspirational quote, or you might carry a picture of your boyfriend or child. One client reported using her transitional object this way:

"I went home with the rock you gave me and tried to figure out how best to use it. At first I carried it in my purse, but it was too hidden. Then I put it by my bed, but then it was only a reminder when I was about to go to sleep. Finally I did the perfect thing: I put it on the back of my toilet, on the tank. I figured that whenever I went in to the bathroom to throw up I would see "you" there. I remember one night in particular when I was feeling out of control and definitely wanted to purge. I went in the bathroom and seeing that rock was like you were there. It was such a shock, really, because I had forgotten about it. At first I felt taken aback, then even kind of angry, but then I laughed and ended up crying. But I did not purge."

—KL

Assignment: Creating a Transitional Object

Explain the concept of a transitional object to someone who is supportive of you and ask if he or she can give you one. You can also find or create one for yourself. Keep it with you as a reminder of the goals you have for yourself, and to help you stay connected to your healthy self.

Using a Recovered Person as a Mentor

Both of us have found that being recovered is a significant factor and tool in our success as therapists. But if you are looking for someone who is recovered to help you, it does not need to be a treatment professional. A recovered person who is willing to help you in a professional or mentoring role can be extremely helpful in a variety of ways. People recovered from eating disorders say that one of the things that helped the most was working with "someone else who has been there." Often a person who is recovered knows how you are feeling without your having to explain in great detail. People who have recovered can share specific strategies they used to help stop their own eating disorder behaviors or to reach out to others. They can share how they got past their resistance to try certain things or how they dealt with slips or relapses. Someone who is recovered can also provide hope and an example for what you can have if you don't give up. We hope we have provided that for you in this book. Mentor Connect provides recovered mentors, and they are listed in the Resources section.

Using Others Who Are Still Recovering or In Recovery

You can also find support from people who say they are "recovering" or in recovery from an eating disorder. Some of these people are free of symptoms while others are still having symptoms, but either way they could be a source of support. People who understand and are going through the same thing can be supportive in many ways. The person may be farther along in recovery than you or not. You need to find out where the person is in the process of recovery and determine whether you think he or she can help you. We see people in groups help each other all the time—both in the group meetings as well as outside of the group sessions. Different group leaders have different rules about this, but we encourage our group members to reach out to each other between sessions to help each other stay accountable, or be there for comfort, companionship, and support.

Personal Reflections:

Carolyn: I knew that a huge key to Gwen's recovery would be helping her to learn to reach out to her husband and friends for support. It was astonishing and sad that she had been living with her eating disorder for 15 years and had never told anyone about it. Her husband and friends knew something was wrong but she was very guarded and very good at keeping people out. She let everyone know that she was not open to hearing what they had to say, nor would she talk to them about herself. Gwen's childhood and subsequent life experience had reinforced her core belief that she had to take care of her own emotional needs, and that sharing herself and being vulnerable was a threat, instead of something that felt comforting or could be helpful. Her complete inability to see others as emotional resources greatly contributed to the development of her eating disorder and the pervasive hold it had on her life.

When we can't connect to people for emotional support, we will find something else to fill that void, and for Gwen it was her eating disorder. Right from the beginning, I tried to connect with Gwen in a way that would help her see me as a resource, trust that she could be honest and not feel judged, and hopefully have the experience of feeling understood and comforted by someone besides herself or her behaviors. I knew that I could not make her reach out to others, but my goal was to make it safe to reach out to me and then help her transfer this skill to others. I knew this was going to be one of the hardest parts of her recovery, but also the very thing she needed the most.

Gwen: When I think about how this key changed things for me, I can't believe I went through so much of my life emotionally isolated. To be honest, it never even occurred to me to reach out to others for emotional support, for help with my eating disorder or anything else for that matter. I wanted others to think I had it all together. My biggest fear was how I would survive if people found out that I had problems or that I needed help. I knew that once I disclosed information about myself, I had no control over how others would feel about me, respond to me, or think of me, and that felt intolerable. When Carolyn suggested that I let my guard down a bit and let my husband in to support me, I thought it was something that therapists have to say, but was totally unrealistic in my situation. I thought that my husband didn't understand me, and how could I expect him to? I thought that he already must feel overburdened, didn't deserve this, and now relying on him to help me seemed unfair, and the thing that would be sure to send him running for the hills. I resisted the whole notion with a lot of intensity and seemingly powerful arguments. The truth was that I was terrified of letting anyone in, and I didn't even know how to let my guard down if I wanted to. In one conversation, Carolyn used a metaphor that made me laugh and stuck with me. She said something like; "Nobody can get inside because you have all these guards at the door guarding the fort. Can't you give them a day off?" We laughed a bit, but it gave me a different perspective on myself that helped me a lot. My defenses had seemed permanent to me and more like an impenetrable brick wall than a guard who could "take a day off."

I slowly started to realize that I could take some risks with people and not feel completely vulnerable and forever exposed. I could let my guard down a little to take a risk and then bring it up again if I needed to. I slowly started to take risks. I was more open with my husband and friends; I let my husband know how he could be helpful and what wasn't helpful. It didn't always work perfectly, but it did work sometimes and I had to admit that it felt good to let someone help me. The fact that he still loved me and wanted to help totally negated and invalidated my deepest fears and was healing in itself. Only after I was willing to risk reaching out to him did I learn that he knew I was sick and needed help but felt confused, scared, and powerless to help me without making it worse. Letting my husband in and then friends had the greatest impact on my eating disorder, and may have been the most important key to my recovery. When I first began reaching out to other people, there was no such thing as texting, so I mostly called people and made plans to be with others so I didn't have too much alone time with my eating disorder. Reaching out to people rather than my eating disorder not only helped me recover, but also helped to prevent relapses. I realized that sometimes just telling someone how I felt seemed to help me stay connected to my healthy self.

I used support people for quite a while to help me expand my food choices. For a long time I refused to go on meal outings with my dietitian, and disliked eating with others. Part of my reaching out for help was scheduling regular meal outings with my dietitian and eventually whoever else would go with me. Allowing my dietitian to be with me when I was struggling instead of faking that I was fine was a big step. The weekly meal sessions helped me break every eating disorder rule, and expand my food repertoire. In the beginning I found it very difficult to eat new foods, a variety of foods, hot foods, and to eat with others. I could tell my dietitian my beliefs and fears about the food, and then let her lessen my anxiety with information, truth, and reassurance. My healthy voice got stronger and soon I started saying those things to myself when I was struggling. Soon, I started calling friends to set up lunch dates a week ahead so they were more likely to happen. If you don't have a dietitian, friends can be helpful as long as they have a healthy relationship with food.

Writing Assignment: How and With Whom Will You Seek Support

Write down your thoughts and feelings about reaching out to others. List any obstacles that are still in your way. Write a list of names of people you are considering as people you would like to be able to reach out to. List some ways of reaching out you think you could try. Make a commitment, in writing, to approach at least one person on your list within the next week. Here are three ideas: a) ask the person if he or she is willing to help you; b) just connect and be with the person, perhaps sharing something about yourself; c) talk to the person about specific ways he or she can help support you. Afterwards, write about any problems and how you could improve things next time, and make your next plan for continuing to reach out.

Reaching In to Yourself

At this point you know how important we think it is that you learn to reach out to others, but we also know that you can't rely solely on others for help. Many people worry that reaching out to others will make them too dependent. Being able to depend on people is important for secure healthy relationships, but the best way to protect against becoming overly dependent is by learning how to rely on yourself as well. You are an important resource—the most important one you have—so instead of just reaching out to others, you also need to be able to reach *in* to yourself. The key is to find the balance between relying on others and relying on yourself. Other people can help you, but they are not there all of the time, and sometimes not even when you think you need them the most. Eventually, even though it may seem unrealistic or impossible, you will need and want to learn how to rely on yourself. It feels good to discover your own resilience and resourcefulness. All of the keys in this book should be helping you to build a stronger, healthy self you can rely on. It is your healthy self that you will need to turn to when reaching out to others is not enough, when others are not available, or when you just want to be there for yourself.

> *"As time went on, I slowly started to add myself as a reason to get better, and then I knew I'd turned a corner. Now, I think things through before doing any of my behaviors and I imagine how I will feel the next day, looking at myself in the mirror. There's no way I can engage in my behaviors anymore. Now my motivation has to do with me and my relationships, and knowing that nothing I want in my life is going to come from spending all day every day in a relationship with my eating disorder."*
>
> —LL

What does it mean to reach in to yourself? You probably already know that you have the capacity to help other people, but applying that same advice to yourself doesn't happen. Reaching in to yourself is allowing your healthy self to guide and help you in the same way that you would advise, challenge, or comfort someone else. Relying on yourself does not mean that you can no longer turn to others; it just means that as you get stronger you will not need them as much because you also have you. It is possible to become overly reliant on others and cause them to feel burdened or even frustrated, so checking in periodically to see how they are feeling is important. Client JM describes her process with this:

> *"I thought reaching out to others was the easy part, but I kept thinking that something 'they' were doing was wrong. Eventually I realized I was overusing people and avoiding dealing with myself. Relying on myself was a lot harder, and seemed pointless, because what I wanted was others. Unfortunately, I would*

ask too much, drain people, and get angry with them if they were not 100 percent there for me. I started to realize that the more I was able to reach into myself, get in touch with my healthy self, and be OK on my own, the more I'd be able to have lasting and real relationships with others. Ironically the only way I could get the love I craved and not push people away was to learn to also rely on myself. When I was looking to other people to do it all for me, it was an impossible request and I was always disappointed. Today I have a healthy balance between relying on others and on myself."

—JM

Tools for Reaching in To Your Self

Throughout this book, we describe various tools that can help you turn inward and strengthen your healthy self. We will briefly go over some of these tools here.

Dialogues

The healthy self versus eating disorder self dialogues described in Key 2 will help you internalize the recovery process and use your own resources. If you find that your eating disorder self seems to be winning all the arguments, or you just feel like your healthy self gets shut down and does not know what to say, then it is time to reach out to someone else for help.

Journaling

Journaling is an important tool for recovery. Writing down your thoughts and feelings is an excellent way of using yourself as a resource, and it helps you be your own support person. Journaling has been one of the most important tools in recovery for many people, and one of the reasons why we have provided many writing assignments throughout each of our keys. If you have not done so already, please go back and read about journaling in the introduction.

Mindfulness

Mindfulness practices are one of the oldest forms of accessing your inner wise self. There are many definitions and variations of mindfulness, but essentially it involves intentionally moving away from thoughts and judgments to a more open, accepting awareness of what is. The concept of mindfulness is so important that we spend a great deal of time with it in the next key, "Finding Meaning and Purpose."

Visualization

Visualization is a way of using your mind to create a mental image of something. Visualization is an interesting skill. When you visualize yourself doing something, you activate the same parts of your brain as when you are actually doing whatever you are visualizing. This is why athletes use this technique to help them train for a sporting event. Visualization can help you to prepare for a challenging event as well, such as eating a new food, or resisting the urge to binge or purge. With visualization you essentially imagine yourself in the situation and see yourself successfully handling it in a healthy way. When you visualize something you are focusing energy in that direction. Visualization helps you access your inner wisdom and creates pathways in your brain that help make your intentions a reality. We will talk more about visualization in the next key.

Writing Assignment: Inner Guidance

The following are three visualization exercises that involve reaching inside for inner guidance. For each exercise, read through the directions first and then close your eyes and try to visualize the whole thing through. After you are finished with each visualization exercise, write about your experience, what you learned if you think it might be helpful, and any questions you have. It helps to have someone else lead you through each exercise and also to discuss any feelings that may arise.

1. Think of something you have wanted to try or something you want to change, but have not been able to. Create a very specific image of yourself in the exact situation you need help with. See where you are, everything around you, and who, if anyone else is there. See what you are wearing. Once you have a clear picture of the entire situation imagine in very specific detail yourself going through the behavior successfully.

2. Think of a time when you were in a bad place emotionally and were feeling the urge to engage in a self-destructive behavior. Bring up an image of where you were, what you were wearing, and who (if anyone) was around. Try to recreate the experience in your mind as if it were happening, but stop at the moment before you actually engage in any disordered behaviors. Now imagine that a wise being who is a mentor or guide, someone you trust, arrives on the scene. It could be someone you actually know or a famous person, like Jesus or the Dalai Lama. Use whatever image works best for you. Imagine your guide is speaking to you

softly and telling you the reasons why you do not want to act out this behavior. Your guide is letting you know what it is you really need instead.

3. *Imagine your guide comes to you and tells you that you are going to look into the future. Your guide then shows you what your life will be like if you continue with your eating disorder. You see specific details of how you look and where you are. Next the guide shows you an image of the future where you are recovered. This image is very specific too. You can see both images of yourself in the future clearly. It is obvious to you that you do not wish to end up with the future that awaits you should you continue your eating disorder behaviors. Now just focus on the image of your recovered self. Take time to see specific details like where you are and what you are wearing. Keep that image in your mind for a few minutes. When you feel you have a good image of your recovered self that you can access when you need to, open your eyes.*

Some Final Thoughts

Whether real or imagined, conscious or not, in one way or another, your eating disorder serves a purpose or function for you. In this key, we explained the importance of using others, and then yourself, to put the eating disorder out of its job. This brings up a variety of questions you might be thinking about.

- What does it mean to "use myself"?
- What will I do without my eating disorder?
- Who will I be if I am not this person with an eating disorder?

- What if life isn't better without my eating disorder?
- What is out there for me?

Our last key, "Meaning And Purpose," turns your attention toward what kind of life is waiting for you when you recover. Symptom remission is not enough to fulfill the longing we all have for a deep and meaningful life. Recovery from your eating disorder involves accomplishing a lot of tasks and takes hard work but you might find yourself periodically wondering, "What am I doing all this for?" Antoine de Saint-Exupéry said, "If you want to build a ship, don't drum up people to collect wood and don't assign them tasks and work, but rather teach them to long for the immensity of the sea." The information in all the previous keys, and the various tools and tasks provided, will help you get better, but the longing for a more meaningful life will help you stay that way. Our next key turns to that longing.

Key 8:

FINDING MEANING AND PURPOSE

The body holds meaning . . . when we probe beneath the surface of our obsession with weight, we will find that a woman obsessed with her body is also obsessed with the limitations of her emotional life. Through her concern with her body she is expressing a serious concern about the state of her soul.

—KIM CHERNIN, *The Obsession: Reflections on the Tyranny of Slenderness*

Women turn to food when they are not hungry because they are hungry for something they can't name; a connection to what is beyond the daily concerns of life. Something deathless, something sacred. But replacing the hunger for divine connection with Double Stuff Oreos is like giving a glass of sand to a person dying of thirst. It creates more thirst, more panic. Combine the utter inefficacy of dieting with the lack of spiritual awareness and we have generations of mad, ravenous, self-loathing women.

—GENEEN ROTH, *Women, Food and God: An Unexpected Path to Almost Everything*

In the previous keys, we have been talking about what you are recovering *from*: restricting, purging, or bingeing your food; hating or not accepting your body; using detrimental methods for coping with underlying issues; and not reaching out to others for help. Key 8 is about what you are recovering *to*. Our final key goes beyond eradicating your symptoms, to find deeper meaning and purpose in your life.

On one level, finding meaning and purpose involves embarking on a new career, beginning a new hobby, or otherwise identifying an endeavor that brings a new sense of importance or meaning to your life. Whether it is making jewelry, painting, working with animals, or becoming a schoolteacher, finding something that gives you a sense of purpose or passion is an important aspect that will help propel you toward getting and staying well. Aside from this however, there is a different level of meaning and purpose that is more spiritual in nature. Key 8 is about this deeper level of meaning and purpose. In this key we move beyond your symptoms to reconnection with the essence of your being, and with the sacredness of life. We said in Key 1 that "When recovered, you will not compromise your health or betray your soul." But unless you have a connection to your soul, why would this even matter?

Canaries in the Coal Mine

Our ability to connect with what is meaningful in life has been hindered by our cultural emphasis on materialism and technology, such that the latest fashion or "iDevice" is more important than spending time in nature or awareness of our breath. Our focus on the external world has been at the expense of our internal world. Image has become more important than substance, and we are bombarded with messages telling us that what we look like is more important than who we are. Our cultural obsession with appearance, and particularly on being thin, has confused the pursuit of thinness with the pursuit of happiness and everyone suffers—some more than others.

The more Westernized a culture becomes, the more the media bombards its population with messages that encourage body scrutiny, dieting, and the idealization of thinness. A good example of this is what happened in Fiji. When television first became available in Fiji in 1995, there was no dieting and no eating disorders. Being large was the standard of beauty for Fijian women, and this had been so for over a thousand years. Three years after the introduction of television, 15 percent of young Fijian girls were vomiting to lose weight! When interviewed the girls explained that they wanted to lose weight to increase their social status (Becker, Burwell, Herzog, Hamburg, & Gilman, 2002). The more Westernized a culture becomes, the more eating disorders become prevalent, and this is not mere coincidence. Through the media and other social networks, Western cultures promote image consciousness, dieting, and the "thin ideal." It is clear that not everyone exposed to an appearance-obsessed, "thin is in" climate develops an eating disorder, but those who do seem to be the ones who are most sensitive to its toxicity.

Individuals who develop eating disorders can be seen as our cultural "canaries in the coal mine." Miners once took canaries down into coal mines in order to signal the presence of toxic fumes. Sad as it was, if the canaries died, the miners knew they were in a toxic environment and had to get out. People who develop eating disorders are our cultural canaries. They are the ones who, for various reasons discussed throughout this book, are more susceptible to the cultural messages that erode body acceptance and self-esteem. They are the ones who take those messages to extremes, and some even die. But everyone should heed the warning that the environment we live in is toxic to our deeper soul-selves, to who we truly are, and it leaves many of us searching for true meaning and fulfillment.

Moving Away From Superficial to Spiritual

If you have an eating disorder you are, on some level, living a superficial life. We are not saying your life lacks meaning, but rather, you have lost track of the *true* meaning of life. Whether it is a number on the scale, a flatter stomach, or some other obsession with food or your body that has caught your attention and stolen your energy, you have lost track of what is truly important. Even if you reach a desired number on the scale, the meaningful problems in life persist: "Am I loveable?" "Do I feel fulfilled?" "Does my life have purpose?" As long as you are striving to achieve love and fulfillment through the pursuit of thinness or the comfort of food, your behaviors may have meaning and purpose temporarily, but they will keep you in a constant state of striving, misery, and unhappiness. With an eating disorder, you fall into the illusion that your worth is tied to the external, to things of the ego such as your looks and your ability to control food or your body. Our goal is to help you tie your worth to your innate intrinsic value as a human being, and your connection to other beings and the world around you. This involves turning your attention to matters of spirituality and soul.

> **Gwen:** I felt nervous and skeptical when I first heard Carolyn using words like soul and spirituality. At that time, I considered myself an atheist, and struggled with esoteric concepts like "higher power," "having faith," "surrendering to God," or "trusting the universe." These concepts felt foreign, hard to believe in, and impossible to manifest. If you find yourself having a similar reaction, this does not mean you cannot explore spirituality. Your exploration will involve finding meaning, purpose, and connection beyond your appearance, and beyond the trials and tribulations of daily life. To connect with spirituality and soul you do not have to believe in concepts that don't feel real, true, or even possible. All you have to do is learn how to give your life depth and value by moving away from superficial adjustment to profound connection with the things you do, the world you live in, and the people you love.

The Four-Fold Way: Simple Spiritual Principles

In our lives and our work with clients, we utilize four main principles that serve as guidelines for living a more spiritual or soulful life. The four principles are adapted from Arrien (1993).

FINDING MEANING AND PURPOSE

As a cultural anthropologist, Dr. Arrien studied the wisdom of tribal cultures and came up with four fundamental principles for living, which she believes support spiritual awareness and social consciousness. The principles are: Show Up, Pay Attention, Tell the Truth Without Judgment, and Don't Be Attached to the Results. In this key, we will explain how to use the four principles as guides to help you connect with yourself, others, and the world in a new and more profound way.

Show Up

Are you showing up for and really being present in your life? You might find you get your body where you want it to go, but do you bring the rest of you along, too? Are you fully present and participating in each moment? Do you often find yourself in your head thinking, planning, comparing, what if-ing? Are you aware of another part of you that needs to be brought forth and cultivated in your life aside from your body and your mind? To help our clients learn to be present in the world in a deeper and more meaningful way we teach them the concept of the "soul self." We know the word "soul" might carry with it connotations which make some people feel uncomfortable. If this is true for you, we believe you will feel more at ease as you read further and come to understand what we mean by the difference between ego and soul. In Key 2, we described two parts of yourself as your eating disorder self and your healthy self. In this key, we are going to talk about your ego and your soul. Learning to distinguish between ego and soul has been one of the most profound aspects of our recovery, and our clients repeatedly report this to be true for them as well. Although we do use the term "healthy self," and you have seen its value, it does not fully capture the innermost, wise, core essence that we all have. Therefore we often use another term, "soul self" that helps us, our clients, and hopefully you, identify and access the deeper sense of who you really are, beyond your body, beyond your thinking mind or ego, to your essence. After reading about the soul self, you can decide if this term works for you. Readers can learn more about ego and soul in Tolle (1999), as well as in other books listed in the Resources section.

Ego and Soul

Most simply put, our ego is our thinking mind. The word "ego" comes from Latin, meaning "I." Our ego is the part of us concerned with personal identity ("I am a therapist"), achievements ("I earn straight A's)", possessions ("My house"), and even our emotions ("I am angry"). All these statements say something about our identity, but they don't really describe who we are underneath all that. If you took away your job or your house, or your grades, you would still be you! Since your ego is what you think of as your personal identity, it is what separates you from others. Your ego compares, judges, and criticizes: "I am ugly," "She is thinner," "I am fat." When you criticize others or feel criticized, know that it is your ego at work. However, you do not need think of your ego as bad or unimportant. Your ego is necessary. You need an ego to live on this planet and effectively interact in the world, to think, plan, prepare, and provide. It might help to think of your ego as the "human" part of human being. The problem arises when you think your ego is all that you are, and you have no connection to your soul self. When you cannot quiet your mind or you feel yourself resisting *what is*, your ego is in charge. When your ego takes over, you cannot stop constantly living in the past or future, expressed in such statements as "I wish," or "If only," which keeps you from being engaged in and appreciating the present moment. If you have an eating disorder your ego has gotten out of control.

Your soul, on the other hand, is the "being" part of human being. Your soul self is the part of you separate from your thoughts and emotions. Rather than "I am this" or "I am that" your soul self is simply expressed in the phrase "I am." To define the soul exactly is impossible because it is not a thing, it is your essence—in other words, you don't *have* a soul, you *are* a soul.

FINDING MEANING AND PURPOSE

Your soul self is your essence, but it is also connected to the essence of all others and the world. Your soul self practices the other three principles: it pays attention to what is meaningful, has no judgment, and is not attached to the results. Therefore, your soul self is not affected by the criticism or judgments of others and is not attached to having things be a certain way. Your soul self is not concerned with numbers or scales, nor does it have any preconceived ideas about how your body should be. The concept of soul self is difficult to grasp because you also have an ego that interferes with your soul's way of viewing and being in the world. Understanding and strengthening your soul self will help you connect with what is truly important, putting your ego back in its proper perspective and helping you to leave things, like your eating disorder, behind.

Consider this Native American story:

> "An elder was talking to his grandson about how he felt about a past tragedy. The elder said, 'I feel as if I have two wolves fighting in my heart. One wolf is a vengeful, angry, violent one; the other wolf is a loving, compassionate one.' And the grandson asked, 'Which one will win the fight in your heart?' And the elder answered, 'The one which I feed.'"

Think of your eating disorder self and your soul self; the one you "feed" will be the strongest. Getting better is about feeding, or strengthening, your soul self. All the principles in the Four-Fold Way are designed to *bring meaning to your life through feeding your soul.* Even if you are recovered from your eating disorder symptoms and thoughts, even if your underlying issues are resolved, feeding or caring for your soul is an ongoing process that will help make your life more fulfilling. Moore (1992) explained that when the soul is neglected it doesn't just go away, but shows up in addictions, depression, meaninglessness, and other symptoms. Care of the soul is not about fixing problems or curing illnesses but about showing up for, paying attention to, and living life as it is, recognizing its sacredness, richness, and value. When you care for your soul, the need to binge, starve, vomit, or reach a number on a scale loses its meaning.

> *"I think honoring what my soul is crying out for when I want to exercise, not eat, or binge and purge, is essential to my healing. I know now when I want to engage in my eating disorder behaviors I have been neglecting my soul self. Listening to my soul self, recognizing what I really want and doing that instead, has helped me reach the level of recovery I have. This feels so much better than any eating disorder behavior I could engage in, and I never thought anything would make me feel better than my eating disorder."*
>
> —ML

We realize just hearing this isn't enough to grasp it. Grasping it takes guidance, a bit of trust or willingness, and practice. As you read through this key, you will gain a better understanding.

Pay Attention

What do you devote the most attention to? What grabs your mind? Where does your focus go several times a day? Are the things you are paying attention to bringing you joy and happiness? Do you focus on things that make you feel better about yourself? You probably have heard the saying, "Do you see half a glass of water as half empty or half full?" Don't be too quick to dismiss this as a cliché, but rather think about the question. If you tend to see the glass as half empty, you might be someone who is prone to pay attention to everything that is missing in your life instead of all that is there. Why is that? How can you train yourself to pay attention to what feels right and good and "fills" your soul? Einstein said, "Energy follows thought," and we agree. Whatever you are thinking about, or paying attention to, like "my thighs are fat" or "my thighs are strong," is where your energy goes and from those thoughts,

FINDING MEANING AND PURPOSE 227

certain feelings are created, which then lead to behaviors. Even though you might not yet understand how to shift your attention, or what to pay attention to we hope that you will begin to see the direct connection between how you pay attention and the quality of your life.

Try a simple experiment in paying attention. Think of a familiar tree in your neighborhood. Get a clear image of the tree and then see if you can answer these questions: Do you know the name of the tree or how old it is? Do you know anything about this tree? Does the tree have a smell? Now imagine this tree is the only one left in the world. Immediately the tree takes on a much greater significance, even though nothing about the tree itself is different and you (along with everyone else) would pay attention to it in a different way. If this same tree were the only one in the world, its importance and value would increase significantly, and it would probably be deemed a world treasure. People would know everything about the tree and would come from all over the world to see it and marvel at its beauty and its ability to turn sun, water, and nutrients into such a magnificent life form. People would celebrate its beauty and magnificence. The once familiar and ordinary tree would become extraordinary, even sacred. If this really happened, the tree itself would not have changed, but your perception of it and how you pay attention to it would have. The next time you see your familiar tree take a moment to pay attention to it and notice it for the magnificent miracle it is.

Learning how to alter your perception so that you can pay attention to the sacred even in the ordinary will increase your appreciation of the world and bring deeper meaning, purpose and re-enchantment to your life. Learning how to take time out of your busy life to pay attention to what matters is part of what makes recovery worth it. Try this experiment as well: the next time you see a friend or neighbor, imagine this person is the only human left in the world, and see if your perception of him or her changes. For a real challenge, do the same exercise but think of someone you are unhappy or angry with. See if you can see that person in this new light. We may be ahead of ourselves here, but the point is, changing the way you pay attention will change and enhance the quality of your life and your relationships.

Mindfulness

Mindfulness is a way of paying attention. Unlike what many clients first think, mindfulness is not an esoteric practice or religious technique; it is a way of being in the world. To be mindful is to pay attention to the present moment with awareness, openness, and non-judgment. *Stop and re-read that last sentence.* What it says seems simple, but is actually difficult to do. Think about what your life would be like if you could really: *pay attention to every experience with openness, acceptance, and non-judgment.* This includes your own emotions, other people's "faults" or transgressions, everything. Mindfulness practices are a way of training your brain to accept what is, so you free yourself to move past it and beyond. Although it may be impossible to be mindful all the time, if you practice, it will start to happen more naturally. We tell our clients that mindfulness practices will help them move beyond the thoughts of their relentless chattering ego and closer to their essence or soul self. In almost every spiritual philosophy you will find a traditional practice of meditation, prayer, contemplation, ritual, silent reflection, or some other way of promoting internal non-judgmental awareness. These are all different forms of mindfulness training. Research in the field of interpersonal neurobiology implies that mindfulness practices actually can change our brains in ways that help us to tolerate and manage our physical reactions and emotional states (Siegel, 2007, 2010). It seems that just as being attuned to children's emotions and needs provides them with a secure attachment and resilience, being attuned to ourselves facilitates our own resilience and stability. Mindfulness practices help you develop the ability to tune in to your inner world and

FINDING MEANING AND PURPOSE

regulate your emotions so that you can respond to, rather than react to, situations, and avoid going into panic mode or automatic pilot. Simply put, mindfulness helps you operate from your soul self rather than your ego.

> *"My ego was 'should-ing' all over my soul. After spending enough time recognizing my thoughts, I was able to observe them, notice them. I saw that they were not the light within. I discovered my thoughts didn't resonate with me, but rather only served to make me feel angry, sad, scared, and confused. I was buried under a pile of shoulds. My ego spun stories, fantasies, and fears. It was only when I stepped back and separated myself from my thoughts that my soul had enough room to breathe and started to grow of its own accord. I didn't have to do anything. That was just a lie my ego told me. All I had to do was wait and listen."*
>
> —VA

Mindfulness can help you not only in dealing with a variety of aspects that contribute to your eating disorder, but also with many other things in your life. There are numerous mindfulness practices that can help increase your awareness of, connection to, and capability of managing your emotions. We will describe two different categories of mindfulness practices. The first category includes traditional mindfulness practices, which involve some kind of physical practice like sitting in meditation, walking meditation, or yoga. All of these are done by focusing your attention on internal awareness of some kind. The second category we call "soul lessons," because they involve concepts or strategies that help facilitate connection to your soul self, but might not be seen as traditional mindfulness practices. Some exercises are easy and take very little time or effort, and others are more difficult and require practice. If you are not interested in a particular practice or exercise just skip it and go to the next one or move around this key. However, having said that, we think you will be as surprised as we were when you learn about the effectiveness of these practices, and hopefully you will learn some new and interesting ways to help both your recovery and your life.

Traditional Mindfulness Practices

We start with paying attention to your breath, because it is the simplest form of mindfulness practice we know and it can have profound effects. Paying attention to your breath increases your awareness of the life force running through your body, but this is where most people think the benefits stop. Your breath is always with you and is rhythmic, so you can close your eyes and easily focus your attention on it. Some breathing exercises involve nothing more than just turning your awareness to your breath. Others involve noticing your breath in specific parts of your body, counting your breath, or other breath-related tasks. When you become distracted, which you inevitably will, simply return to your breath and any related exercise.

Mindfulness Assignment: Learning To Pay Attention To Your Breath

See if you can count to twenty breaths. Sit in a quiet, comfortable place where you can spend a few undisturbed minutes. Close your eyes, settle yourself into a comfortable sitting position, and pay attention to your breathing. Notice that you are paying attention to your life force. Begin counting each breath. Count each cycle of an inhale and exhale until you get to twenty. If you lose track, simply start over. The idea is to focus on the inhale and the exhale twenty times and tune out all other activity and thoughts. See if you can do it. You will be surprised how hard this is.

Another breath exercise is to reflect on your breathing and to focus specifically on the turn-around point where the inhale stops and the exhale begins. See if you can do this for five minutes. When you get distracted, which you will, simply return your focus to your breath. It is easy to try this out. Just set the timer on your phone or watch and get started. On the other hand, it is very hard to do.

We are not used to slowing down, turning our focus inward, and paying attention to things such as our breath. Over time, you will find that this kind of practice becomes easier and develops your ability to feel calm and centered, not just while doing it, but at other times when you need to be calm and centered in your life. You may also become more aware of your internal self, a presence that you are normally not in touch with. The books in the Resources section for this key will give you more information about breathing and mindfulness. Meditation is what seems to come to mind when most people think of mindfulness. It is also usually thought of as difficult to do. Many people don't really know what meditation is, think it is mysterious, or believe they can't do it because they don't know how to "empty the mind." There are many forms of meditation, but they all involve shifting from thinking to awareness, and learning to separate your ego (mind) from your inner essence (soul). Meditating is simple in concept yet difficult to do. If the word "meditation" brings up negative connotations, try substituting the phrase "going inside," which is a good way of thinking about what meditation really is. Viola Fodor (1997), who recovered from a severe case of bulimia, describes in her book, *Desperately Seeking Self: An Inner Guidebook for People with Eating Problems*, how "going inside" helped her recover.

On the simplest level, meditation is sitting quietly, eyes closed, with the goal of letting go of, or letting pass, any thoughts that come to mind. When thoughts do come in, as they always do, just notice them, let them go, and return to just being aware and present with yourself and any sensations. Getting lost in your thoughts does not mean you are doing it wrong or are unable to meditate. The point is to notice the distractions and perhaps even say to yourself, "I am distracted" or "I am thinking" and let the thought go by. Trying this for 10 minutes will likely demonstrate how simple but difficult this practice is. Learning how to just be still and aware is a way of gaining access to, and building a relationship with, your soul self. The goal of meditation is not just whatever benefits you achieve while meditating, but to help you become more open, aware, and attuned with yourself, your emotions, and your world during all the other moments of your life.

Various health benefits of meditation have long been recognized. Meditation is now widely accepted as an effective way of reducing both physical and mental stress and promoting psychological well-being. Specifically, meditation has been shown to enhance higher-order cognitive functions and reduce anxiety, chronic pain, high blood pressure, serum cholesterol level, cortisol levels triggered by stress, substance abuse, and symptoms of post-traumatic stress (Rubia, 2009). Meditating has also been shown to alter brain activity and increase gray matter in the brain, which might account for greater focus, emotion regulation, response control, and mindful behavior (Luders, Gaser, Lepore, Narr, & Toga, 2009).

If you want to practice meditation, we suggest you start by finding a time to do it that works best for you. Choose a time when you are least likely to be interrupted and have a special place to go to meditate. You will soon begin to associate this place with meditating, and your mind and body will begin to relax just by entering the space. Don't have any expectations; remember there is no right or wrong way to do it, meditation is a practice. Make commitments in time increments, times of the day, and days per week you can reliably maintain. For example, start with five minutes twice a week. Practice this same schedule on a regular basis until you are able to do it fairly easily and then you can increase the minutes or the days, but go slowly. If you attempt to do too much you risk becoming frustrated and may want to give up. If you are still unsure about the practice of meditation or just want more information, we suggest Dan Siegel's book, *Mindsight: The New Science of Personal Transformation*, as well as *Real Meditation in Minutes a Day: Optimizing Your Performance, Relationships, Spirituality, and Health* by Joseph Arpaia and Lobsang Rapgay.

Personal Reflections:

Gwen: It's easy to feel like we are just victims of our minds as we helplessly perseverate on whatever thoughts, conversations, fears or problems are spinning around in there, especially when there is an eating disorder voice chiming in all day. When I first heard about meditation and mindfulness I thought it was all some New Age wishful thinking, but as I was searching for ways to heal and grow I kept running into this same concept in different forms and arenas. I began to wonder if maybe there was something to these practices. I was skeptical, but viewing meditation as a way of taking my mind to the gym was a helpful analogy in increasing my understanding and openness to trying it out. I am proof that even if you don't initially believe in it, you can learn to actually shift your mind away from all the chaos and chatter to a calmer and more peaceful place.

I was first introduced to the idea of mindfulness and meditation at Monte Nido, so I was somewhat open to the idea when someone encouraged me to enroll in a mindfulness-based meditation course. Meditation was not natural or easy for me. During the first couple of weeks of the course, I became anxious and agitated during many of the exercises and fell asleep on more than one occasion. I wanted to quit, but I kept going in the hope that it would get better. As a person who is rarely silent and loves to talk, sitting in total silence was a grueling task. At the end of the ten-week class, I received the award for "most improved" on the final day of class, which was a whole day spent together in total silence—a heroic feat for me. Today I continue to practice breathing and mindfulness techniques that help me stay focused in the present moment and give me a break from my busy mind.

For various reasons, meditating may not be a fit for you. For many people, closing their eyes to meditate makes them uncomfortable or they "get too lost inside" their head. There are other mindfulness practices we suggest. You might prefer a more active kind of mindfulness practice, like a walking meditation, where you simply focus your awareness and attention on a certain part of your body as you walk, perhaps shifting your focus from one part to another. Monitoring awareness and intention is the essence of all mindfulness practices. Doing things like gardening, hiking, or spending time in nature can be a mindful or meditative experience. Being in nature has a way of bringing mindfulness to you. There are also specific body-oriented movement activities, such as tai chi or yoga, that for millennia have been known to support internal awareness and mindfulness. Because we have found it so effective in our personal lives and the lives of our clients, we will explore yoga here in more detail.

Carolyn: As already mentioned in Key 6, I began yoga under the duress of running injuries. As unsure as I felt about it, I stuck with it, and before too long found that the practice of yoga gave me a way to be in my body and be calm and mindful, using my awareness and intention to set and accomplish goals. Yoga not only helped my body, but it helped my mind stay fit and flexible. When I opened Monte Nido I knew yoga had to be a part of what I would offer. When Gwen was first introduced to yoga, she too did not take to it right away. Now we both practice yoga as a part of our lives. Yoga is an ancient practice, and the word itself means "yoke" (as in yoking together) or "union" of mind, body, and the divine. Over the last few years, research on yoga and eating disorders has been increasing and is promising, showing that practicing yoga can lead to less self-objectification, greater body satisfaction, and fewer eating disorder symptoms. Clients consistently tell us that introducing them to yoga helped them immensely in a variety of ways, as described by the following clients:

"Yoga allows me to experience connection on many levels. I feel connected to my breath, I feel connected to my body, and I feel strength, both mental and physical. I know my body's limitations and I listen to my body. I feel at one with my breath. I am living in the moment and am fully present. I am not thinking about calories. I am not feeling fat. I am not thinking about food. I am actually living."

—JL

"Yoga was the first time I could do any exercise without trying to calculate calories burned. In yoga, I found myself for the first time being really interested in how my body felt, not how it looked. It was as if I noticed it for the first time. I began to pay attention to my body in class without judging it and this helped me pay better attention in that way in all areas of my life."

—JW

Soul Lessons

We use the term "soul lessons" to describe various exercises, activities or assignments we use to help our clients become mindful of and connect with spirituality and soul. One of the simplest and easiest ways to connect with soul is to pay attention to what we call "soul moments." A soul moment is a moment that touches you deeply, and you experience awe or reverence that is hard to describe in words. We often ask our clients to remember and report back to us different "soul moments" they experience during the week. Asking clients to share soul moments helps them to connect to their soul self. Here are some examples of soul moments clients have shared with us:

- Participating in ritual or ceremony
- Singing or chanting with others
- Watching the sunset
- Gazing at the moon and/or the stars
- Staring into someone's eyes
- Witnessing a child being born
- Feeling the spray of a waterfall
- Listening to music or a choir
- Sitting quietly in a forest

Keeping track of soul moments is keeping track of life's sacredness. Soul moments remind us how easy it is to find a way to be moved, and reminded of the connection to something greater than ourselves. Keeping track of soul moments will help you remain grateful for things that might be ordinary in some sense, but are still full of wonder when you take the time to fully pay attention to and appreciate them.

Writing Assignment: Soul Moments

Make a list of some soul moments you have experienced. Describe what made it a soul moment. Think about a world where the things on your list are no longer possible to experience. This will help you grasp the sacredness of these moments.

Beginner's Mind

Seeing with our soul self rather than our ego is seeing with a beginner's mind. Many of our soul lessons are essentially mindfulness practices, which involve learning to see and experience things as if you were seeing them for the first time, or with "beginner's mind." Using a beginner's mind means learning to rid yourself of preconceived notions and see things in a new, fresh way. This is similar to the tree example described earlier, but in the tree example you imagined that the familiar tree became rare, and with beginner's mind you imagine seeing something as if for the first time. In both cases you are paying attention in a new way and making the ordinary sacred. If you have ever watched the awe and delight of a child discovering ice cream or sand for the first time, you have witnessed beginner's mind. We hope the following examples and assignments will help bring this concept to life.

Writing Assignment: Sunrise or Sunset with Beginner's Mind

Bring your journal with you to watch the sun set or rise. After you watch the sun set or rise, write down a description of the sun and what is happening. Describe everything: the colors, the changing light, the clouds, and anything else you can think of. Try to avoid using the word "sun" and instead describe what the sun actually is. Read what you wrote. Hopefully both your experience of watching and then writing about this earthly event will bring you a renewed appreciation of it.

Writing Assignment: Discovering an Apple

Imagine you have arrived on earth from another planet and have come across an apple tree. You are told that apples are food and given one to taste. Write about what an apple is and what it looks and tastes like.

Our next beginner's mind assignment comes in two parts. The first part involves describing a flower and the second part involves describing your body. If you decide to skip this part now, we encourage you to come back to it later. This assignment is important and will illustrate how beginner's mind will help you with your eating disorder and other areas of your life.

Writing Assignment Part 1: Describing a Flower

For this assignment you need your journal and a flower. Pretend you are from another planet and you are asked to describe your flower to the people back home so they will know what a flower on Earth is like. Describe color, sight, smell, touch, and anything else you sense. You can use analogies or metaphors. Here is a short example from one of our clients:

> "My flower is called a rose. It is light pink, almost peach, and pink. It is an imperfect circle, made up of petals, which resemble irregular, slightly round, velvet droplets, flattened out. The petals on the inside are the color of the sun just as it sets over the ocean. There are about four rows of open petals surrounding a tighter bud. The rose is beautiful and fragrant. Each petal itself is not beautiful or very fragrant; only when all of the petals are combined together does its beauty and fragrance show."

After you have written about your flower, read what you wrote to yourself and just take it in. For a moment imagine a world where flowers compared themselves to each other, because one had a fatter stem, or larger petals. Remember comparing our bodies is a learned behavior, but we can also unlearn it if we work really hard.

Writing Assignment Part 2: Describing Your Body

As this assignment might be more challenging, we encourage you to take time and give it your full attention. You are once again a being from another planet inhabiting a human body, or your "earth suit," for your time on Earth. Just as you did for the flower, write a description of the human body using your body as the model. Write about what the body looks like, the many parts and how they function, what purpose the body serves, and how it works or moves. If you find yourself writing anything derogatory, stop and write that part again. Just like when you wrote about the flower, use detailed, objective descriptions, not judgments, when describing your body. Here is an excerpt from a client's description:

> "My body is a vehicle for my soul, my spirit, my energy. I have four appendages, which carry me through life. The two lowest, the legs, support me, ground me, and connect me to the earth. They enable me to run, jump, walk, they are strong, and they are curvaceous and feminine. My torso, the core of my body, holds messages of love, connection, creativity, and spunk. From my torso extends the two other appendages, my arms. My arms give and take, they have five-fingered hands at the end, which grasp, touch, caress, feel, and help. My arms are strong, they are connected to my torso by my shoulders, also durable, but they have the tendency to tighten when I experience emotional fluctuations. The other extremely feminine parts of my body are my breasts. They give life-sustaining nourishment to my offspring."
>
> —KM

After you have written about your body, read over your description and perhaps share it with someone else. As you reflect on this experience, consider these questions: What was it like to describe your body without any negative words? How did you feel before you began writing and how do you feel after reading over what you wrote? What is it like to describe your body in terms of all that it does for you from a beginner's mind, instead of focusing on its appearance and size, comparing it to others, and pinpointing all the things you dislike?

Seeing first a flower and then your body with a beginner's mind, appreciating it for all it is and all it can do for you is an important aspect of living a more soulful life and healing your body image. Over identification with the body is one of the most basic forms of ego; you begin to think of it as who you are. We hope you are coming to understand your body as special and unique to you—your precious "earth suit" that allows you to run, jump, hug, play, and a myriad of other things. It's OK if you have a hard time with this. Changing the way you think about your body and developing a new relationship with it can take a long time, so be patient.

Negative body image is known to be the most difficult symptom to treat and the last to heal in recovery from an eating disorder. Healing your negative body image is a very important aspect of your recovery. We do not use traditional body image assignments, such as body tracing, or estimating your body size to show you have distorted body image, because we don't find them helpful. To illustrate this point, suppose we said, "Don't think about a white horse." If you are like most people, the first thing that came to your mind was just that, a white horse. Traditional body image exercises often keep the focus on your body, when it seems wiser to turn your focus to what is more important, or what truly matters. In terms of negative body image we agree with Ben Franklin: "Instead of cursing the darkness, light a candle."

Remember that one of the criteria for having an eating disorder is that your *self-evaluation is unduly influenced by body weight and shape*. Rather than "working on" your body image,

FINDING MEANING AND PURPOSE

we prefer to bring in some light by helping you transfer your self-evaluation to matters of the heart and soul. When your life is filled with soul moments, mindfulness, and seeing the ordinary as sacred, you will find yourself focusing less on your body image and more on who you are and the world around you. Our goal is not that you stop caring altogether about your appearance, but that you come to accept what you can and can't change *without compromising your health or betraying your soul.*

Valuing your soul means that inevitably your body gets valued too, but valuing doesn't mean changing; it means honoring. The goal is not to detach from your body, but rather to attach a soulful meaning to it. By caring for your soul, you are healing your body image. As you work on mindfulness practices and soul lessons you will rediscover the sacred in everyday life, and find connection, appreciation, and even love for your body.

Writing Assignment: A Letter to Your Body From Your Soul Self

Now that you understand the difference between your ego and your soul, write a letter to your body from your soul self. See how your soul self thinks about, describes, and treats your body. We suggest you put this letter on your mirror or keep a copy with you for difficult times.

Tell the Truth Without Judgment

"Truth Without Judgment" is the third guiding principle. It is an important concept we follow in our own lives and teach to our clients. If someone hurts your feelings or upsets you, it is your ego that has been hurt. Your ego might react by wanting to hurt back. When you react and lash out at another person with anger and judgment, it is always your ego reacting to that other ego, and a battle of egos ensues. Understanding the concept of ego and soul provides you with the insight you need to realize when you are reacting from your ego, and to redirect yourself to connect with your inner wisdom or "soul self," which will help you decide how you really want to respond.

Telling the truth without judgment is easy when you are happy with a situation, or want to tell people how much you appreciate them or something they have done. It is far more difficult to tell the truth without judgment when you are dissatisfied, upset, or want something to be different. To accomplish truth without judgment you will need to step outside of your ego, bring your soul self forward, and honestly communicate your thoughts and feelings without negativity or judgment. This allows other people to better hear the message and take it in. Truth without judgment is often a very hard thing to convey.

Imagine you find out that a friend lied to you. Your ego gets hurt and you react with judgment and negativity, by yelling and calling her names. None of these reactions are likely to get you what you really want. To practice truth without judgment you first ask yourself, "what is my goal?" and then "how do I want to feel about myself after the conversation?" If your goal is to make your friend angry with you and perhaps end the relationship, then yelling and screaming will likely accomplish this goal. If your goal is to have a better relationship, but at the same time to tell her how you feel, and get her to look at her behavior and perhaps change it, then truth without judgment is a better approach. Telling the truth without judgment allows you to be honest about how you are feeling without blaming others, which makes it much more likely your message will be heard rather than ignored or defended against. The first and very crucial step to making this successful is working to calm and neutralize any anger or strong feelings you have inside you before you attempt to communicate. It's not just about the words you say; it's very much about the energy and emotion behind them. To get any negative energy out of your body, go for a walk, listen to some music, journal, meditate, or do one of the mindfulness exercises—whatever helps you to get calm and back to neutral. When you feel balanced, calm, and connected to your "soul self," you are ready to approach your friend and communicate your truth without any judgment.

> **Carolyn:** Practicing truth without judgment has improved my own life and relationships. This practice reinforces itself when you do it because people actually hear you without judgment or negative energy interfering with your message, and you leave the situation having accomplished your goal. Buddha reminds us of the importance of practicing truth without judgment with these words: "Holding onto anger is like grabbing a hot coal with the intention of throwing it at someone else. You are the one who gets burned."
>
> Truth without judgment is important but difficult to practice, especially with people you are close to. The people with whom we have the greatest emotional history can easily trigger negative energy and activate our egos. I find it most difficult to stay calm and communicate from my soul self when I have a conflict with my sister or my husband. They are the two people in my life whom my ego will react to immediately, before I even know it. My best approach to this challenge has been to view them as my highest spiritual teachers, because learning how to *respond* to them rather than *react* to them provides me the greatest opportunity for growth. A tactic I use when I am feeling angry or critical, and I am unsure how to respond to someone without being judgmental, is to ask myself, "What would the Dalai Lama say?" Thinking of what he would actually say helps me tap into my soul self. We encourage you to think about the people who trigger your ego the most, and then try to evoke a "teacher" you can call on to help you know what to say in those difficult moments.

Writing Assignment: Practicing Truth without Judgment

Think of a person with whom you are upset or have unfinished business. Write down your feelings about the situation, and then come up with what you can say to the person without any negative comments or judgment. For example, in the case of a friend who has lied to you, instead of saying, "You are such a liar and a terrible friend," you could say, "It hurts that you didn't trust me enough to be honest. I thought we were better friends than that." Next, write what you would like that person to know and what you would specifically like to ask for. "I am having a hard time with this and feel strongly that we need to tell each other the truth no matter how hard it is." Make sure that you leave out any name-calling, labeling, or blaming. Practice saying what you wrote without any anger or strong emotion attached. If you still get angry or upset, you aren't quite ready yet. You may need more time. When you are first learning this skill, it sometimes helps to read what you want to communicate to the person.

You might be thinking, "What if truth without judgment doesn't work?" You can't be sure of, or control, how other people will react to anything. You can only do your part to be the best person you can be. Just like a tuning fork that sends out a certain vibration, we have found that when you stay connected to your soul self, you help bring out the same in others. Practicing truth without judgment will help improve the quality of your interactions and relationships. We have yet to find anyone who says otherwise. The following illustrates how these concepts have helped one of our clients.

> "I know now that my ego reacts but my soul responds, and as hard as that is to remember, more times than not I am able to take a step back and ask myself—how do I want to be in this,

and which part of me is showing up? I now know that being "right" isn't always winning an argument or being the one with the most evidence to prove the other person is at fault, but rather it is the person who stays connected to who they truly are and knows when to step back and bring that soul self in the room. It's really hard at times not to react when I know I'm right (which of course is my ego talking), but I've gotten to the point where I want to be heard, not feared, and if I don't come from a place where my soul self is driving, and tell the truth without judgment, that won't happen."

—CR

Not Being Attached To the Results

The fourth guiding principle for living, "Not Being Attached to the Results," is difficult to grasp at first. People often think that not being attached means not caring about what happens. Caring about what happens is important, but so is accepting the things you cannot change or that are not worth the energy, money, or effort to change. Not being attached means letting go of the past and being open and hopeful about the future, but accepting what is now and whatever happens. Non-attachment is learning how to live a life of acceptance, as opposed to resistance.

There are only two ways to deal with something: acceptance or resistance. Think about that for a minute. There really is no other way. When you realize the truth in this fundamental principle and keep it in mind, it can change how you experience your life. Here is an example: Let's say you have been planning all week to be outside on Saturday and enjoy a nice sunny day. When you get up Saturday morning you realize clouds have come in and it has started to rain. You have two ways of handling this turn of events. You can resist the situation by feeling deprived, angry, and upset. You might say you can't believe this has happened and curse the rain.

Some people in this situation would be so unhappy about the rain they would allow it to ruin their day. Or you can *not be attached* to having a sunny day, and *accept* the rain. Acceptance is realizing things are as they are and not resisting. When you accept that it's not the rain that is awful, but *your reaction* to the rain that is awful, you begin to see how you create your own happiness and unhappiness. Once you accept that the rain just is, you can decide what to do about it. You can create a whole new plan for your Saturday that incorporates the fact that it is raining. You may not be able to accept the situation immediately (for example, you might need to express your sadness and disappointment about having to change your plans), but when you do reach acceptance you will be released from your negativity and unnecessary unhappiness. Of course, it is easier to accept rain on a day planned for sun, than accepting a betrayal by a friend or getting into a car accident, but the underlying concept is the same. The important things to do in any situation are to feel your feelings, accept what you can and can't do about it, and proceed accordingly. For example, in the case of a car accident, non-attachment would be: 1) letting yourself feel your feelings, like anger or sadness, knowing they will pass; 2) accepting that it happened and you can't undo it; and 3) doing what you can do, such as making sure you are OK, calling the police, and calling a friend. Attachment and resistance would look like: 1) berating yourself repeatedly for not taking an alternate route ("Why didn't I go the other way?"); 2) blaming the other person and name calling, ("You are an idiot, why didn't you look, you are so stupid!); and 3) not accepting and doing what you *can* do, but instead continuing to argue and blame, keeping yourself stuck.

The principle of non-attachment can be applied to every area of your life. Imagine doing what you can and then letting go. The next time you get into a fight with your best friend or partner ask yourself, "How long do I want to be mad?" Non-attachment can help you let go of anger or a need to have it your way. A text message from a client illustrates how the prin-

FINDING MEANING AND PURPOSE 247

ciple of not being attached and acceptance verses resistance can help you out even in the simplest of situations that could otherwise ruin your day:

> *"Here I sit in a traffic jam on the freeway. I can't move my car at all. I was starting to get mad and frustrated and then I remembered, "acceptance versus resistance," and I started to laugh. I turned on the radio and started singing. Thank you for this concept; it has changed my life."*
>
> —CR

Non-attachment and Your Body

Hopefully you are beginning to think about how you can apply the concept of non-attachment and acceptance versus resistance to your life. Our clients repeatedly tell us that this principle helps them in numerous ways. We have found that one of the most profound uses of this principle and one of the hardest areas to apply it to is in relationship to your body. If you are having a difficult time with your body or body image, consider how not being attached to the results could help. Just like the rain in our earlier example, your body is not awful. It just is. It is your resistance to your body and the emotional reaction created by that resistance that is awful. Believe it or not, you are in control of your happiness and unhappiness in this area. True happiness is rarely (if ever) achieved by changing something external, or outside of you. Our inner states of consciousness are far more influential than our outer circumstances. The way we experience life is created by the state of mind with which we meet it. Try to imagine what your life would be like if you were truly able to practice acceptance versus resistance. Imagine what your life would be like if you were truly able to accept your body's natural size and shape. Imagine what it would be like to let go of any attachment you have of forcing your body into a weight or shape that you have to be sick and unhappy in order to achieve. Think about what your life *will* be like when you live with acceptance rather than resistance to your body every day. This can be done and you can get there.

You have come to the end of our exploration of the four principles for living. We hope you can already see how showing up, paying attention, telling the truth without judgment, and not being attached to the results can not only help you recover but add necessary meaning and purpose to your life, making it all worth it to do so. We often suggest that our clients create a special place, such as an altar, in their home where they can place special objects to remind them on a daily basis of the four principles for living or something else that is meaningful to them. You could also just have a special spot where you can put a poster or a sign where you write out the four principles of living or the 8 keys to recovery or special quotes that you change periodically. Our clients tell us that just being reminded of these things helps them stay connected to the concepts or things in life they find meaningful.

Assignment: Creating an Altar

This assignment is for you if you are interested in creating a special place or altar to display items that remind you of what you find meaningful and important. The place should be quiet and private, like your bedroom or some similarly personal area. You can use the top of a dresser, an end table, or a shelf. Using a special piece of fabric helps to designate the area as a separate and sacred space. The fabric can be anything from a favorite scarf, to a piece of lace, or a piece of cloth cut from the old clothes of someone you love.

You can use things that symbolize the four principles of liv-

ing or the 8 keys or items that remind you of your soul self or taking care of your earth suit. Use objects that mean something to you such as photographs, a favorite quote, or a personal item from a loved one. For example, one client used a small mirror to represent "Show Up" and another used a picture of an angel to represent "Truth without Judgment." To represent Key 1, motivation, you could use a picture of a hiking trip you want to be well enough to take or for Key 7, reaching out, you can use a list of phone numbers or photographs of people you will call when you need support.

It is often suggested that traditional altars display the elements of earth, air, fire, and water. For example, a stone or crystal for the earth, a feather for air, a candle for fire, and a seashell or small bowl of fresh water for water. Many people like to display things that represent the senses (sound, smell, taste, touch, and vision) such as a bell or chime, a fresh flower, incense, a mint, a piece of chocolate, a piece of velvet, or anything else that you think belongs and engages your senses. People often like to light candles or incense to evoke a more sacred feeling. Do only what feels meaningful to you. The important thing is that you have things in this special place that remind you of meaning and purpose in life and help get you connected to your soul self and to that which you value. Spending time with your altar is a healthy ritual.

You can use your special place or altar in any way that feels right for you. You can just look at it periodically to remind you of what you find important, or you can sit near it, contemplating an important decision, or just in gratitude. This space and the objects displayed are your reminder of your connection to that which lies beyond the daily concerns of life. Let it be an external representation of your internal world. Your altar is a daily whisper to remember soul.

> **Gwen**: I experienced firsthand most of the assignments in this key and I know how helpful and meaningful they can be. Carolyn has been cultivating them like a garden for many years. I

also remember that while I was still deeply entrenched in my eating disorder, I was pretty numb and unable to connect on a spiritual level. I was disconnected from my body, my feelings, and from others, so it's not surprising that I felt disconnected from the deepest part of me, my soul. If you are struggling with this key, here are some things that will help. *Get some distance from your behaviors.* You don't have to be symptom-free, but if your eating disorder is taking up all the space, there is not much room for anything else to get through. My eating disorder was like a shroud covering or blocking my ability to connect. *Share experiences with someone.* Find a friend who would be interested in doing some of the exercises with you. Doing something soulful with someone else is like infusing the experience with an extra dose of meaning. If I couldn't connect to something at all, I told myself "I'm not there yet." Nothing more. I didn't judge the activity as stupid or meaningless and I didn't judge myself as bad or soul-less. If a thought like that popped in, I immediately countered it with "I'm not there yet."

We are near the end of this key and the end of our book. We want to share with you hopeful words from a client that illustrate several of the four principles and 8 keys at work in her recovery process.

"Each day has its challenges, but I show up and I am free of my old behaviors. Once I challenged the behaviors and was abstinent from them for a significant period of time, it became easy to see the core issues underneath because my attempts to divert attention from those issues manifested themselves in new ways. The point is, life can only be viewed with clarity and approached without fear when I pay attention. I must own my emotions, notice them in my body, feel my feelings and express them. I must accept my body without judgment. I must act in honest ways, telling the truth without judgment to others. If I am constantly acting and doing rather than "being," I will never know

FINDING MEANING AND PURPOSE

where my intentions are rooted. I am still employing mindfulness *in my everyday life and this is what connects me to my* soul self.

At one point I wrote a good-bye letter to my eating disorder self *and in the last paragraph I wrote:* "I feel your fear, I see you as a small and fragile child. I reach out my hand to you and embrace you. I won't ignore your fear; I will help you trust the world. You will not need to use eating disorder behaviors because this does not serve us and together we will find other ways to get what we need. The strange reality is, once I started feeding my body and soul, we began to fuse in a harmonious way. Right now there are still some small remnants of you as a distinct eating disorder self *separate from my* healthy soul self *that is back in control. The goal is not to get rid of you. However, through caring for my soul, your energy was and still is being neutralized and transformed. You are now my* alarm system *telling me when something needs to be attended to. We are the same person. I exist because you exist. In some ways this letter is a good-bye, but it is also a welcome home to where our true* integrated self *lives an honest and full life."*

How did I get to this place? I began to work on a picture of my essence, or soul self. Who am I without a physical form? I worked on this daily and would picture this essence or soul self when I was eating consciously, exercising, and doing any activity. I got used to living life without referencing my physical body but with a strong reference to my soul self. I began to meditate on my physical body. This was sad and painful at first. I would scan my body, part by part, noticing the thoughts and beliefs that came up. I would do this at times where my negative and distorted thoughts ran high such as after meals. However, I also created an inventory of positive thoughts and beliefs from my essence or *soul self and got better and better at* challenging and counteracting the negative thoughts with healthy soul self statements. *I would have long* dialogues with my two parts of self *and when it was too difficult or I just wanted help, I would* reach out to others for support.

I came to realize that my body, my earth suit, *is a gift meant for living life and also for deriving pleasure from life. I try to love and* accept it unconditionally. *If I feed and nurture my body, heal it and continue to respect it, my eating disorder has no place in my life. There are other things to which I turn my attention now, things that bring my life* true meaning *rather than the illusion of meaning and purpose my eating disorder had given me before."*

—KM

Our Final Thoughts

We hope this key and this book have inspired you to leave your eating disorder behind and find deeper meaning. You have the ability to make more soul-led choices. Perhaps you just needed someone to point you in the right direction and encourage you to pay attention to what will bring your life more connection and joy. Taking the time to practice mindfulness skills, participate in soul lessons, see things with a beginner's mind, and bring reverence and sacredness to yourself and those around you will help you create a more spiritual and soulful life. You cannot control everything that happens to you, but you can control how you react to what happens. Living in acceptance helps you decrease needless suffering and let go of unnecessary attachments you may have. This does not mean you have to just sit by and accept everything that happens without ever trying to make changes. It means you first have to pay attention, accept things for what they are, and then determine what you can do. You can live your life in resistance to things or learn when to accept, change, or move on. Letting go of your eating disorder will help you to live a more meaningful life and, on the other hand, living a more meaningful life will help you let go of your eating disorder. Both are true and up to you.

After reading through all the keys, you might now have a

better idea of what it might be like for you when, like us, you can look back and see your eating disorder as a thing of the past. When that time comes you will be recovered. You will no longer have an eating disorder self but instead will be living your life as a fully whole integrated person. You will understand your issues but no longer use eating disorder behaviors to cope. You will feel your feelings and know how to challenge your thoughts. You will eat freely — but consciously — what you want, and no longer use scales or diets to dictate your eating. You will continue to be aware of and work on any problematic behaviors that need to change. You will get your needs met from your relationships rather than your eating disorder and live a soul-led life that brings you meaning and purpose.

Writing Assignment: A Day in My Life When I am Recovered

We have come to our last assignment in the book. By doing this last assignment, you will have the opportunity to write your own final thoughts and create a personal ending of this book for you. In Key 1 we asked you to write about a day in your life when you are recovered. Take some time to visualize once again a day in the future when you are free from your eating disorder. Where are you and who are you with? Get very specific in your imagery. What are you wearing? What is going on in your life at this time? Are you working or going to school? Are you in a relationship? Imagine yourself sitting down to have a meal. Are you with someone or by yourself? Where are you having this meal? What are you eating? How does it feel to be free of negative or fearful thoughts about the food and your body? What kind of friends do you have? What brings meaning to your life? Spend some time with this visualization and then write it down. Remember, having a clear image of what your life will be like and writing it down is an example of setting an intention for where you are headed. Carry a copy of this assignment with you and hang a copy of it somewhere where you can see it every day. You can even send us a copy if you would like.

Our best to you on this journey.

Namaste, Carolyn and Gwen.

"We are not human beings having a spiritual experience. We are spiritual beings having a human experience."

—Pierre Teilhard de Chardin

EPILOGUE

When clients are at the end of their treatment at Monte Nido they have a graduation ceremony. We ask them to write and read out loud an "Eaters Agreement" which is a concept taken from a book called *Nourishing Wisdom* by David Marc. Writing an eaters agreement is making a vow to yourself and setting intentions for the future. At some point you might want to write one yourself. But for now we wanted to share with you some of the agreements clients have written. We hope that they will shine a light of encouragement and inspiration on whatever darkness might be lingering within.

"Many times I've said I wish my body could be a separate person from me so that I could apologize to it for the pain I've put it through for the last 15 years. I would tell it that it has never done anything to deserve the punishment it's received and all along it's only been an innocent victim to the darkness in my head. And I imagine my body looking me straight in the eye with a knowing look and asking, 'What do you plan on doing now?' and this is what I would say... I plan on restricting, not my food but the part of me that lived on self-hatred. I will starve, but only my shame, guilt, and fear. I will continue to purge, not the food I eat but my feelings. I will let them all tumble out when they need to, instead of letting them build until I don't know what to do with them and the feeling is unmanageable. Over-exercising is going to be a given, but not in the gym or by moving my body. I will over-exercise my right to exist, be seen, heard and most importantly to love who I am. I will do the best I can and reach out for help when I feel like I don't have it in me to keep going or I falter in believing in myself.

I promise to stay awake and present during this process. I promise to discover who I am and start to accept that I have more in me than I knew. I will not settle for less in food, life, or love."

—CR

"I begin with choosing to own and take responsibility for the eating disorder that I have lived with and now, after twenty years, I choose to let go. *I choose to live my life that has been blessedly given specifically to me and only me with the feelings, the emotions, the pathways, and the choices that are uniquely mine yet universally understood. I choose to no longer merely survive, but to awaken to the moment, to evolve and to live in the grace of life itself. I choose to live my life with self acceptance and compassion, committed to truth without judgment, without deprivation and without egoistic control. I will take my seat at my family's table forgiving those who have hurt me. I choose to take refuge in the present moment, freeing my soul from the bondage of the past and the anxiety of the future.*

I choose to let go of the desired sought-after skinny girl, and all that comes with her. I choose to let go of the skinny jeans, skinny lattes and the skinny mentality, for I choose a life that is full and fat. I choose the body that I am in and I am excited to live in that space. Therefore, I will eat when I am hungry and stop when I am full. I not only deserve this nourishment, but to do anything else would be to deprive, restrict or abuse my body, spirit, and soul. I will let food satiate my physical hunger and love fulfill my emotional hunger. I choose to not only fuel my earth vehicle, so that she may carry my soul in this world, but also to allow her adequate rest. I let go of compulsive and manipulative exercise regimes that once served me. I choose to let go of all that does not serve me anymore. I will reach out for help when I am confused, lost, and scared. Lastly and yet perhaps most importantly, I choose to dance wildly with others who enter into my life and to trust and engage not their egos, but their souls. I choose to surround myself in a circle of women who are brave enough to bare the truths of their own souls and to hold a space so sacred that mine can do the same. And I promise to hold such space for others to walk the path that leads to wisdom just as others have and will continue to do for me. I will not be in this body forever, so, for the time that I am in it, I choose to celebrate and fully live."

—JS

EPILOGUE

"It's time, time to start thriving rather than surviving. Time to value friendships over food, emotions over apathy, and future over the past. Eat food. Not too much. Don't throw up. That's the eating philosophy I followed after birth, and the one that served me best. I ate when hungry, ceased when full, and followed the physiological cues of my ancestors. I will no longer abuse my body. I will no longer use food and exercise as punishment or reward. I will no longer degrade myself for the shape of my thighs, the size of my hips, the roundness of my stomach, the swell of my chest, because I don't need to anymore. I'm no longer searching for something perfect, so I don't have to make my body conform to my will. Instead I will use love to comfort my feelings of doubt, friends to soothe my sadness, and mentors to alleviate my confusion. As I've learned to respect the child I once was, I've learned to feed the woman that I am. I may have been damaged and lost as a girl, but I have all the power to change. I know where I'm headed is where I've always belonged. It's time."

—AS

"Today I agree to choose relationships over compulsion, happiness over thinness and love over guilt... *I choose independence, freedom, and control. I agree to love and appreciate my body for all that it does for me, rather than resenting it for areas in which it fails, criticizing it, judging it, or trying to change it. I was given this body for a reason—not to run fast, to get A's or to look beautiful—but to feel pleasure, to experience life, and to bring happiness to myself and others. I recognize that my opportunity to live is a blessing, and will no longer take it for granted.*

I acknowledge that love and respect for my body will come with love and respect for my inner being. I am proud of my body as the vehicle and protector of my soul. I will use it to bring comfort and love, to heal, to touch, to feel, to hug, jump, and dance. I agree to treasure my body rather than destroy or deprive it in order to numb my emotions and pain. I refuse to push it to its limits just to see what it can accomplish, in a perpetual search for perfection and success. I refuse to depend on exercise and eating for self-definition and mood stabilization. I am not loved for the number of push-ups I can do or the miles that I can run, those are just things that I do, yet they are vastly inadequate to describe the multi-faceted person who I am. I refuse to live as a ghost in the shadow of my eating disorder. Darkness will no longer obscure my being. I myself light up a room, and not even the greatest dark-

ness can obscure the energy and vitality that shine from within. I no longer need to look for something better, something more, I am whole—it was the eating disorder that was taking away a part of me, eating away at my soul.

I give myself permission to ask for guidance and support, to hold a friend's hand in times of struggle. I agree to celebrate life, not diminish it. I will not wither it down into a compulsion, an addiction, a disorder. This is the beginning of a new life, a new outlook on the world, where the possibilities can be endless if I do not let the eating disorder hold me back; recognize what I am capable of when I am freed from its chains that deprived me for so long. I am a strong, independent, competent, intelligent, beautiful woman. I deserve to take a breath, to look up at the stars, to live in the moment, to be loved, to be free. I deserve and I choose to live a full life."

—CF

"**I became bulimic because I had something to hide, because I was dying from the pain of being numb, because I didn't know the difference between eating my feelings and feeling them.** It didn't work, though. The difficulty is: when I numb pain, I numb joy; when I try to make the uncertain certain I wind up with nothing; when I hide in my attempts at perfection no one can see me. It is in loving relationships, truth without judgment, and living a soul-led life that I learned to be seen. I know now that that's the only way to live and it's the only way to love. And I am grateful. I am also grateful for me and my illness which forced me to pause, to examine, and to give myself the space to realize that I love myself fully and deeply. I agree to keep traveling into myself and into the world. I will tell the truth. I will trust myself. I will laugh when I want to, not when I need to. I will remember that pain ends and so does everything else. I will feel and I will crumble. I agree to remind myself every day that what makes me vulnerable makes me beautiful, that I am imperfect and because of that I am worthy of love. Seven weeks ago I gave myself away daily; there was nothing sacred or gentle or present. I ran around town in red dresses with a car full of parking tickets, not giving a damn. Yesterday I sat outside watching the bunnies and breathing. I felt a sharp gust of wind hit my right cheek, I am alive."

—LS

"**By the time I got to Monte Nido, I was a fatalist in the true sense of the word, resigned to my fate as a career anorexic, destined to be just another eating** *disorder statistic. I didn't much understand the point of trying to get well if it simply was never going to happen for me. I believed fervently that I was a passive victim of the eating disorder, a force stronger than myself, with bigger weapons and tricks up its sleeve. I was lonely and sad and sick of watching life pass me by. Still, I did not understand, would not accept, that it was an active choice I had made all these years to have given my life to the eating disorder rather than some kind of passive surrender. I was resigned to the fact that I was nothing more than an eating disorder, that it was the only thing that made me interesting, that if I tried to fight it I would lose. I remember feeling that it would be easier and far more congruent to just occupy that identity. I was a walking, talking eating disorder. I felt that, since I had not willfully chosen my eating disorder I was therefore a prisoner to it. What I learned, through others who had been there before me, was that even though I had not chosen an eating disorder I could chose to recover. Victor Frankl, in his book,* Man's Search for Meaning, *says about men in concentration camps that, "Even though conditions such as lack of sleep, insufficient food, and various mental stresses may suggest that the inmates were bound to react in certain ways, in the final analysis it becomes clear that the sort of person the prisoner became was the result of an inner-decision, and not the result of camp influences alone. Fundamentally, therefore, any man can, even under such circumstances, decide what shall become of him—mentally and spiritually" (Frankl pg. 65–66)... "Our answer must consist, not in talk and meditation, but in right action and in right conduct. Life ultimately means taking responsibility to find the right answer to its problems and to fulfill the tasks which it constantly sets for each individual" (Frankl, pg. 77). And so I choose to decide what will become of me. No more games, no more hiding food or using eating disorder behaviors or acting like an eating disorder instead of a human being—an interesting human being, with things to say and places to get to and interests to pursue and a family to build. No more wasting time or wasting my life. I have simply had enough. It doesn't matter that the eating disorder chose me, that it has clung onto me without mercy for over half my life and tricked me into believing there was nothing I could do about it. I am taking my power back. I am choosing life. And I am ready for the challenge."*

- *I agree to move forward, not backward.*
- *I agree to never be a slave to the scale or the tyranny of numbers again.*

- *I agree to maintain the pride I feel for myself at this very moment.*
- *I agree to remember that the instant I realized it was possible for free will to usurp fatalism, my life became infinitely simpler and more manageable.*
- *I agree to choose the right thing.*
- *I agree to choose the harder thing.*
- *I agree to choose life.*
- *I agree to celebrate my liberation."*

—JA

References

American Psychiatric Association. (2000). *Diagnostic and statistical manual of mental disorders* (4th ed., text rev.) Washington, DC: Author.

Arrien, Angeles. (1993). *The Four-Fold way: Walking the paths of the warrior, teacher, healer, and visionary*. San Francisco: Harper SanFrancisco.

Arpaia, J. & Rapgay, L. (2008). *Real meditation in minutes a day: Optimizing your performance, relationships, spirituality, and health*. Boston: Wisdom Publications.

Astrachan-Fletcher, E. & Maslar, M. (2009). *The dialectical behavior therapy skills workbook for bulimia: Using DBT to break the cycle and regain control of your life*. Oakland, CA: New Harbinger Publications.

Becker, A. E., Burwell, R. A., Herzog, D. B., Hamburg, P., & Gilman, S. E. (2002). Eating behaviors and attitudes following prolonged exposure to television among ethnic Fijian adolescent girls. *British Journal of Psychiatry, 180*, 509–514.

Brewerton, T. (2004). *Clinical handbook of eating disorders: An integrated approach*. New York: Marcel Dekker.

Brewerton, T. (2007). Eating disorders, trauma, and comorbidity: Focus on PTSD. *Eating Disorders: The Journal of Treatment & Prevention, 15*(4), 285–304.

Brewerton, T. (2004). Eating disorders, victimization, and PTSD: Principles of treatment. In Timothy Brewerton

(Ed.), *Clinical handbook of eating disorders: An integrated Approach* (pp. 509–545). New York: Marcel Dekker.

Bulik, C. M. (2010). Specialist supportive clinical management for anorexia nervosa. In Carlos Grilo & James E. Mitchell (Eds.), *The treatment of eating disorders: A clinical handbook* (pp. 108–128). New York: Guilford.

Burns, David D. (1980). *Feeling good: The new mood therapy*. New York: Morrow.

Chernin, Kim. (1994). *The obsession: Reflections on the tyranny of slenderness*. New York: HarperPerennial.

Costin, Carolyn. (2007a). *The eating disorder sourcebook: A comprehensive guide to the causes, treatments, and prevention of eating disorders*. New York: McGraw-Hill.

Costin, Carolyn. (2007b). *100 questions and answers about eating disorders*. Sudbury, MA: Jones and Bartlett Publishers.

Costin, Carolyn. (1997). *Your dieting daughter: Is she dying for attention?* New York: Brunner/Mazel.

DiClemente, Carlo C., & Velasquez, M. M. (1991). Motivational interviewing and the stages of change. In William R. Miller & Stephen Rollnick (Eds.), *Motivational interviewing: Preparing people to change addictive behavior* (pp. 191–202). New York: Guilford Press.

Fodor, Viola. (1997). *Desperately seeking self: An inner guidebook for people with eating problems*. Carlsbad, CA: Gurze Books.

Free, C., Knight, R., Robertson, S., Whittaker, R., Edwards, P., Zhou, W., Rodgers, A., Cairns, J., Kenward, M. G., and Roberts, I. (2011). Smoking cessation support delivered via mobile phone text messaging (txt2stop): A single-blind, randomised trial. *The Lancet, 378*, 49-55.

Geller, Josie. (2002). Estimating readiness for change in anorexia nervosa: Comparing clients, clinicians, and research assessors. *International Journal of Eating Disorders, 1*, 251–260.

Keel, Pamela K. (2006). *Eating disorders*. New York: Chelsea House Publishers.

REFERENCES

Keys, Ancel Benjamin, et al. (1950). *The biology of human starvation* (2 vols.). Minneapolis: University of Minnesota Press.

Luders, E., Gaser, C., Lepore, N., Narr, K. L., and Toga, A. W. (2009). The underlying anatomical correlates of long-term meditation: Larger hippocampal and frontal volumes of gray matter. *Neuroimage, 45(3),* 672–8.

Maine, M. (2000). *Body wars: Making peace with women's bodies: An activist's guide.* Carlsbad, CA: Gurze Books.

Moore, T. (1992). *Care of the soul: A guide for cultivating depth and sacredness in everyday life.* New York: HarperCollins.

Rorty, M, & Yager, J. (1993). Speculations on the role of childhood abuse in the development of eating disorders among women. *Eating Disorders: The Journal of Treatment & Prevention, 1*(3–4), 199–210. doi: 10.1080/10640269308251 1605.

Roth, G. (2010). *Women, food and God: An unexpected path to almost everything.* New York, NY: Scribner.

Rubia, K. (2009). The neurobiology of meditation and its clinical effectiveness in psychiatric disorders. *Biological Psychology, 82,* 1–11. doi: 10.1016/j.biopsycho.2009.04.003.

Siegel, D. J. (2007). *The mindful brain: Reflection and attunement in the cultivation of well-being.* New York: W. W. Norton.

Siegel, Daniel J. (2010). *Mindsight: The new science of personal transformation.* New York: Bantam.

Smeltzer, D., Smeltzer, A. L. (2006). *Andrea's voice—silenced by bulimia: Her story and her mother's journey through grief toward understanding.* Carlsbad, CA: Gürze Books.

Strober, M. & Peris, T. (2011). The role of family environment in etiology: A neuroscience perspective. In Daniel Le Grange & James Locke (Eds.), *Handbook of assessment and treatment for children and adolescents with eating disorders.* New York: Guilford.

Tolle, E. (1999). *The power of now: A guide to spiritual enlightenment.* Novato, CA: New World Library.

Wade, T. D., Bulik, C. M., Neale, M., & Kendler, K. S. (2000). Anorexia and major depression: Shared genetic and environmental risk factors. *The American Journal of Psychiatry, 157*(3), 469–471.

Resources

Key 1: Some Ways To Connect

Beyond Hunger (http://www.beyondhunger.org/) is a nonprofit organization that offers support groups, workshops, and education for adults and adolescents with eating disorders. Eating Disorders Anonymous (http://www.eatingdisordersanonymous.org) is a nonprofit organization which promotes fellowship and community support among persons in recovery from eating disorders. MentorCONNECT (http://www.mentorconnect-ed.org/) is a global eating disorders mentoring community that connects members individually and in groups with mentors, to share experiences, provide guidance, and help each other through the struggles and triumphs of their journeys. National Association of Anorexia Nervosa & Associated Disorders (http://www.anad.org/) is a nonprofit organization dedicated to promoting public awareness of eating disorders, encouraging research on the treatment and prevention of eating disorders, and providing resources and referrals to persons affected by eating disorders.

Key 3: Trauma Therapy

Bass, E., & Davis, L. (1998). *The courage to heal: A guide for women survivors of child sexual abuse*. 3rd ed. New York: HarperPerennial.

Leitch, L., & Miller-Karas, E. (2010). *The trauma resiliency model workbook.* Claremont, CA: Self-published. www.traumaresourceinstitute.com

Rothschild, B. (2010). *8 keys to safe trauma recovery: Take-charge strategies to empower your healing.* New York: W. W. Norton.

Key 4: Trauma Therapy

Levine, P. A. (1997). *Waking the tiger: Healing trauma.* Berkeley, CA: North Atlantic Books.

Key 5: Conscious Eating

Hennes, R. (2007). *One day at a time: Food journal and fullness monitor.* New York: RJ Communications, LLC.

Koenig, K. R. (2005). *The rules of "normal" eating: A commonsense approach for dieters, overeaters, undereaters, emotional eaters, and everyone in between!* Carlsbad, CA: Gurze Books.

Tribole, E., & Resch, E. (2003). *Intuitive eating: A revolutionary program that works.* New York: St. Martin's Griffin.

Key 6: Compulsive Exercise

Powers, P. S., & Thompson, R. A. (2008). *The exercise balance: What's too much, what's too little, and what's just right for you!* Carlsbad, CA: Gurze Books.

Key 8: Spirituality and Soul

Kornfield, J. (1993). *A path with heart: A guide through the perils and promises of spiritual life.* New York: Bantam Books.

Lelwica, M. M. (2009). *The religion of thinness: Satisfying the spiritual hungers behind women's obsession with food and weight.* Carlsbad, CA: Gürze Books.

Appendix

Example of a Food Journal
Date _____

Time	Food and Amount	Hunger (Fullness)	Feelings	Urges/Purge
8:00	1 cup yogurt, an orange, lots of granola	3–7	Feeling hungrier in the a.m.	N/N
10:30	Luna bar, coffee latte	3–5	Needed something, stressed	N/N
12:30	Turkey sandwich	3–6	Not quite satisfied, feeling anxious	N/N
4:00	small bag of trail mix, apple	2–7	Lunch wasn't enough, got too hungry	Y/N
7:00	bean and cheese burrito, chips (lost count) salsa, guacamole	3–8.5	Out with friends, too many chips, feeling guilty and frustrated with myself	Y/Y

Example of a Weekly Contract

Name _____
Date _____

A. Eating/Nutrition Goals (meal plan commitments, food challenges, plans to eat with others)
   1. I will try a new breakfast this week.
   2. I will keep my food journal up to date.

B. Weight and Weighing Goals
   1. I will not weigh myself.
   2. I will work on maintaining my weight.

C. Exercise Goals
   1. I will go to yoga class instead of running three times a week.
   2. I will take a rest day where I do no exercise.

D. Behavior Goals
   1. I will write in my journal if I feel like bingeing or purging.
   2. I will write a healthy self versus eating disorder self dialogue at least three times this week.

F. Relationship/Family Goals
   1. I will ask a friend to have diner with me one night this week.
   2. I will call someone if I feel like bingeing or purging.

Index

100 Questions and Answers About Eating Disorders, 16
12-step model, 65–67

AA, 67
abdominal pain, 169
"about the food". *see* food
abuse, 74–75
 see also laxative abuse
acceptance, of self, 188–89
 see also not being attached to the results
achievement, high, 84
action, as a motivation level, 20, 21–22
actions, as part of chain, 97
addiction, exercise. *see* exercise, compulsive
all-or-nothing thinking, 66–67, 98–99
altar, 248–49
ambivalence, 12, 41–42, 43, 201
 see also motivation
American Psychiatric Association, 68
ANAD. *see* National Association of Anorexia Nervosa and Associated Disorders (ANAD)
Andrea's Voice (Smeltzer and Smeltzer), 168
anorexia nervosa
 12-step model and, 66
 bingeing and, 162
 body image disturbance, defined, 68
 control and, 39
 diagnostic criteria, 149
 food addiction and, 65
 genetic predisposition and, 77
anxiety. *see* feelings; weighing
Arpaia, J., 233
Arrien, A., 222–23
automatic thoughts, 100, 103
AWARENESS app, 122–23

Barrett's esophagus, 168
beginner's mind, 236–40
 see also mindfulness
behaviors, body-checking, 182–84
behaviors, changing, 181–90
behaviors, compensatory, 172
behaviors, overt. *see* bingeing; purging; restricting

behaviors, recovery-sabotaging, 171–81
behaviors, tracking, 182–84
bingeing
   12-step model and, 66
   abuse, as a risk factor and, 74
   causes of, 162–65
   cognitive distortions about, 100
   control and, 39, 42, 126
   feelings and, 83, 85, 164
   food addiction and, 65
   as habit, 95, 165
   hunger and, 136
   strategies for overcoming, 163–64, 165
   thought-feeling-urge-action chain, 96
   trust, lack of, and, 85
   weighing and, 152–53
   writing assignments, 165–66
   see also eating disorder self; restricting
biology. *see* genetics; interpersonal neurobiology
birth control pills, 174–75
black and white thinking, 66–67, 98–99
blaming, 99
body awareness, 115–17
body-checking behaviors, 182–84
body image disturbance
   body-checking behaviors and, 182–84
   comparing self to others and, 180
   cultural climate and, 67–71
   definition, 68
   healing of, 240–41, 247–48
   writing assignments, 70–71
   see also weight, body
body relaxation, 119
body stances, 119
body therapies, 118–20
body weight. *see* weight, body
bone density, 174, 175
bowel dysfunction, 169
brain function
   bingeing and, 164
   body stances and, 119
   compulsive exercise and, 174
   distorted perceptions and, 102, 105
   food rituals and, 179
   meal plans and, 137
   meditation and, 232
   mindfulness and, 228
   Name It To Tame It, 114, 198
   visualization and, 31, 214
breathing, 230–31
Buddha, 243
bulimia, 168, 172
   see also bingeing; purging
Burns, D., 98

calorie counting, 178–79
calories. *see* metabolism
canaries in the coal mine, 221
Carson, R., 140
CBT. *see* cognitive-behavioral therapy (CBT)
change
   of behaviors, 181–90
   feelings during, 25–27
   persistence for, 34–35
   see also motivation

INDEX

Chernin, Kim, 219
cognitive-behavioral therapy (CBT), 98
cognitive distortions, 96, 98–105
　see also perceptions, distorted
colectomies, 169
commandments, thin, 127
comparing, self to others, 180
compassion, 188–89
conscious eating, 132–37, 179
　see also hunger scale
consequences and rewards, 187–88
constipation, 169
contemplation, as a motivation level, 20–21
control
　anorexia nervosa and, 39
　bingeing and, 39, 42, 126
　calorie counting and, 178
　food labels and, 131–32
　food rules and, 127–29
　hunger and, 136
　meal plans and, 142, 143
　need for, 84–85
　purging and, 39, 42, 126
　resistance to change and, 181–82
　rigid versus chaotic, 126
　see also eating disorder self; healthy self
coping mechanisms, 83, 85, 94, 95, 120
　see also bingeing; eating disorder self; purging
Costin, C.
　on cognitive distortions, 101–2
　on exercise goals, 177
　on feelings and vulnerability, 111–12
　on genetics, 76–78
　laxative abuse, 170
　on meal plans, 145–46
　overview of, 3–5
　on "real issues", 86–87, 88
　"recovered", 16–17
　on relationships with people, 208
　on risk factors, 72–73
　on thin commandments, 126
　on truth without judgment, 243
　on two selves, 46–47
　on vulnerability, 25
　on weighing, 155–58
　on yoga, 176–77, 234–35
counterarguments, to not reaching out, 196–203
creative assignments, 122, 206, 248–49
critical voice, 89–91, 113, 188
　see also cognitive distortions
cultural climate, 67–71, 76, 180, 220–21

DBT. *see* dialectical behavior therapy (DBT)
dehydration, 167, 169, 170
Desperately Seeking Self (Fodor), 231
dialectical behavior therapy (DBT), 117
dialogues, between two selves
　automatic thoughts and, 103–4

overview of, 53–56
writing assignments, 41, 52, 55, 61, 104–5, 241
see also integration, of two selves
dichotomous thinking, 66–67, 98–99
DiClemente, C., 19
diet. *see* food; meal plans
dietitians
between-session policies, 194
conscious eating and, 133, 137
intuitive eating and, 144
meal plans and, 142, 143
as supporters, 210
transitional objects and, 205
weighing and, 152, 153
discounting positives, 99
distortions, cognitive, 96, 98–105
see also perceptions, distorted
distraction, as coping skill, 83, 94, 111, 120
diuretics, 170
see also purging

Eaters Agreements, 255–60
eating
conscious, 132–37
intuitive, 144
permission to, 162
eating disorder self
contributing factors to, 82–89
control and, 39, 42, 50, 54, 73, 112
genetics of, 75–79
as habit, 95
healthy self versus, 41–47, 50–52

overview of, 37–40
reinforcement of identity as, 66, 94, 225
responsibility for, 40–41
risk factors for, 71–75
transformation of, 49–52
writing assignments, 13, 41, 52, 55, 61, 91–92
see also dialogues, between two selves; integration, of two selves
ego, 224–26, 231, 236, 240, 242
see also critical voice
Einstein, A., 226
electrolyte and mineral disturbances, 168, 169, 170
emotional eating, 164
emotional reasoning, 99
emotions. *see* feelings
emptiness, filling up, 83
encouragement, personal reflections about, 32–34
enemas, 170
environment. *see* cultural climate
esophagus, 168
exercise, compulsive, 172–75, 177–78
exercise, normalizing, 175–78
exercise goals, personal reflections on, 177

fasting. *see* restricting
fat gram counting, 178–79
Feeling Good (Burns), 98
feelings
of being fat, 108–9
bingeing and, 83, 85, 164

INDEX

body-checking behaviors and, 182–84
body image disturbance and, 67–71
exercise and, 175–76
identification of, 114, 115, 116
journaling and, 9
motivation and, 25–27
opposite action and, 117–18
overview of, 105–6
ownership of, 106–8
processing of, 198
purging and, 85, 110
regulation of, 109–18, 228–29
as response to thoughts, 115–17
transference of, 94–95
validation of, 199
vulnerability and, 110–13
worse during recovery, 107, 192–93
writing assignments, 107–8, 109, 114, 187, 193
see also eating; pay attention; thought-feeling-urge-action chain
Fiji study, 220–21
Fodor, V., 231
food
journaling about, 138–41
reasons why it's not about, 65–80
relationships with, 129–32
writing assignments, 81–82, 128–29, 130–31, 162
see also eating
food labels, 131–32
food rituals, 179
food rules, 127–29, 163–64
Four-Fold Way. *see* spirituality
Frankl, V., 259
Franklin, B., 240
fullness, 145
see also hunger scale

Geller, J., 19
genetics, 75–79
goal management, 181, 184–86
going inside. *see* meditation
Grabb, G.
on cognitive distortions, 101–2
on critical voice, 89–90
on feelings and vulnerability, 110–11, 112–13
on genetics, 78–79
on meal plans, 144–45
on mindfulness and meditation, 233–34, 249–50
on motivation, 23–25
overview of, 3, 6–8
on "real issues", 87–89
on relationships with people, 208–10
on risk factors, 73–74
on spirituality, 222
on two selves, 45–46
on weighing, 154–55, 156–58

habits, 95, 165
happiness. *see* not being attached to the results
healthy self
control and, 55–56
eating disorder self versus, 41–47, 50–52

overview of, 37–38
strengthening of, 47–49
writing assignments, 55, 60–61
see also dialogues, between two selves; integration, of two selves
healthy self statements, 48–49, 60–61
homeostasis, 95
hope, 32–34
hormone levels, 148, 149, 174–75
hunger, 134, 135, 136
see also eating
hunger scale, 139–41

impulsivity, 79
inner guidance visualization, 215–16
integration, of two selves, 44–45, 56–60
see also dialogues, between two selves
internet assignments, 122–23
interpersonal neurobiology, 198, 228
intuitive eating, 144
inward focus. *see* spirituality
iPhone app, 122–23
issues, real. *see* "real issues"

journaling, 9, 49–50, 53, 138–41, 213–14
see also writing assignments

Keel, P., 68
Keys study, 160

labeling, 100, 131–32
laxative abuse, 168–70
see also purging
life force, 230–31

magazines. *see* cultural climate
magnification, 99
Maine, M., 172
maintenance, as a motivation level, 20, 22
Mallory Weiss Syndrome, 168
Man's Search for Meaning (Frankl), 259
Marc, D., 255
mass media. *see* cultural climate
meal plans, 137, 142–46
meaning and purpose, finding, 219–22
see also mindfulness; spirituality
meditation, 78, 229, 231–34
see also mindfulness
menstruation, 71, 148, 174
mental filter, 99–100
mentors, 193, 199, 206–7
metabolism, 136, 160–61, 166, 167, 174
mindfulness, 214, 228–41, 249–50
mind-reading, 99
Mindsight (Siegel), 233
mineral and electrolyte disturbances, 168, 169, 170
minimization, 99
models. *see* cultural climate
Monte Nido Eating Disorder Treatment Center, 3, 29, 233, 234, 255

INDEX

Moore, T., 225
motivation, 13, 17–23, 25–27
   see also hope

Name It To Tame It, 114, 198
National Association of Anorexia Nervosa and Associated Disorders (ANAD), xi
Native American story, 225
neurobiology, interpersonal, 198, 228
non-attachment and your body, 247–48
not being attached to the results, 245–48
Nourishing Wisdom (Marc), 255

opposite action, 117–18
over-generalization, 99

parotid glands, 168
pay attention, 226–28
perceptions, distorted
   eating disorder self versus healthy self and, 42
   feeling fat as, 108–9
   resistance to change and, 181–82
   writing assignments, 100–101, 104–5
   see also cognitive distortions; pay attention
perfectionism, 83–84, 101–2
   see also shame; traits, as liability or asset
"perfect storm", 76, 78
personality. *see* traits, as liability or asset

personalizing, 99
policies, between-session, 194, 204
positives, discounting, 99
pre-contemplation, as a motivation level, 20
preparation, as a motivation level, 20, 21
prevalence statistics, xi, 221
progress, 188
purging
   12-step model and, 66
   abuse, as a risk factor, 74
   cognitive distortions about, 100
   control and, 39, 42, 126
   feelings and, 85, 110
   methods of, 166–70
   reinforcement of, 94–95
   thought-feeling-urge-action chain, 96
   weighing and, 152
purpose, finding, 219–22
   see also mindfulness; spirituality

Rapgay, L., 233
"real issues", 82–89
Real Meditation in Minutes a Day (Arpaia and Rapgay), 233
"recovered", 16–17, 147
   definition, 16–17
recovery
   12-step model and, 67
   ambivalence during, 12, 41–42, 43, 201
   behaviors that sabotage, 171–81

changing behaviors during, 181–90
feeling worse during, 107, 192–93
hope during, 32–34
meaning of, 16–17
motivation during, 13, 17–23, 25–27
nonlinear process of, 27–28
phases of, 14–16, 17, 30
success factors in, 2, 29–30
writing assignments, 17, 31, 181, 253–54
relapses. *see* recovery
relationship, with food, 81–82, 129–32
see also eating; food rules
relationship, with self, 211–16
see also integration, of two selves; self-reliance
relationships, with people, 81–82, 191–211
relaxation, 119
resistance, to change, 181–82
resource box, 122
restricting, 160–62, 163–64, 167
rewards and consequences, 187–88
risk factors, 71–75
see also traits, as liability or asset
role play, between two selves, 55–56
see also dialogues, between two selves
Roth, Geneen, 219

de Saint-Exupéry, A., 217

scale. *see* weighing; weight, body
self-acceptance, 188–89
see also not being attached to the results
self-care methods, 119–23
self-concept. *see* eating disorder self; healthy self
self-esteem, 83, 84, 85, 86
see also critical voice
self-reflection, 91
see also mindfulness
self-reliance, 202–3, 211–16
self-soothing, 121–23
setbacks. *see* recovery
shame, 112–13, 197
see also perfectionism
shape. *see* body image disturbance
"should" statements, 100, 229
see also thin commandments
show up, 223–24
see also spirituality
Siegel, D., 233
Smeltzer, A., 168
Smeltzer, D., 168
Smeltzer, T., 168
somatic therapy, 118–19
soul lessons, 229, 235–36
see also mindfulness
soul self, 229, 231–36, 241, 242, 243, 244
see also healthy self
spirituality, 222–48
support system. *see* dietitians; relationships, with people; therapists

television. *see* cultural climate

INDEX

texting, 204–5
therapists
  between-session policies, 194, 204
  goal setting and, 181
  opposite action and, 117
  reaching out to, 193–94
  self-disclosure of, 3, 5, 28–29
  transitional objects and, 205
  weighing and, 152, 153
thin commandments, 126, 127
thinking, dichotomous, 66–67, 182
thought-feeling-urge-action chain, 96–97
thoughts
  automatic, 100, 103
  belief in a myth, 83
  of eating disorder self, 43, 44–45, 47, 50–52
  feelings following, 115–17
  transference of, 94–95
  see also cognitive distortions
Tolle, E., 224
tooth damage, 167–68
tracking behaviors, 182–84
traits, as liability or asset, 76, 77, 79, 80–82
transitional objects, 205–6
trauma. *see* abuse, as a risk factor
trust, lack of, 85
truth without judgment, 241–45
two selves, integration of, 44–47, 56–60
  see also dialogues, between two selves

urges, 97, 117–18, 165–66

Vasquez, M., 19
visualization, 31–32, 214–16
  see also mindfulness
vomiting, 166–68
  see also purging
vulnerability, 25, 110–13
  see also feelings

walking meditation, 229, 234
Weekly Contract form, 181
weighing, 151–58
weight, body, 146–49
  see also cultural climate
weight loss, as a relinquished goal, 149–51
weight restoration, 153, 175
Weight Watchers, 73
writing assignments
  on bingeing, 165–66
  on body image, 70–71
  on changing behaviors, 186
  on dialogues between two selves, 41, 52, 55, 61, 104–5, 241
  on distorted thinking, 100–101, 104–5
  on eating and hunger scale, 141, 162
  on eating disorder experience, 13, 91–92
  on exercise, 173, 177–78
  on feelings and vulnerability, 107–8, 109, 114, 187, 193
  on food goals and rules, 128–29, 130–31

on healthy self-statements, 60–61
importance of, 8–9
on inner guidance visualization, 215–16
on mindfulness, 237–38, 240
on motivation, 23
on "real issues", 86
on recovery, 17, 31, 181, 253–54
on relationship to food and people, 81–82
on seeking support, 196, 203, 211
on traits as liability or asset, 81
on truth without judgment, 244
on weight loss as relinquished goal, 151

yoga, 78, 176–77, 229, 234–35
Your Dieting Daughter (Costin), 83, 126